BLACK PERFORMANCE AND CULTURAL CRITICISM
Valerie Lee and E. Patrick Johnson, Series Editors

D1569704

Reimagining the Middle Passage

Black Resistance in Literature, Television, and Song

Tara T. Green

THE OHIO STATE UNIVERSITY PRESS | COLUMBUS

Library of Congress Cataloging-in-Publication Data
Names: Green, Tara T., author.
Title: Reimagining the Middle Passage : Black resistance in literature, television, and song
/ Tara T. Green.
Other titles: Black performance and cultural criticism.
Description: Columbus : The Ohio State University Press, [2018] | Series: Black performance
and cultural criticism | Includes bibliographical references and index.
Identifiers: LCCN 2017055652 | ISBN 9780814213650 (cloth ; alk. paper) | ISBN 0814213650
(cloth ; alk. paper) | ISBN 9780814254714 (pbk. ; alk. paper) | ISBN 0814254713 (pbk. ;
alk. paper)
Subjects: LCSH: American literature—African American authors—History and criticism.
| Slave trade in literature. | Slavery in literature. | African Americans—Intellectual life.
Classification: LCC PS153.N5 G72 2018 | DDC 810.9/896073—dc23
LC record available at https://lccn.loc.gov/2017055652

Cover design by Angela Moody
Text design by Juliet Williams
Type set in Adobe Minion Pro

CONTENTS

Preface   vii

Acknowledgments   ix

INTRODUCTION   Death and Rebirth in the Middle Passage   1

PART I   IN THE MIDDLE PASSAGE

CHAPTER 1   Understanding the Middle Passage   21

CHAPTER 2   Alex Haley's Roots of Resistance   40

CHAPTER 3   Middle Passage Legacies in Charles Johnson and HBO's *Treme*   68

CHAPTER 4   Calling Marie Laveau   90

PART II   LEGACIES OF THE MIDDLE PASSAGE

CHAPTER 5   Deadly Waters, Southern Blues, and Richard Wright   109

CHAPTER 6   Katrina Sings the Blues in Jesmyn Ward's *Salvage the Bones*   126

CHAPTER 7   Telling of Return and Rebirth in Marshall's *Praisesong for
            the Widow*   144

CONCLUSION Acts of Redemption through Forgiveness: Remembering
            Charleston in the Post–Middle Passage Era   162

Works Cited   169

Index   176

PREFACE

WATER IS always near me. Not simply for drinking or bathing, but as a part of my upbringing. That's how it is for those of us who are reared in coastal areas. Before he retired, my dad was a machinist who made parts for ships. For years, my mother's brothers worked in the shipping industry in New Orleans. When I was younger, my absolute favorite activity was to ride the ferry from the Westbank suburban area of New Orleans into the city, especially on Mardi Gras Day. That the Mississippi River holds the pain of importing enslaved Africans and their descendants into what we now call the United States was not something that I knew as a child. Water has always been near me, but I was unaware of how it had been a part of me.

Water's presence in my historical DNA called me to this project, but it would take me at least seventeen years to complete the book. It began when I lived and taught in Baton Rouge, Louisiana. Moving to the mountains of Arizona disrupted my connection to water, but that was also when Hurricane Katrina came. Images of people stranded on the streets and their roofs in the August heat streamed nonstop on local and national news outlets. Viewing them told the story of a city I did not recognize even though I had been there just a week and a half before. I felt disoriented.

Most of my family had left the area. One of my uncles who lives in the Third Ward of New Orleans, however, had a different experience. Concerned about what would happen to his home if he left, he decided to stay in the city. He nearly drowned in fast-moving floodwaters but was saved by some folks, maybe first responders, who came by in a boat. I can still recall the pain in his voice as he told me his survival story twelve years ago. I hear it now in remnants: "I was walking home from a friend's house. It was hot. I heard a woman in a tree screaming to me for help. I turned the corner and hit a wall of water. I couldn't breathe. They pulled me out. At night, the mosquitoes ate me alive. I couldn't see my hand in front of my face. I've never fought in a war before, like Vietnam, but I imagine what it was like." Several days later, he left the city. I hear him tell his story multiple times. More details sometimes. Less other times. But always with an emotion that is both unfamiliar yet familiar. He brings me where I don't want to be. I listen with pained intensity. If he can still tell his story, the word is made flesh.

This is not his story. This is not my story. It is ours.

ACKNOWLEDGMENTS

SPECIAL THANKS to the College of Arts and Sciences at the University of North Carolina at Greensboro for providing the support needed for my 2014 research leave and travel to the Urban League of Greater New Orleans's "State of Black New Orleans: 10 Years Later" conference. I am also thankful for support provided through my appointment as Linda Carlisle Excellence Professor of Women's and Gender Studies. Thanks also for major funding provided by Vanderbilt University's Callie House Center for the Study of Global Black Culture and Politics.

A book cannot be written without the support of a community of talented and patient people. I am thankful for mine. I cannot express how much I value the encouragement and expertise of my sisters in the Fugitive Writer's Group. Appreciation is also given to Mark Rifkin for always listening to my ideas in their rawest forms and helping me to craft them into words. I also appreciate the reading provided by Robin Cheeley Adams.

I am thankful to Chester Fontenot Jr. and Jacob Gordon for their supportive words and helpful suggestions during the development of the manuscript. Jerry Ward Jr. and Brenda Marie Osbey's writing and fondness for the beauty of New Orleans is simply inspiring. Thanks to them for their presentations at the National Endowment for the Humanities (NEH) poetry seminar hosted by University of Kansas, where many strands were tied together by the poets, participants, and the organizers, Maryemma Graham, Howard Rambsy III, and Evie Shockley.

I am also indebted to the external reviewers who gave of their time and offered helpful comments for revision as well as those at The Ohio State University Press, especially Lindsay Martin, Valerie Lee, and E. Patrick Johnson.

As always, special thanks to my parents and family, including Uncle George. Your love and your stories are empowering.

Death and Rebirth in the Middle Passage

SEEKING REFUGE from threats of high winds and moving floodwaters, New Orleans residents are encouraged to take shelter in the Superdome. As a local, you know it as the "home of the New Orleans Saints" and the site of the annual Essence Music Festival, but that night it is to be a safe haven for those of you who live in the lower-lying areas that are more likely to flood. During the night, you huddle in the seated area with your family together with blankets and various items. You squeeze the hands of your loved ones as the lights flash off and on and then, finally, turn off. This means that the air conditioner is no longer working in the space that has no windows and that relies exclusively on coolant. The bathrooms began to overflow hours ago. Access to sanitary conditions is not an option. Fear of what is to come unsettles you as you try to comfort yourself and the others. "As long as we stay together, we will be okay," you reason. Thunder and lightning rages outside the dome and the sounds give rise to uncertainty, and a sense of powerlessness and vulnerability plagues your imagination. Water begins to pour through cracks in the dome and you begin to wonder just how safe you are in this dark enclosed smoldering hot space. What is going on outside? And, when will it end? In the hallway, you hear people singing and know that you are not alone in your fear and misery. They resist this feeling of powerlessness and vulnerability, stop wringing their hands, and begin to shake them in defiance.[1]

---

1. Description of events visually documented in *Trouble the Water* (2009).

In this contemporary age, two centuries after the last ship with enslaved persons is known to have sailed to the Americas, people of African descent remain haunted by forced engagement with the Atlantic, especially the leg of the journey known as the Middle Passage. Assessing the history of the African diaspora requires consideration of the role the Middle Passage has played in forming the diaspora and the collective consciousness of the survivors' descendants. Capturing emotions associated with the journey, Kamau Brathwaite, a contemporary Barbadian poet, expresses shared pain and fears of African descendants[2] stemming from collective historical memories of the Middle Passage: "& the sea between us yields its secrets / silver into pellables into sheets of sound / that bear our pain" (6). Brathwaite is not alone. Stories told by African-descended peoples (i.e., people of the African diaspora who are of various nationalities) emerge from memories of Middle Passage experiences, where, according to the Transatlantic Slave Trade Database, an estimated 12.5 million Africans were transported from their homeland and dispersed to areas of the Caribbean and the Americas. The Middle Passage in the African diasporic imagination has come to represent a site of suffering (i.e., physical atrocities) as much as it has a release from suffering (i.e., freedom through death). Inspired by memories borne out of suffering and oppression, *Reimagining the Middle Passage: Black Resistance in Literature, Television, and Song* probes the historical and symbolic meaning and legacy of the Middle Passage as explored by African-descended artists[3] in their literature, music, film, television performances, and art. By engaging storytelling as passed down in writing, orally, or in song, hearers of the word are able to find themselves in memories of the past and to decide what power the stories will have in crafting their own identity as they navigate and resist oppressive forces.

African-descended artists surmise that in the Middle Passage, Africans were introduced to the idea that they were "Black" and that "Black" has meaning, meaning that was significantly opposed to their identities as members of various ethnic groups and communities. As "Black" as a state of being emerged, so too did white supremacy, which depended on a myth that Whites are superior to Blacks and that God had deemed it so. V. Y. Mudimbe's analysis of the effects of African colonization examines the Inter Coetera Bull, an influential doctrine issued in 1493 by Pope Alexander VI:

---

2. Although the body of this work emphasizes African American experiences, I use "African descendants" to note that the ideas that emerge in this study may also apply to members of the African diaspora who live outside the United States. At times, I use "African descendants," "Black," and "African Americans" interchangeably.

3. Unless otherwise specified, I often use "artists" to refer to the creators of multiple forms of creative work, including music, fiction, and poetry.

Among other works well pleasing to divine majesty and cherished of our heart, this assuredly ranks highest, that in our times especially the Catholic faith and the Christian religion be exalted and everywhere increased and spread, that the health of souls be cared for and that barbarous nations be overthrown and brought to faith itself. (30)

To be Black and no longer African required submission to white supremacy ("exalted" White Christians) and to see the self, through the eyes of the oppressor, as valueless "barbarians," except when the Black body was exploited to make money. However, it stands to reason that African captives, facing unbelievable, unexpected, strange, and foreign threats, would have come to value their lives even more. In this state of understanding, African captives' resistance to this new experience was inevitable. African-descended artists' revisions and reimaginings seek to make legible the untranslatable, the painful, the emotional by isolating and narrating moments in the Middle Passage where the humanity of the African captive clashes with the inhumane acts of white supremacy.

Some of the 10.6 million who survived the journey—fraught with physical and mental abuses and constant threat of death—employed ways of resisting oppression en route and upon arrival in the New World. As I argue that the artists recognize the Middle Passage as a site for, if not the origin for, both blackness (a state of being) and white supremacy (a social myth), I recognize death as a part of the evolution of the diaspora. Therefore, death emerges as a major intersecting theme in African descendants' creative engagements with the Middle Passage. Sociologist Orlando Patterson and literary scholar Abdul JanMohamed inform my exploration of the meaning of death as symbolic, social, and physical.[4] By extension, my work emphasizes the meaning of life to African descendants when threatened with death through violence and as a form of power. African American religious studies scholar Albert Raboteau's definition of conversion provides a lens through which I analyze the role of resistance in the construction of a transformed identity resulting from engagement with the vast presence of water—a bridge between life and death in their various forms. Death, I argue, is simultaneously a pause in the life cycle, the beginning of a transformed state of life, while social death indicates a life status based on perception. My focus on the individual acts of African

---

4. Tenets of Afro-pessimism as an extension of social death may be relevant here—a theoretical lens for "situating relations of power, at the level of the political and the libidinal" (*Afro-Pessimism: An Introduction*). My intent here is to look more directly at the meaning of social death as a lens to discuss African descendants' experience. In other words, what happens when the slave as object affirms the self as an individual (as opposed to a member of a movement) and does not acknowledge the self as socially dead?

descendants (both real and imagined) moves us from perception to the reality of how the individual affirms life, humanity, and personhood.

In *Reimagining the Middle Passage,* I am concerned with how the Middle Passage is both historic and symbolic. For African descendants, it is not merely a geographical space in the Atlantic Ocean. Within the Middle Passage, water acts as a symbolic medium or conduit between the captive who is deemed as socially dead and the captives' attempt to reconstruct the self as a converted or transformed person. It is there that the African captives came to understand for the first time that they were not considered human by their strange-looking captors. Having no previous sense of this, we can imagine that many would have begun to see their lives differently, to embrace what they knew as truth—that they were human and wanted to be treated as such. As a fluid space, temporality shifts from the past to the present, for the very act of moving over the Atlantic as a captive incites a new identity and understanding of freedom. Artists find that the Middle Passage and the experiences associated with it have purpose that begs descendants to look beyond the trauma. I argue that African-descended writers and artists recognize the Middle Passage as a historical and figurative place for discovery. By returning to it, they exorcise the idea that fueled the transatlantic slave trade, that Black life does not matter then or now, as they express that it does. To be sure, it was there—in the Middle Passage—that forms of Black resistance to social death were born.

SOCIAL DEATH AND THE MIDDLE PASSAGE

For the purposes of this study, social death has to do with the ways in which Black folks have been (mis)treated in society, the ways in which they have been denied access, the ways in which they have been silenced or their human desire for equal treatment ignored. Patterson identifies three facets of power that make it possible for supremacists to assign Black folks to social death status: (1) the use of threat to exert control, (2) the ability to persuade a person's perceptions, and (3) the exertion of authority by equating obedience with duty (Patterson 1). Patterson argues that once a person acquiesces to the power, he becomes to the people in power a "nonperson" (1). As such, he has a choice to either consent to these forms of power wholeheartedly or to resist the treatment in one form or another. Further, the enslaved or socially dead individual, according to Patterson, "differed from other human beings in that they were not allowed freely to integrate the experience of their ancestors into their lives, to inform their understanding of social reality with the inherited meanings of their natural forbears, or to anchor the living present in any conscious community of memory" (4). Contemporary writers' and artists' reclamation of the past and revisioning of the meaning of the historical narrative challenges Patterson's assertion that disruptions of cultural linkages were a sign of social death. *Reimagining the Middle Passage* uncovers the many ways in which African descendants did and do recover a "right or claim of birth" as they "integrate the experience of their ancestors into their lives" (Patterson 4). I argue that memory, often in the form of storytelling but also in everyday living, replicates too often the horrors of the past and causes an excavation of ancestral living to survive the present. In sum, sequential connections to the past make the Middle Passage always present. As such, African descendants (must) remain in resistance.

Exploring the meaning of death as a major theme in the works of Richard Wright, who published during the mid-twentieth century, Abdul JanMohamed builds on the work of Patterson to construct his idea of the death-bound subject, which he defines as "the subject who is formed, from infancy on, by the imminent and ubiquitous threat of death" (2). He expands further to note that there is power or the "effectivity of the threat of death as a mode of coercion" that results in the death-bound-subject (3). Presenting his summation of "Patterson's analysis," JanMohamed finds that "the slave is socially dead in that he has no sociopolitical presence as a subject or citizen in the master's society, and he is socially dead in the sense that he constitutes 'bare life,' life that can be killed without commitment of a homicidal or sacrilegious transgression" (3). JanMohamed advances his assessment of the characters "if the slave is willing to die, if he is willing to risk actualizing his postponed death, then that actualization will totally negate his social-death or his enslavement" (17). While JanMohamed makes a compelling case regarding the meaning of social death, I depart from his study by emphasizing the significance of life for African descendants. It is my contention that African descendants' belief in the value of life is what compels resistance, and not a willingness to die. Moving beyond both JanMohamed and Patterson, I argue that measuring the value of the life of the oppressed through the lens of the oppressor serves to overlook the ability of the oppressed to redefine the meaning of power and to assert the self as a person.

It is precisely the presence of violent death or "killing" that interests me, at least as much as probing the existence of social death to African descendants. To add some clarity and to expand on the ideas presented by JanMohamed regarding the threat of death, I argue that true coercion is powerful when there is not simply a threat that physical life will cease to exist, but when the threat is rooted in the violence that will precede death. In fact, to be sure, the act of killing is what an individual responds to. The threat of killing assures the oppressor that social death status is possible. In some ways, the threat is an acknowledgment of the oppressed's humanity even as the oppressor shows no respect for that humanity. In the literary works, songs, and visual media that I analyze, African descendants, like those who jumped into the Atlantic, resist succumbing to physical and social death and thus affirm the value of their lives as they submit to a conversion experience. Following cues of contemporary African-descended storytellers, including writers, filmmakers, and performers, I explore forms of death in their work and the ways they show resistance to facets of power and subsequently an identity as a "nonperson."

Although I focus primarily on twentieth and twenty-first century African American artists in *Reimagining the Middle Passage,* the slavery era, at times, figures prominently as a means for analyzing the intervention of power in Black lives. Looking back at the era becomes necessary to revisit the meaning of life and the Middle Passage as a symbol for death and as a site conversion. For African-descended writers of the Atlantic South, social death involves alienation as a sociopolitical status. Black people, regardless of their social status—for example, their economic status or educational background—may seek to embrace life, but the people in positions of power will not allow them equal access. In other words, life becomes a privilege as social death is a consequence of the lack of a privileged life. White citizens who are in positions of power economically and politically enjoy privileges that place their lives at an elevated social value. Moreover, they deem themselves socially supreme (as opposed to intellectually or spiritually supreme) and assume the right, usually by force, to kill members of the African-descended community or threaten to kill members of the community. In this context and under these circumstances, a "nonperson" is treated and perceived as not being worthy of equal treatment, for example, having access to education, clean water, well-paying jobs, health care, rescue from disasters, and so on. They are treated like a body—dispensable and replaceable by another body; undeserving of access and, in too many cases, deserving of a violent death/killing, if the body refuses to work or to follow the rules. Some may also come to think of themselves as inferior, as Patterson suggests. However, treatment based on the perception that leads to the status of social death means that the one considered a socially dead (non)person has to either accept this status or reject it. This study illuminates the moments and various forms of rejection and resistance expressed by African descendants when their lives are threatened and their humanity negated.

For the African descendants placed in the position of subjugation, there is an opportunity to redefine the meaning of life in opposition to the status of social death and to affirm personhood. Consider Frederick Douglass, who rejected social death status as he affirmed the humanity of African descendants in his speech "What to the Slave Is the Fourth of July?" He presented the limits placed on African descendants, ones that relegate them to the status of socially dead within the white supremacist paradigm: "Are the great principles of political freedom and of natural justice, embodied in that Declaration of Independence, extended to us?" (63). He goes further to reveal the privileges that he and Blacks do not enjoy: "The rich inheritance of justice, liberty, prosperity and independence, bequeathed by your fathers, is shared by you, not by me. The sunlight that brought light and healing to you, has brought stripes and death to me." Shifting his attention to establishing that indeed, the subjugation that occurs is of one human over another, he assesses the purposes of relevant laws:

> Must I undertake to prove that the slave is a man? That point is conceded already. Nobody doubts it. The slaveholders themselves acknowledge it in the enactment of laws for their government. They acknowledge it when they punish disobedience on the part of the slave. There are seventy-two crimes in the State of Virginia which, if committed by a black man (no matter how ignorant he be), subject him to the punishment of death; while only two of the same crimes will subject a white man to the like punishment. *What is this but the acknowledgment that the slave is a moral, intellectual, and responsible being? The manhood of the slave is conceded. It is admitted in the fact that Southern statute books are covered with enactments forbidding, under severe fines and penalties, the teaching of the slave to read or to write.* When you can point to any such laws in reference to the beasts of the field, then I may consent to argue the manhood of the slave. When the dogs in your streets, when the fowls of the air, when the cattle on your hills, when the fish of the sea, and the reptiles that crawl, shall be unable to distinguish the slave from a brute, then will *I argue with you that the slave is a man!* (65; italics mine)

I have highlighted where Douglass boldly pointed to the hypocrisy of white supremacy by describing the practice of enacting laws that can only govern people and not animals. Douglass succeeds in reminding his White listeners that the privileges they enjoy and the rights that they have ascribed only to themselves are an act against humanity. To be sure, he gives an analysis of white supremacy. Their actions, as Douglass points out, are against "moral, intellectual, and responsible" beings, which are humanistic values (66). He leaves no doubt that the maker of the laws acknowledges that the subject of the laws is, in fact, a person and cannot be considered otherwise. Social death status has much to do with not simply how a person is treated, but

how the person perceives the self. As Douglass, a man freed by his own voli-
tion, refused to swallow wholesale the idea of a socially dead nonperson by
challenging the idea of social death, so did others. Douglass shows that being
treated as though a powerless nonhuman does not make it so.

Douglass's ability to write and speak in public is an exercise of prophecy.
Through his resistance of social death, he gives voice to the dead. As M. NourbeSe Philip emphasizes, the case of the Zong did not deal with the humanity
of African people but focused on the loss of cargo. Laws that protected the sale
of people as commodities did not provide protection otherwise. Within a five-
year period, high-profiled killings of African Americans—such as Trayvon
Martin (2012) and Jordan Davis (2012) in Florida; Renisha McBride (2013) in
a Detroit suburb; Eric Garner (2014) in New York; Tamir Rice (2014) in Cleve-
land; Michael Brown (2014) in Ferguson, Missouri; Philando Castile (2016) in
Minnesota; and Alton Sterling (2016) in Baton Rouge, Louisiana—inspired
national and international questions about the value of Black people in the
United States (and other countries)[5] and the devaluing of Black life. In so
doing, within Black consciousness, a contemporary fear of death at the hands
of White fellow citizens has surfaced that psychically connects one generation
of African descendants to the past, and, like them, the younger generation
begins to assess just how precarious life is, especially their lives. Although
their threat of death is not from contact with water, the American consciousness taps into the historical narrative and judges these Black bodies as punish-
able, valueless, replaceable, a theme emerging from events that occurred long
before they were born.

RESISTANCE IN THE MIDDLE PASSAGE

Water's presence in the historical lives of African descendants signals the
moment when beginnings and endings collide. Humans' resistance to this
moment is inevitable. To be sure, resistance to captivity occurred often and
in some cases, as soon as Africans were taken from their homes and then
dragged aboard ships on the African coast. In a comprehensive study on
shipboard insurrections by African captives, Eric Robert Taylor finds that
there were "hundreds—perhaps thousands—of . . . incidents that took place
throughout the history of the slave trade" (1). He goes on to note that he found

---

5. Inspired by the Black Lives Matter movement in the United States, movements began
in Toronto, Canada, Ghana, and London and among Ethiopians in Israel and Palestinians in
Garza. For one source, see Janaya Khan's article "Black Lives Matter Has Become a National
Movement" in Root.com.

at least four hundred cases that occurred in the eighteenth century alone and that "it is highly likely that revolts of varying magnitude occurred on slave ships at least once a month on average" (3). One of the most well known is the case of the *Amistad*. In violation of international treaties that were in place in 1839, Africans were taken from Sierra Leone on a ship bound for Cuba. During the voyage, the enslaved killed the ship's captain and a crewman. Not knowing how to properly navigate, they veered off their desired destination and ended up off the coast of New York, where they were seized and detained until U.S. courts decided who had authority over their bodies. A remaining thirty-five were eventually allowed to return to their homeland. Taylor notes, "Insurrection is shown to have been one of the only viable options for resistance open to slave rebels on ships, in spite of the seemingly overwhelming array of obstacles set up to defeat it" (4). Surely the loss of home and a longing to return home—a place of belonging and comfort—motivated acts of resistance and would continue to from one generation to the next. I would argue further that there was absolutely no barrier that could prevent the captives' desire to maintain their identity as people deserving of freedom.

As a consequence of the Middle Passage and related beliefs, social death is challenged by conversion. Conversion is possible as a form of resistance to social death. In particular, literature of the African diaspora preserves attempts to "reclaim" alienated rights as a form of rebirth. From the stories of ancestors passed down from generation to generation until written, a dialectic forms that allows the oral and written forms to converge. The result is a confrontation of this traumatic history. Writers of African descent have found ways in their fictional work and poetry to deal with the tensions largely resulting from the movement over the Atlantic. Writers, in particular, help us to understand that rebirth may also entail a reconstruction of a personal narrative that involves connecting the present self with whatever self still exists from the past through family history, memories of stories, and so on. What is commonly seen in the body of work produced by authors of African descent who engage water thematically is the changed self, or as Daniel M. Scott III puts it, "a re-configuration of the self" (645).

For the purposes of this study, I refer to the re-configuration as a conversion experience. Albert Raboteau defines conversion as being "not just a change in behavior but metanoia, a change of heart, a transformation in consciousness—a radical reorientation of personality, exemplified in the stories of St. Paul the Apostle and the St. Augustine of Hippo as a life changing event" (152–53). While mine is not a religious study, especially not the study of Christianity, religious studies scholarship provides me with appropriate language for probing the meaning of the "re-configuration of the self," or the changes detected in identity from one point of life or in life to another. Once removed from the place of origin, the "travelers" were not the same. In truth, conversion results in a rebirth of identity, a transformation of the self that may encompass some aspects of the past identity. Further, based on a moment of a revelatory experience, identity evolves into a new identity. Raboteau's understanding of conversion speaks to the construction of the African diaspora in the Atlantic world—its various cultures, religious practices, and languages that developed as a result of the transatlantic voyage and the peoples' survival through the treacherous Middle Passage. Conversion, spurned by trauma in this context, is analogous to transcendence—the mind's ability to move from its present state to another merged state, making it possible to move beyond one's pain and suffering, perhaps to shift the pain and trauma to another space where creativity and/or resistance resides, for instance. Those who reimagine what occurs in the Middle Passage and as a result of the Middle Passage experiment with a double consciousness probe the reality of existing in one state while simultaneously experiencing another state. Ultimately, conversion or transformation is the result of resistance that represents the longings of humanity and its capacity to survive being present in multiple states at the same time.

African descendants recognize water as a medium for the "transformation of consciousness." As I will discuss further, conversion has been documented as occurring within the Middle Passage—a historical and/or symbolic site, including the Atlantic Ocean and its connection to Africa to the global Atlantic South and the presence of floodwaters in Black communities. Engagement with water can lead to social change just as submersion in water can lead to spiritual redemption. Conversion or rebirth is a mental, psychological experience that has spiritual implications. Documenting African spiritual beliefs in the intersection of God, water, and death, Robert Farris Thompson explains the cosmology of the Kongo (a kingdom located in west central Africa) and the survival of their beliefs in the African diaspora. Quoting scholar Wyatt MacGaffey, he describes the Kongo Cosmogram:

> The simplest ritual space is a Green cross marked on the ground, as for oath taking. One line represents the boundary; the other is ambivalently both the path leading across the boundary, as to the cemetery; and the vertical path of power linking "the above" with "the below." This relationship, in turn, is polyvalent, since it refers to God and man, God and the dead, and the living and the dead. The person taking the oath stands upon the cross, situating himself between life and death, and invokes the judgment of God and the dead upon himself. (Thompson 108)

He goes on to note that the fork in the road, or the crossroads, is the "point of intersection between the ancestors and the living" (109). Finally, for our purposes, "God is imagined at the top, the dead at the bottom, and water in between" (109). In this vein, it is possible to see how Africans, seeing their experience from a different lens, may have seen the Atlantic as a "middle passage" linking the spiritual space between God and man, the living and the dead. While I am not suggesting that African-descended writers or artists knew of or used specific Kongo beliefs and practices to construct their work, it stands to reason that those beliefs and similar ones that survived the Middle Passage have had their influences on the songs and folklore that are present in some form and that have found their way to written stories and other forms of Black art.

OVERVIEW

If the Middle Passage emerges as a major recurring theme in works by writers of the African diaspora, then scholars are compelled to identify and analyze the significance of the theme in such works. In addition to Patterson and JanMohamed, *Reimagining the Middle Passage* is in conversation with Anissa Janine Wardi's *Water and African American Memory: An Ecocritical Perspective,* which "takes into account the politics and the poetry of water in the African American expressive tradition" (4). To achieve this, she uses ecocriticism to explicate African American literature and films to critique, among other issues, "the connection between racism, colonization, and environmental degradation" (16). Wardi's study is useful in its discussion of water: by "tracing a connection to the past, African American writers evoke a transatlantic history in which language, and by extension their literary works, are given life through water" (10). However, even though my interdisciplinary study briefly overlaps with hers in our interest in Hurricane Katrina (Wardi dedicates her conclusion to this event) and Wright's "Down by the Riverside," our theoretical interests differ significantly, showing the myriad of approaches and perspectives on the impact engagement with water has had on people of African descent. Indeed, our studies open inquiry into the impact and significance of water within historical African diasporic imaginations.

Reimagining the Middle Passage has a particular focus on the region I refer to as the Atlantic Global South, which includes, for our purposes, the coastal states of Louisiana, Mississippi, and South Carolina and, to a lesser degree, the Caribbean—regions that have been considerably impacted by the transatlantic slave trade. In his consideration of the American South's connection to the

Caribbean, John Lowe observes, "One of the salutary effects of transnational-ism/globalization has been the rethinking of nation and national boundar-ies" (*Calypso Magnolia* 54). While Lowe argues for the conceptualization of the American South as the "northern rim of the Caribbean," I see the "salu-tary effects" as stemming from the transportation of African bodies over the Atlantic (54). Historical movement between West African coastal ports, the Caribbean, the U.S. eastern shore, and the southern coastal areas of the United States has resulted in the relocation of African peoples who have made their homes in the Atlantic Global South. Consequently, regions that were once exclusively occupied by indigenous peoples—who had their own set of values and traditions—have been transformed by the influence of European coloniz-ers and African peoples, making the coastal region a place where old cultures merged and new cultures emerged.

To probe the presence of the Middle Passage and its historical and con-temporary meaning to African descendants, I am interested in the intersec-tion between literature, song lyrics, films, documentaries, and television to tell complex, overlapping stories. However, literature anchors this project. Con-version is most obvious in literature, where conflict and development occurs. Further, as this is an interdisciplinary project, I draw upon critical literary theory, African American cultural studies, and Atlantic world history, as well as concepts from religious studies, to inform my close analysis of the pri-mary texts. Such an approach allows for consideration of how written, visual, and oral texts dialogue with one another to show the fluidity and emergence of diverse cultural identities, and to facilitate consideration of how identities across the Atlantic Global South are interdependent at certain points. In con-versation with songs, African-descended writers from across different times and places—whether conscious or unconscious—use storytelling techniques to explore states of being, where life lingers in the physical state but longs for a connection to the spiritual state. Song and narrative act as markers for what is past, and what fades, but is never completely gone. In other words, memory keeps the narrative of the one passed on in existence.

This study is divided into two parts based on the Middle Passage recre-ations and reimaginings and the legacy of the Middle Passage, through engage-ment with water in the South. From the introduction through chapter 4, I examine African descendants' representations of the Middle Passage in work set in and influenced by the history of enslavement in the U.S. South. I begin with the period of transformation by water, where its intersection with death and suffering emanates hauntingly from the subconscious and the conscious-ness of African descendants. In chapter 1, I engage with select poetry, fiction, film, and art that is rooted in the Atlantic Global South and that attempts to capture the horrific experience of travel through the Middle Passage. Olaudah Equiano's *The Interesting Narrative of the Life of Olaudah Equiano or Gustavus Vassa* serves as an ancestral text for contemporary fiction writers and poets whose work reimagines the meaning of the Middle Passage to the descendants of those who survived. Equiano makes prominent, through the writing of the narrative itself, forms of resistance as he speaks to the humanity of African captives, for example, their ties to family, governing practices, purpose in naming, relationship with their land, and so on. Therefore, chapter 1 provides historical and theoretical context for considering just what the Middle Passage is and why it is that the voyage figures so prominently in work by twentieth- and twenty-first-century African-descended writers and artists.

In chapter 2, I begin with the first novel known to revisit the Middle Passage and to return African Americans to an African home. My concern in this chapter is to explore Kunta's story, not as a work of fact, but as Alex Haley's attempt to use storytelling to create one's self as an act of resistance. Haley's groundbreaking historical novel, *Roots: An American Saga,* was the first to place Blacks in American history and to introduce Blacks into the popular imagination as contributors to the development of America when it debuted in 1976. The following year, its television adaptation introduced millions more to an African American experience that they otherwise may not have thought about had it not been for Haley's interest in tracing his paternal ancestral line and constructing a historical story for public consumption. In May 2016, cable television presented a "reimagining" of the story of Kunta Kinte and his ancestors, proving that Haley's attempt to connect Blacks with a heritage that would make them proud was still a concern for the Black Lives Matter generation in the twenty-first-century age of mass protests stemming from the public murders of unarmed Black men by police. Movement through the Middle Passage is certainly a transformative experience for Kunta, but it does not make him a slave disconnected from his past. Kunta's resistance to social death through his attempts to deny his status as an American slave under a new name resonates as a theme from the novel to the adaptations.

Chapters 3 and 4 focus on African descendants' resistance to social death and the subsequent meanings of life that emerge from contact with the Middle Passage and its connection to New Orleans, a southern port city with African influences and a gateway to the Atlantic Global South in America. Relying on historical memory to construct lived experience, Charles Johnson and Jewell Parker Rhodes present characters as being empowered and transformed, rather than irretrievably oppressed by the Middle Passage experience. More specifically, my concern in chapter 3 is to explore how a return to the Middle Passage as a geographical space and temporal space of metaphorical discovery serves as a site for the development of Black masculine identity, which emerges from the overlapping perspectives and experiences of fathers and sons, despite the threat of social death as represented in Johnson's novel and the series *Treme*. In chapter 3, Charles Johnson's *The Middle Passage* responds to and expands Equiano's narrative. Johnson's protagonist, Calhoun, converts from a self-centered man who was abandoned by his enslaved father and feels that he has little self-worth to become a father figure and sensitive hero. I place him in conversation with the HBO series *Treme* and its depiction of a father and son relationship set against the backdrop of jazz and masking in New Orleans culture in the four years after Hurricane Katrina. Although the writers of the show are mostly White, they draw from a culture highly influenced by Africans who survived the Middle Passage and the experiences of those who survived Katrina. Christina Achman argues that "black television artists and producers . . . locate effective resistance in an effort to control black images" (xv). To some extent, this may be true of HBO's *Treme* where Black performers depict how some Black residents worked against the trauma of being treated like they are socially dead by engaging in African-influenced practices (e.g., jazz, Mardi Gras Indian masking) as they also work to recover their damaged homes and fractured communities.

While chapter 3 offers up men's experiences, chapter 4 focuses on the popular cultural icon Marie Laveau. In this chapter, I argue that Marie's act of seeking her identity and finding that she is a legacy of the Middle Passage, in fact is a cultural medium between Africa and the enslaved in America, shows a successful attempt to defy social death, but this is only made possible when she understands her possessed performance in relation to the story of her maternal past. In her novel, Jewell Parker Rhodes uses African-based religious practices of Voodoo to highlight the ways in which Black women relied on these practices to assert forms of liberation that resisted racism and gender oppression in an early nineteenth-century New Orleans. Marie resists social death as she searches for her identity and insists on following her ancestral calling for the good of the African descendants in her community.

In her poem "History," Brenda Marie Osbey's anonymous speaker states, "and so we begin again our weary wearied and wearying lessons / because we have not learned them well" (190). Part I takes up the question of what happens when lessons are not learned as I probe the Middle Passage as a metaphor, more specifically its implications and consequences to African descendants in the South. In this section, I look at African descendants' resistance to social death in response to the deadly presence of water in Black artistic work set in the twentieth and twenty-first century. Links to the Middle Passage as a traumatic space, or where "for us / all oceans are red" (Osbey, "History" 190), become evident when used as a lens to analyze more recent events, such as the neglect of Black people during the aftermath of Hurricane Katrina, over fifty years after the floods that ravaged communities in 1927, inspiring the emergence of flood blues by Black artists. This section probes how they define their lives at a critical moment of realization despite the oppressors' attempts to belittle their lives. It also probes the deliberate use of storytelling by Black folks as testimony, as creative form, and in song to immortalize life and to move beyond death. In these works, we find that what has a beginning does not necessarily have an end. Contemporary writers show how the Middle Passage is still in motion.

Chapters 5 and 6 probe how flooding uncovers race and class disparities, which, I argue, emerge from the Middle Passage. As with the Middle Passage, residents find themselves losing their homes and, possibly, members of their families. In chapter 5, I argue that flooding and its impact on poor Black communities shows the legacy of the Middle Passage. If the Middle Passage shows racism as the devaluing of Black life in favor of valuing Black bodies, then stories documented in Wright's "Down by the Riverside" and flood blues serve as twentieth-century reminders of that history. More specifically, I analyze blues songs and literature that deal with Blacks' traumatic contact with water as the result of flooding and the physical deaths that occur as a consequence of the lack of adequate preparation for such natural disasters. Here we see the relationship between white supremacy and social death as experienced historically and remembered by African descendants in music and literature. Richard Wright's "Down by the Riverside" depicts Mann, a father who desperately tries to save his family when the flood of 1927 drives them from their home and who must undergo a conversion experience in the process. Further, I place Wright in conversation with flood blues that emerged in response to the impact water had on poor Black communities of the South in 1927.

Wright calls to Jesmyn Ward. In response to Wright, Ward presents a novel that begins with the absence of a mother who died in childbirth, just as occurs in Wright's short story. Undergirded by testimonies of African descendants who faced Hurricane Katrina floodwaters, chapter 6 places documentaries, such as Spike Lee's *When the Levees Broke,* in conversation with Jesmyn Ward's novel *Salvage the Bones,* set in rural Mississippi during Hurricane Katrina. Ward and the documentarians show the transformative impact of flooding on the potentially socially dead residents of segregated, poor, southern Black communities and highlight the significance of their experiences. Lee's documentary provides testimonies and observations from African Americans who survived Katrina. Through Lee's lens, we find what Herman Gray argues: "cultural representations by African Americans, while occasionally myopic and exclusive, are also crucial political moves against racism and white supremacy, sexism, and class inequality" (3). In flood narratives and songs, I argue that spaces of destruction become symbolic of the Middle Passage site of trauma.

Chapter 7 is particularly congruent with Haley's *Roots*. His work asks, What does storytelling do for people of African descent? What is the relationship between storytelling and transformation? In the age of DNA ancestry testing, chapter 7 returns to these questions more specifically as I analyze the meaning of the myths that deal with return to Africa by flight over the Atlantic. I argue that Paule Marshall's Aunt Cuney uses myth to present a counter-discourse to the Middle Passage experience in an effort to reset the lens from victimization to empowerment. Further, Marshall's work *Praisesong for the Widow* makes use of the idea of return and a re-configured self as a form of resistance, I argue, to social death. Her characters, Avey and Aunt Cuney, embrace an African identity that has been suppressed as a result of the slave trade. In an effort to resist this history, they "return" "home" to Africa in memory through storytelling and dancing. Focusing on storytelling in the American South and its connection to the Caribbean symbolically helps to recover history from the perspective of African descendants. Marshall's return and her transformation to a "re-configured self" echoes the work of Alex Haley and recalls the purpose Haley undertook in the writing of *Roots*.

I conclude by exploring the act of forgiveness as a response to racially motivated trauma. Just two days after the 2015 mass shooting at a predominantly Black church in Charleston, South Carolina, occurred, the victims' relatives expressed forgiveness for the killer. Forgiveness, I argue, is a tenet of humanity and is in direct opposition to the idea that social death has pervaded the consciousness of African descendants. Further, forgiveness is a sign of conversion and an expression of resistance. It requires a change of consciousness from anger to compassion for one who, particularly in this case, hoped to incite a "race war." Forgiveness, then, is a choice to empower the African descendant and to disempower the white supremacist agenda.

My primary concern in this book is to map the ways in which the Middle Passage serves as a historical and symbolic site for physical and spiritual travel and as a catalyst for destruction and creation. As such, African descendants acknowledge that the Middle Passage has not only developed and shaped Black communities, cultures, and identities in the Americas but that language has been carefully extracted from the Middle Passage to voice the painful process of survival and change. At such times, African descendants express their humanity through subtle and overt acts of resistance. This study is an analysis of (1) how writers of the African diaspora rely on and depart from oral traditions; (2) how literature, in conversation with visual and audio media, gives voice to oppression and forms of resistance and; (3) the purpose of the experience to its descendants. As they depict refusals to stay in states of oppression, we may also discern patterns of healing from the writers and their characters. African-descended artists, writers, and performers query the purpose of the Middle Passage experience in an effort to move forward. *Reimagining the Middle Passage: Black Resistance in Literature, Television, and Song* considers how and why.

PART I

IN THE MIDDLE PASSAGE

CHAPTER 1

Understanding the Middle Passage

RELIVING the horrific experience of those housed in the Superdome during the peak hours of Hurricane Katrina and several days after requires a visceral imaginary moment that has been documented as reality by those—mostly African descendants—who were in New Orleans. Just a few blocks from the Mississippi River, where Africans were brought into the city and generations of their descendants were sold, the loss of life that occurred as a result of the floods and the circumstances that sent people to the location of "the 'dome,'" unfortunately, are eerily resonant of the Middle Passage. It is no wonder, then, that contemporary African-descended writers and artists continue to see water as an iteration of the Middle Passage and as a site for forms of death. Seeking to understand its meaning, to exorcise the consciousness of trauma, is a major part of resistance and the movement toward rebirth.

The Middle Passage is a mappable, geographical site, a watery pathway over a vast ocean that people used to transport goods from Africa, Europe, the Caribbean, and the Americas. Yet, it is more, and this study intends to analyze the nuances of the long-ranging impact of what occurred within the geographical space and the legacy of the occurrences. My purpose here is to look at the physical, temporal, and psychological experience of the Middle Passage. Expanding the work of Maria Diedrich, Henry Louis Gates Jr., and Carl Pedersen, I see the Middle Passage as extended past the transatlantic slave trade that ended in the nineteenth century. In the introduction of *Black Imagination and the Middle Passage,* the authors argue,

Instead of looking at the Middle Passage as a phenomenon of constricted space and limited time, the essays collected here extend its meaning to the relationship of African Americans to their past, from the hierarchical spatial relationships of above/below (deck of the slave ship and its hold) and center/periphery . . . to the syncretic space-in-between that links geographical and cultural regions. (9)

While there may be a discernible beginning to the historical Middle Passage, the ways in which it has had an impact on those involved and their descendants cannot be measured by a linear time paradigm. Michelle Wright argues, "It is this continuity that is the problem, the linking of events through a logic bound by cause and effect that ties the past to the present and provides direction for the future" (19).

In the creative reimaginings, answers to two questions emerge. First, what is the Middle Passage? Historians have provided numerous studies on the physical aspects of the Middle Passage, including when it occurred and what, according to ships' logs and other documents, occurred during the Atlantic voyages. Yet, what is missing from those is an understanding and acknowledgment of the interiority of the African captives, considered Black cargo, who were rendered voiceless and valued only for their bodies. Contemporary writers and artists have sought to fill in the gaps of the missing voices by imagining human engagement with terror. Through their work, we can begin to "construct a cultural map of African America [that] would arguably reveal the varying degrees of cultural survival" (Diedrich et al. 8).

Second, what is the purpose of theorizing the Middle Passage, particularly in artistic forms? I would argue that the writers and artists map Black survival, but advocate for moving past a stage of survival to actual living. In other words, how do you move past the pain of trauma that is designed to keep a person stagnant in merely surviving through a series of negotiations with traumatic experiences? In searching for an answer to this question, the writers and artists rely on cultural practices. "An African American concept of space had its beginnings in the holds of the slave ships during the Middle Passage and appears in different settings, such as the relationship between clandestine slave religious practices and the dominant center of the plantations in the United States and Caribbean" (Diedrich et al. 8). What rises out of the space of trauma gives voice to pain and allows descendants to go to where it happened to understand how the ancestors dealt with the reoccurring moments at the site of trauma, moments that would continue long after movement through the geographical space. I am not arguing that the authors and the artists seek to know why, for this may be impossible to ascertain, but they do discover "what" happened and "how," and in some instances, through naming, they can give voice to these aspects through a "who." Perhaps more importantly, they seek to find meaning in the reality. Yes, government-sanctioned Christian-approved atrocities occurred, but what does that mean for the survivors and their descendants? Giving voice, then, empowers the writer and artist as they give evidence of some form of triumph, even if it is through the conversion experience and how the subject refuses to be defeated by trauma, even if changed by it. The overview of fiction, poetry, and film that I provide in this chapter illuminates works that stand as legacies of empowerment.

THE MIDDLE PASSAGE

African descendants in America owe their existence largely to the survival of those Africans who were brought through the Middle Passage—the journey between West Africa and the Americas. Without question, traveling across the Atlantic, regardless of the circumstances, particularly at a time when maritime travel was still in its infancy, could result in the deaths of some of the ship's inhabitants, Europeans and Africans alike. Stephanie Smallwood summarizes the kinds of conditions that led to illness and death:

> Exhaustion, malnutrition, fear, and seasickness resulted in depressed immune systems and increased vulnerability to disease. Particularly among the African prisoners, crowding, poor hygiene, and often contaminated food and water supplies, together made the slave ship a breeding ground for airborne pathogens (smallpox and tuberculosis) as well as those spread via fecal-to-oral pathways (bacillary and amoebic dysentery) or by direct physical contact (yaws). (136)

Perceived as sites for death among West Africans, the "slave ships were appropriately called 'tumbeiros' in the eighteenth-century Angolan trade," translated as "floating tombs" or "undertakers" (Smallwood 137). Fear of death on the vessels that took captives on an unknown journey, then, was prominent among African communities by the time the slave trade reached its peak in the eighteenth century.

Staving off death for the purpose of making as much profit as possible from the sale of the human cargo was a priority for the captain. To meet their goals, captains devised ways to preserve the lives of all involved. Using records from the *Diligent,* a ship that transported West African captives to the Caribbean, Robert Harms provides details of how the ship's captain followed the maritime recommendations. Best recommendations mandated that enslaved Africans, while chained together on the "slave deck," have access to a toilet in the form of a bucket that was to be emptied twice during the night. They were to be provided with three meals and a small amount of drinking water at least three times a day. At times, water seeped into the area during storms, bringing with it the possibility of drowning. Ironically, some scientists have come to believe that the African captives who were able to retain water are the ones who survived the journey.[1]

Harms and other scholars make clear that as early as the Middle Passage journey, Africans were forced to act as laborers and to participate in their degradation. Two to three days a week, they were given access to water for bathing and cleaning the slave deck. Exercise on the deck occurred frequently and was designed to avoid depression and melancholy. As such, captives were required to dance to the music played by the sailors, which often emanated from African instruments. Surely the cacophony of confused, chaotic sounds added to the agony felt by African peoples who had been abruptly taken from their homes. All of these measures could not be confused as attempts at humanity; they were meant to prevent the loss of profit for the self-proclaimed owners of the Black bodies.[2]

Based on perception of threat, men and women were treated differently. Depending on the commander, enslaved men were not shackled once they were on the high sea as it was believed that they were not likely to rebel. Believing that women were not capable of overwhelming the ship's crew, they were not shackled either. However, they were subjected to cruel experiences as they were made to serve the men in various ways, including sexual gratification through rape. Mistreatment is immeasurable. It is difficult to imagine the long-term psychological and spiritual effects of being perceived as nonpersons in human form and its impact on those African captives. Death on some level is almost certain.

WATER AND THE SPIRIT

What does water mean within the context of the Middle Passage? For African people, travel across the ocean distorted the meaning of water to African

---

1. A legacy of this, according to Damon Tweedy's study on race and medicine, is that these survivors suffered from major health disparities as they "passed on their genes, which later proved problematic in the modern world" (72).

2. Yet, rebellions—a form of resistance against eminent death—occurred at least 30 percent of the time (Harms 315).

societies. Bodies of water have significant meaning in African religious beliefs. For example, the Ogbuide of Oguta Lake in Igboland of Nigeria believe that the water goddess could provide life through fertility to those who respect and worship her. She could also sustain life by, for example, watering the banks of the river for the nourishment of the soil. If feminine beings are thought to produce life, then it makes sense that the river would often be considered a mother figure, as in Mammy Wata, who has similar characteristics as Ogbuide and is part of African spiritual beliefs on the continent and across the diaspora. The Akan of Ghana saw the Atlantic as a deity as well and honored it by not fishing on a day of the week. For many enslaved Africans, bodies of water were sacred and held a special place in the lives of the people who relied on the water to sustain their physical and spiritual lives and, more importantly, their communities.

Therefore, as they traveled across the Atlantic, we can imagine that some may have seen the Atlantic as a connection to the sacred. Robert Farris Thompson's work on Kongo beliefs confirms this. They may not have been consumed by a sense of physical danger, but may have thought that they were in the constant presence of a supreme being that was watching out for them as they dealt with alien threats, in the form of Europeans, to their lives. Jewell Parker Rhodes draws on beliefs in Damballah, a father figure who resides in bodies of water in the form of a snake that traveled from Africa to America (see chapter 4). Bodies of water continued to represent a connection to home (West Africa). As I discuss in chapter 7, there is evidence that some Africans had no sense that they were geographically disconnected from their homeland when they reached the United States, but instead physically sought to return to Africa, a home that was with them in their mind and spirit. Transmigration of the soul, also a means for return, may occur by attempts to let go of the physical self and to move through a gateway, perhaps by falling overboard into the Atlantic, allowing the soul the opportunity to walk or fly back to Africa. Such an act is resistance to a physical state of being.

As time passed on the ship, a process of conversion occurred. Smallwood notes that "the slave ship at sea reduced African captives to an existence so physically atomized as to silence all but the most elemental bodily articulation, so socially impoverished as to threaten annihilation of the self, the complete disintegration of personhood" (125). Humans, including the captives, kept time by the rising of the sun at day and the moon at night. In Africa, they marked seasons by the rise and fall of the river, which signaled the time for planting and picking. The meaning of water to the everyday life of the captives would have been absent. However, water had meaning—its significance evolved into a layer of feelings and emotions steeped in trauma and renewal. On board the ship, days would have passed without a sense of seasons. Monotony would have led to a sense of loss and disorientation. And, as a result, mental death would occur, not to be confused with social death. Survival itself is an act of resistance. Consequently, the captive has not lost a connection to the origin of birth.

RELIVING THE MIDDLE PASSAGE

Memories become rooted to the water and the past associations with water and time merged with the present engagement with water and time. Morrison explores this in *Beloved* as Sethe tries to explain the relationship between memory and place:

> Some things go. Pass on. Some things just stay. I used to think it was my rememory. . . . Some things you never forget. Places, places are still there. If a house burns down, it's gone, but the place—the picture of it—stays, and not just in my rememory, but also out there in the world. What I remember is a floating around out there outside my head. I mean, even if I don't think it, even if I die, the picture of what I did, or knew, or saw is still out there. Right in the place where it happened. (36)

Whether historical events are acknowledged or not, they continue to exist in the place where they occurred. Nature never forgets, and the same can be said of humans who rely so heavily on water and land to survive physically. As seen in the work of African descendants, water as a spiritual site that stores memories makes its connection to human emotions tangible and remarkable.

African-descended artists and writers provide us with opportunities to engage the significance of death on a personal level and the subsequent need for resistance to forms of death; they call to us to tap into certain emotions and to imagine that the experience of one just may be our own experience too. Olaudah Equiano, in *The Interesting Narrative of Olaudah Equiano or Gustavus Vassa* (1789), provides the earliest written memory of the Middle Passage. Through writing, Equiano projects an emotional appeal that stands as a form of resistance to the horrific experience suffered not only by him as an individual but also by others who endured what became known as the Middle Passage. His talent, among others, is his ability to connect the senses; he moves effortlessly from expressing a child's fear to describing why that fear is reasonable. He describes the suffocating "closeness of the place, and the heat of the climate" to help readers to understand the feeling of closeness in the hold of the ship, where "each had scarcely room to turn himself" (Equiano 159). We can imagine, then, that there was a profound sense of claustrophobia as people who did not know each other were forced to share an enclosed space that had no respect for its human inhabitants. He moves from touch to "the sounds and the smell" by noting "the shrieks of the women, and the groans of the dying" (Equiano 159). Equiano issues a call, an invitation to share a painful, harrowing memory.

Beyond the sounds of the torture and the emotions of the enslaved, there is resistance. According to Equiano,

> when we had a smooth sea and moderate wind, two of my wearied countrymen who were chained together (I was near them at the time), preferring death to such a life of misery, somehow made through the nettings and jumped into the sea. (159)

Equiano offers a counter-discourse to suicide as a reaction to the trauma of enslavement. His description appears as a slight reference to suicide, especially to Western readers, but when viewed within the context of the literature and cultural experiences of people of African descent, as discussed earlier, the water may serve as a medium for crossing over to another life. Monica Schuler observes,

> The narratives' and rituals' symbolism locates the slave and immigrant experience in the context of West and West Central African beliefs in parallel worlds of the living (blacks) and the dead (whites), separated by a mirror-like surface or a permeable body of water which empowered people could cross. (193)

We may believe, then, that this reference to those who chose to live by jumping rather than to face a certain death is not simply an escape from misery, but the opportunity to "cross over" to a "world of living." Poet and cultural critic Brenda Marie Osbey sees death in New Orleans Voodoo in a similar way:

> As a child, I was taught that in the Land of the Dead, all of my own family was waiting to welcome me. It didn't matter that I didn't know them before because they knew me and always had and would not fail to claim me. That's the thing about Death. Through it we are restored to our True People, our True Place, our True Home, our Ideal City. We are made whole. And that's the point. ("Why" 9)

Equiano shows an embrace of the ancestral home, as his "country men" defy threat of physical death and potential social death. Logically speaking, they only knew of their present state, and their reaction is likely more to the tortures they were facing in that moment. Fearing an unknown future would certainly prompt a need to control the outcome, to seize power in the assertion of choice. If only empowered by enacting their preference, the nameless Africans memorialized in the personal narrative of the impressionable Equiano chose to sacrifice themselves to the water goddess and to cross from one world to the other, where family awaited them.

Although his narrative gives voice to the 12 million, what if this was not his own experience? Vincent Carretta argues that there is evidence that Equiano was not born in Africa and therefore did not have the Middle Passage experience that he describes as his own. Carretta demonstrates this by referencing documents that state Equiano's place of birth as South Carolina and not Africa.[3] Equiano's narrative is not just the prototype of the American slave narrative, as Henry Louis Gates Jr. has convincingly argued, it is also part of the tradition of memories that are told as a form of resistance against social death status projected upon the captives by European oppressors and as a means to empower the subject of the story. Of the debate, historian Marcus Rediker provides a compelling conclusion:

> If he was born in South Carolina he could have known what he knew only by gathering the lore and experience of people who had been born in Africa and made the dreaded Middle Passage aboard the slave ship. He thus becomes the oral historian, the keeper of the common story, the griot of sorts, of the slave trade, which means that his account is no less faithful to the original experience, only different in its sources and genesis. . . . He was the voice for the voiceless. (109)

Storytelling cannot rely on absolute truth to determine authenticity. Arguments about whether or not he was actually born in Africa and endured the experience of being kidnapped from his home at the age of eleven and surviving the brutality of the transatlantic journey firmly places his text, I argue, in the tradition of storytelling. Whether or not Equiano had this experience, I do not know, and neither do the African-descended writers and artists who have relied on his work to construct theirs. What is important to the ongoing

---

3. In a detailed response, Paul E. Lovejoy in his article "Autobiography and Memory" challenges Carretta by establishing that Equiano's knowledge of Iboland authenticates his African identity. Without dismissing Equiano's narrative as inauthentic, Rediker succeeds in establishing him as a voice for the African presence in the South, particularly South Carolina.

Middle Passage narrative is the method and purpose of return, which writers would take up more regularly in the twentieth century as a form of resistance. In Equiano's case, his narrative shows the formerly enslaved writer's "return" to Africa through the written word. He calls to African descendants to deal with this traumatic experience through collective memory. Writing his narrative shows his conversion experience, from an Ibo to one influenced by British Christian teachings, as much as it shows his resistance to the belief that the transatlantic slave trade is justifiable. In other words, Equiano defies the idea that he is socially dead. Equiano's 1789 narrative is a foundational text that begins the conversation that contemporary Black writers and artists continue to engage. To return to my question of whether or not it is his own experience, is it possible for it not to be his?

REVISITING THE MIDDLE PASSAGE

Most important to the study of the Middle Passage is the presence of memory. From memory, African descendants feel the fear of death and the pressure of power generations later. Indeed, memories are passed down through both captives and captors, causing the tension of the trauma, the series of documented and undocumented acts to thrive in various ways. No one had to be *there* to know something about *there,* to feel something of the emotions associated with *there.* Middle Passage narratives are not derived from the writer's or artist's memory, but from historical documents that are partially composed from memories, such as captains' logs and other eyewitness accounts. Melvin Dixon notes, "Memory becomes a tool to regain and reconstruct not just the past but history itself" (19–20). Further, Pierre Nora provides a more comprehensive link between memory and history:

> Memory is life, borne by living societies founded in its name. It remains in permanent evolution, open to the dialectic of remembering and forgetting, unconscious of its successive deformations, vulnerable to manipulation and appropriation, susceptible to being long dormant and periodically revived. History, on the other hand, is the reconstruction, always problematic and incomplete, of what is no longer. Memory is a perpetually actual phenomenon, a bond tying us to the eternal present; history is a representation of the past. (285)

In the absence of recordings from African captives, Black artists and writers probe this bond when they tell the memories in form of a story, which empowers not only the storyteller but the subject(s) of the story. If, as Patterson argues, power is a way to exert control and to persuade a person's perception, then storytelling in written, visual, or oral forms places the storyteller or performer in a position of power.

In the brief overviews of historical creative renderings to follow, the authors, visual artist, and filmmaker rely on history and use various angles, such as voices of the dead in *Beloved, Zong!,* and *Middle Passage,* to revisit fear, trauma, and resistance—human emotions that take readers and viewers to a place that is sacred and forbidden. Jennifer Griffiths probes the intersection between trauma, memory, and testimony. Testimony is the act of telling a story to a willing listener. It "depends on a relationship and a process between the survivor and the witness, as memory emerges and reunites a body and a voice severed in trauma" (Griffiths 2). It "exposes the vulnerabilities of listeners," who must "face their limitations . . . through the story of another's trauma" (Griffiths 2). In this chapter, I am interested in how storytelling exorcises trauma for the participant. African-descended writers and performers ultimately ask us, as reluctant participants, to take leave of the safety of our present space and then to stand in a space of death and wrestle with the meaning of death in its various forms. They remind us that time is distorted, and within this distortion we experience the tension between longing and reality. We do not receive times of day or night when events occur and rarely do we know the year or time of the year. Trauma cannot be measured in increments of time, not when one second of pain can feel like an eternity.

Honoring the connection between history and memory, Robert Hayden takes his cue from Equiano and reconstructs a historical moment with his now iconic poem "Middle Passage." According to Osbey, Hayden's poem was the first to nod to poets, like her, to look at the Middle Passage as more than a maritime event but as a traumatic experience of captivity and enslavement.[4] First published in 1945 and republished with changes in the 1960s, Hayden's poem captures particular historical experiences mired in severe oppression at a time in the twentieth century when oppression had taken on different forms. Carl Plasa observes,

> Hayden's poem is in this respect both timely and prophetic, setting up a certain resonance between the past it recalls and the present in which it initially appears, as well as the future in which it is reworked and recirculated: its slave-ship dramas of white male oppression and black male counter-violence

---

4. After reading selections of her poetry, Brenda Marie Osbey shared this with participants of the "Black Poetry After the Black Arts Movement" National Endowment for the Humanities (NEH) seminar hosted by the University of Kansas in the summer of 2015.

find their echo in the racial conflicts cross-cutting the civil rights campaigns from the 1940s onwards and culminating, in the mid- to late 1960s, in the formation of a militant and male-centered black nationalism, whose "cultural arm" (Gayle 364) is the Black Arts Movement. (558)

While the poem may have been lost on an America that was preoccupied with World War II, it resonated among African descendants in the 1960s. The civil rights and Black Power movements had ushered in an era of Black resistance, and African independence movements were well under way. As a form of resistance to American nationalism, Raphaël Lambert observes, "It is this soothing, self-congratulatory narrative of heroism and national grandeur that Hayden's poem disrupts. 'Middle Passage' *is* counterhistory in that it challenges national history by shedding a new but unflattering light on the past" (332). Poets of the 1960s and later began to make direct connections between the diaspora and Africa as African nations declared their independence from Europe and took historic steps to develop their own governments. Thus, Hayden's desire to revisit the troubling period that was responsible for the creation of Black life and culture outside Africa resonates with Black people as they began to wrest themselves from political and/or social confinement.

Hayden's "Middle Passage" is the first known literary work to document Black resistance on the Atlantic. The poet interweaves historical studies of the *Bella J,* a Spanish slave ship that burned at sea, and the *Amistad,* a ship that was overtaken by Africans, to tell the story of death and fear of death on the Atlantic. Sections I and II are told in the voice of a captain with twenty years' experience who perishes in the fire along with the "shrieking negresses" left behind by the crew. Some "five hundred blacks" were taken from the Guinea Coast for sale. Through his observations of the "rebellious" Blacks, we find indications that the captain is fully aware that the cargo of "nonpersons" is capable of responding in a variety of ways to their treatment. Hayden finds beauty in the midst of tragedy. The ship's captain notes that "their moaning is a prayer for death / ours and their own" (lines 10–11). Hayden's line break allows for an emphasis on how the experience of the African is joined to the experience of the European. It may also suggest a contrast. What kind of death are they praying for? Do they wish for the same sort of death for themselves as they do for their captors? Translation of experience is distorted by limited perception. Hayden's linguist hardly qualifies as a trustworthy translator of experience, regardless of ethnic origin. Nevertheless, for the captain to glean this translation from a "linguist," Hayden deals directly with the treatment of the "black gold, black ivory, black seed" (line 16). He goes on to speak of three leaping "with crazy laughter / to the waiting sharks, sang as they went under" (lines 12–13). Again, the captor cannot so easily interpret the purpose of singing and laughing.

Placing the fear of death in the voice of the crewman who lost control of the *Amistad* to Cinquez and the other African captives allows readers to imagine what losing power means to White captors when they become the captives. As I explore above, a sense of disorientation may cause a disconnect between the person and the land, but it certainly does not disconnect the person from home. Enslaved Africans deemed "rebellious" defied social death, even under the worst of circumstances, and made efforts to physically return to their place of origin. In the turn of events, Hayden invites readers to imagine that their inability to navigate properly on the Atlantic is a shared experience that was meant only for the captives, "Cinquez was forced to spare the two of us / you see to steer the ship to Africa, / and we like phantoms doomed to rove the sea / voyaged east by day and west by night, / deceiving them, hoping for rescue" (III.53–57). Despite their dire situation, the European voice can only note the loss of control and power on the ship: "we were no match for them" (III.39). It was not to be so. Each side grasped for life, but grappled with a sense of death. Hayden ends the poem as it began: "Voyage through death / to life upon these shores" (III.82–83). Through poetry, Hayden reminds us why such ships were called "tumbeiros," or floating tombs, as he describes resistance to their treatment.

Tom Feelings's *The Middle Passage: White Ships/Black Cargo* is a well-known artistic narrative of the transatlantic slave trade. Inspired by his desire to know a history that was not taught to him in art school, Feelings sought to reclaim that history and make a place for it in art for Black audiences. His work is intensely personal, as he clearly states in the introduction of his book: "You have to engage the past, she [Paule Marshall] said—to deal with it—if you are going to shape a future that reflects you" (1). Feelings notes that it was the early 1960s, at the time of the civil rights movement and African and Caribbean nations fighting for independence, that marked the time when he "became the most emotionally, spiritually, and creatively involved with depicting images of [his] own people" (1). Feelings goes on to list what he saw, such as Black Americans being assaulted as they demanded equal rights. By acknowledging a link between his contemporary moment and the past, Feelings writes himself into the history as he revisits the era in art and word.

In the pages that follow his thoughtful introductory biography, Feelings provides emotional renderings of the Middle Passage as he imagines it and based on his transatlantic slave trade research. Often, his drawings show people or events in motion, allowing him to map the interior feeling of loss through external physical expressions. He begins with a representation of

Africans before the arrival of European captives. The focus is on a man and a woman who appear as a royal couple, as suggested by the ornate figures above their heads. Their faces are looking forward and before them is an eagle, signifying freedom. Flip the page and a village is in the process of being overcome by Europeans who have guns and are aiming them at Africans who hold spears. Resistance occurs at several places in the artistic narrative, particularly on the ship. In one rendering, an African man can be seen with his arm around a captive's neck. In another, it appears as if some are jumping off the ship. The jumpers' extended arms suggest a deliberate movement of the body. Following this one, a clear revolt is occurring, but the brandishing of guns by the Europeans informs us that the African captives will not succeed. In contrast to their resistance, Feelings depicts bowed-down heads of the captives crowded in the hold, skeletons of bodies in the Atlantic, babies taken from crying mothers. Pain has words and a face. While there is no triumph in the revolt, the act of survival is not lost.

By isolating personal moments in public settings, Feelings seeks not to simply revisit the agony of the Middle Passage experience, but, like the writers, to probe it for a better understanding of African descendants' lives in the present moment and in the future. He ends with a poignant statement: "My struggle to tell this African story, to create this artwork as well as live creatively under any conditions and survive, as my ancestors did, embodies my particular heritage in this world. As the blues, jazz, and the spirituals teach, one must embrace all of life, both its pain and joy, creatively. Knowing this, I, *we,* may be disappointed, but never destroyed" (4). Feelings's statement emphasizes the importance of Black life, even as he depicts the killings of Blacks.

In conversation with Hayden's poetry and Tom Feelings's art, many African-descended writers and artists of the Atlantic Global South have undertaken the charge of revisiting the Middle Passage and placing the horrific experience into contemporary context. Their work exhibits what Feelings identifies as a "race memory"—a story shared by "Africans all over the world, . . . who [share it] consciously or subconsciously" (2). In addition to those I examine in this study, descendants of the African diaspora such as Gloria Naylor, Elizabeth Alexander, Kamau Braithwaite, Jamaica Kincaid, and Caryl Philips, among others, have revisited the Middle Passage in their creative work.[5] Indeed, there is an abundance of sources on this era of history. However, I will deal briefly with a few writers and artists here, choosing from works that focus more specifically on the theme of the Middle Passage and

---

5. In her essay "Going Overboard: African American Poetic Innovation and the Middle Passage," Evie Shockley provides more information about contemporary poems that focus on the Middle Passage.

its legacy in the contemporary work and that are not set in the southern region of the United States. If, as Melvin Dixon states, reconstruction is possible, and the one engaged in the reconstruction is in possession of power to craft and (re)create the self and the self's own history, then, as established by Equiano, facing the Middle Passage allows writers to journey through a space of horror in the mind and of the body in order to take possession of a new self on the other side. It also allows for an opportunity to identify the remnants of the Middle Passage and to try dealing directly with what the past has brought forward.

Toni Morrison's *Beloved*[6] is a work that shows the intersection of death and water as she revisits the Middle Passage and probes its lingering effects among African descendants. Through her text, we see the interconnectedness of memory and history. Sethe's own personal experience with enslavement—an experience so traumatizing that she left Sweet Home Plantation on the verge of giving birth to her fourth child and without knowing the whereabouts of her husband—led to her decision to try to kill her four children when it seemed certain that they would be taken back to Kentucky by the tormentors she tried to leave behind. Crossing over the Ohio River, shortly after giving birth, signaled for her the possibility of a new life. Moreover, the promise of that new life was granted, until Schoolteacher and the others came.

Sethe's crossing of the river gave her a sense of freedom, at least for twenty-eight days, before their crossing brought the reality of death. Her attempt to affirm her humanity and that of her children's by escaping Sweet Home meant that she placed herself in the position of resisting social death status. When she attempts to kill her own children, she finds herself defining the children's worth through an act that not even her oppressors could fully comprehend. Their sense of power—to coerce or threaten death with the expectation that they could control the enslaved—disintegrated when she took the life of her daughter. They found that Sethe did not fear death; it was living that she feared.

Before Sethe crossed the river to freedom, her mother endured the Middle Passage. Sethe is a direct descendant of the Middle Passage, and she knows too well the connection between water and death. Her existence is born from the decisions her mother made en route, as Sethe learns from her mother's friend, who was "together" with her "from the sea," where they were raped by the crewmen (62). Refusing to mother babies that came as the result of rape either on board the ship or elsewhere, Sethe's mother chose to keep the one

---

6. I am providing a brief analysis here because much of the plot occurs in Ohio, outside the Atlantic Global South.

child who was conceived by consensual union with a Black man. Unable and unwilling to mother children who reminded her of her state of oppression, Sethe's mother clearly made significant efforts to define herself as a mother who chose to be a parent rather than one forced into motherhood. Although an unwilling agent of life, she understood her position to serve as a progenitor of death and "threw away" her babies. Mothers, even enslaved mothers, show the fragility of life and death, for they have the power to give it and to take it away.

Similar to the Kongo cosmology, Morrison sees water as the border between life and death. Morrison teases the reality that water is a site for life and death. "A fully dressed woman walked out of the water," writes Morrison (50). Anissa Janine Wardi notes, "The woman who emerges from the stream completely dressed is the site of water immersion and a conduit to water memories" (66). A woman figure birthed by the water, Beloved represents death, violence, and trauma. Trauma is analogous to the unknown and unspoken. She narrates her memory of the world of the dead, a place that some scholars have argued is the Middle Passage. Beloved crosses over a bridge to get to 124 after she has put in an inestimable amount of time looking for Sethe's face in the water. She also describes fear of the men "without skins" who hurt her (215). Vincent O'Keefe argues,

> Morrison's narrator recreates perceptual confusion through memories made present by techniques such as jumbled syntax and lack of punctuation, pronoun slippage, and shifting verb tenses. Significantly, these narrative techniques are fully amplified in the section of the novel that most directly evokes the traumatic Middle Passage seemingly experienced by Beloved. As a result, readers experience a perceptual middle passage, a liminality that in many (inevitably limited) ways conveys the horror, disorientation, and lack of control suffered by slaves during the actual Middle Passage. (640)

Although Sethe herself did not travel through the Middle Passage as a direct descendant of the experience, she feels the impact of the trauma associated with the journey. Dealing directly with Beloved and all that she embodies gives Sethe an opportunity to exorcise trauma through confrontation. Is it possible that the same may be said of African descendants' engagement with the Middle Passage in their creative works?

History and memory are motivating guides for Philip's *Zong!* Born in Tobago, M. NourbeSe Philip uses poetry to look closely at the meaning of humanity as she relives the inhumane acts of throwing African captives into the Atlantic. Evie Shockley takes note of contemporary poets' use of history in their poetry. In her article about M. NourbeSe Philip's *Zong!* and Douglas Kearney's "Swimchant for NiggerMer-Folk (An Aquaboogie Set in Lapis)," Shockley observes,

> These poems argue that the Middle Passage was a rupture that has been and continues to be inscribed in multiple discourses informing and shaping the subject position of African Americans, even in the first decade of the twenty-first century. Any healing to be found in these poems will be produced not through a textually manufactured wholeness, but through a reckoning with the discursive evidence of that rupture. (86)

Philip's *Zong!* is a powerful revisitation of the murders of 150 enslaved West Africans who were thrown overboard a ship bound for Jamaica for the purpose, perhaps, of claiming insurance for the lost cargo. Philip, an attorney and poet, excavated the British legal case *Gregson v. Gilbert* and has been lauded by critics for giving voice to the intricacies of traumatic death. Voice, itself, becomes a witness and offers testimony for those who were relegated as commodity, as socially dead nonpersons rather than as human. Of course, if they were valued for their humanity, they never would have been subjected to kidnap, torture, and transport to a new land. Understanding this, Philip undertakes a daunting challenge—intervening in a historical event by interjecting language—namely English—to place readers of the twenty-first century as witnesses to mass murder in the eighteenth century. In an interview she states, "I believe that this is a lesson poetry offers us—freedom within limitation" (Saunders 65). For people who could only see and experience, unlike Equiano, there was no possibility of recording or documenting what was seen, felt, or heard.

Philip uses language and form to speak and to dissect the occurrence leading to death on the Atlantic, similar to the way Beloved, who cannot drink enough water, comes to life through language. *Zong!* #1 places us in the position of inhabiting the body of the subject-speaker. Setaey Adamu Boateng may be the one who is telling the story to the author, but *Zong!* #1 also suggests that Boateng is not speaking as one. Visually, readers see the vastness of the Atlantic through the spacing of the letters spread across the page. Additionally, as the eyes move from one letter to the next to connect one sound to the other in an attempt to achieve a coherent understanding of what idea is being transmitted, movement occurs. Such movement of the words, the sense of confusion, causes readers to interact, to become actively engaged with the movement of the ship that is implied by the scattering of the letters. In conversation with Smallwood and Morrison, Philip does not overlook the feeling of disorientation and the subsequent attempts to orient the self to an experience of floating in water aboard a vessel bound for the unknown.

Ironically, the utterance of the word "water" sheds light on the multiple meanings of water for Africans of the Middle Passage. First, Smallwood's study documents water was scarcely provided to quench thirst. Africans had to rely on captors to provide the water, and when it was provided, it was only done so at specific times of the day. In the case of the Zong, the captain's errors in navigation caused the trip to go unexpectedly long. Provisions were low, which reportedly had an effect on the crew and the captives. In any case, learning the word "water"—whether in English or another language or multiple ones, depending on the ship's crew—signaled a moment when the African captives' struggle to stay alive went on for hours and days longer through the provision of a small amount of water or for the "want" of water, as the poem shows. Morrison makes this clear as well. Beloved's immediate request is for water when she meets Sethe and the others. Humans need water to live. Second, the speaker captures the fact that water surrounds the ship. Such a site, with no experience or background in which to compare, could leave one grasping for words, literally in a verbal state of incoherence confused by the repetition of site—water, everywhere, day after day.

What exactly does the speaker "want"? "Want" is used at least three times in the first five poems, and it proceeds a reference to death—a desire to recover not just the voice but the loss of the bodies, or the "bones," as Philip states, that were not buried but discarded. Consequently, recovery of the story may be possible, on some level, but the loss of the Black body is permanent. Shockley remarks, "Philip's text unlocks her source text, the *Gregson* case, in order to release a story of the Zong massacre—not to tell that story, which must tell itself, as she reminds us again and again in the notanda section" (85). Death's meaning is not clear or translatable within the historical context, according to court records and the captain's log that privileges loss over death and, more importantly, loss of cargo over death of humans. In this case, water plays a dual role. It is restorative as much as it has the capability to destroy if withheld or if given in large quantities. Philip recognizes this in the construction of the lost narrative of the African's testimony: "If you have something that is dried, when you put it in water, the water restores the dried fibers— and if you think about this, this two-page account of *Gregson v. Gilbert* that I found, squeezed out the lives that were at the heart of this case" (Saunders 69). In telling the story, Boateng, Philip's fictional testifier, names the dead in defiance of social death. Naming is a right of birth and a claim of life. By being a voice of those who were murdered, the speaker and writer testify to satisfy the want or desire to define the physical loss not as death, but as the taking of life without cause. Rebirth of the dead becomes possible through the act of speaking/writing the word.

Along with Philip, African descendants of the Caribbean share in the reimaginative conversations about the Middle Passage. In their film *Middle Passage*, director Guy Deslauriers in collaboration with African American novelist Walter Mosely present the horrific voyage from the perspective of a man who is kidnapped from West Africa by the Dahomey. He was sold for a barrel of gunpowder and placed on a ship bound for Martinique. His body has crossed over, but his voice lives in order that his name and experience will not be forgotten or buried in the Atlantic grave. Deslauriers places a focus on close-up shots of African captives, mostly men, whose vacant eyes portray their grief. Although the only voice heard is that of the narrator, in the voice of Djimon Hounsou, viewers know that everyone has a story, a past, hopes, and dreams.

Resistance comes in various forms. When brought on deck and forced to dance, the men dance. The narrator gives a description of a pastoral testimony, and the camera focuses on the movement of the feet and isolates the sounds of drumming, presumably African drumming, that drown out the chaotic, unfamiliar sounds of Europeans playing insignificant (in this space) instruments. What the players did not know is that the captives had returned, become one with the other, and joined fellow captives in calling on the spirits. Feeling as though they were in charge, that white supremacy was working as it should, they overlooked the moment. One captive converts by jumping overboard into the water, an act of return through an act of resistance. "Death will free our souls. Once free we will find a way back home" (Deslauriers). If embracing physical death is the gateway to freedom, the path home, then there is no space or consideration of social death. Realizing the power of dancing, its significance to the captives, the captors do not allow dancing anymore. Walking becomes the captors' mandated form of exercise. In the hold, the camera focuses on the blank stare of a captive as the narrator offers a prayer:

> Spirits of the sea be merciful to us. We offer you our bodies, our speechless suffering souls. Accept this offering of our sorrows for the appeasement of your wrath. (Mosley)

Offering this prayer suggests that the vacant look and silence of the captives do not properly depict the inner thoughts or the humanity of the African captives. Through engagement with the history and memories of the Middle Passage, Mosley and Deslauriers discern that African ancestors were spiritually connected to the water that threatened their bodies. Life exists beyond the moment of suffering.

Death, for some, can be a morbid subject that many would hope to avoid. Yet, it is a theme that emerges in the creative work of African descendants and that is traceable to the Middle Passage. In the twenty-first century, the Black Lives Matter movement[7] has addressed the disparity of convictions in the deaths of African descendants by Whites. A major tenet of the movement is to deal directly with the threats to Black life by speaking to the value of those lives as a human. Their website clarifies the basic purpose of the movement: "When we say Black Lives Matter, we are broadening the conversation around state violence to include all of the ways in which Black people are intentionally left powerless at the hands of the state. We are talking about the ways in which Black lives are deprived of our basic human rights and dignity." Stemming from the transatlantic slave trade, the fear of violent death has a particular resonance for African descendants. Looking at the Middle Passage and its legacy from African descendants' creative perspectives is a painful but necessary exercise. Historical creations may indeed work as part of the process of healing the trauma stemming from the atrocities sustained by the oppressed's oppressors, as Shockley states, but art in its various forms most certainly works as a means to show connections from one era to another as it also provides a means by which the treatment of literature as global and universal can form connections across time and space.

---

7. Black community activists Alicia Garza, Patrisse Cullors, and Opal Tometi established a hashtag in response to the acquittal of George Zimmerman, who had killed Trayvon Martin in 2012. In response to the killings of Michael Brown and Eric Garner in 2014, protestors responded to a call to action and organized as Black Lives Matter activists.

CHAPTER 2

Alex Haley's Roots of Resistance

I climbed down successive metal ladders into her deep, dark, cold cargo hold. Stripping to my underwear, I lay on my back on a wide rough bare dunnage plank and forced myself to stay there through all ten nights of the crossing, trying to imagine what did [Kunta] see, hear, feel, smell, taste—and above all, in knowing Kunta, what things did he think?

—Alex Haley, speaking of his time on a freighter trip he took from Africa to the United States (*Roots* 884)

I'm hoping that the conversation around *Roots* when it airs [May 2016] will fill in the gaps so that it is absolutely, unavoidably clear that America today is directly related to America of the antebellum South and the slave trade. And that some of the issues that we still grapple with have their roots in slavery and its attendant legacy of racism.

—LeVar Burton (qtd. in Bell)

IN 1976 at the country's bicentennial, Alex Haley, who had established a reputation as a journalist and the writer of *The Autobiography of Malcolm X*, published *Roots: The Saga of an American Family.* His historical novel appeared in the decade after the emergence of the civil rights and Black Power movements as well as the assassinations of President John F. Kennedy (1965), Malcolm X (1966), and Martin Luther King Jr. (1968). Additionally, the 1964 Civil Rights Act and the 1965 Voting Rights Act had been signed. In the 1970s, as U.S. racial tensions began to fade from nightly television news, the nation focused on U.S. troops in Vietnam. By the time the Watergate scandal dominated the news, leading to the resignation of President Richard Nixon in 1974, the nation found itself occupied with an unstable presidency as bicentennial plans were under way. Anticipating the release of *Roots,* President Gerald Ford appointed Haley to participate in the planning.[1] If the bicentennial was about celebrating freedom and commemorating the "founding fathers," Black America would

---

1. According to Robert J. Norrell, Haley accepted the appointment intent on making sure Blacks' contributions were made known (149).

not be denied their connection to a father and acknowledgment of their role in the making of America.

Segments of society were still calling for change as the aims of the Black Power movement (1960s–1970s) remained prominent. Emerging from the movement, student protestors demanded that university curriculum include the contributions that the people of Africa and their descendants had made to the development of Western civilization.[2] More specifically, Stephanie Athey finds that "at least three major anthropological studies were published between 1970–76, rejuvenating a field that had seen little activity since Herskovits's *The Myth of the Negro Past* was published in the 1941 [and republished in 1969]" (172). In addition to Herskovits's work were John Blassingame's *The Slave Community* (1972) and Eugene Genovese's *Roll, Jordan, Roll* (1974), both studies on slavery. By the time *Roots* hit the shelves, universities had begun to offer Black studies courses, and writers and activists, such as Sonia Sanchez, taught some of those courses. Enter Haley's *Roots,* which told stories of slavery from the perspectives of the enslaved. As a historical novel published approximately two hundred years after Olaudah Equiano penned the story of his life in Africa, captivity, and freedom in *The Interesting Life of Olaudah Equiano or Gustavus Vassa* (1789), *Roots* delved into the psychology of humanity to tell a story of captivity and a journey toward freedom.

Alex Haley was fully aware of America's interest in stories told by African Americans about their lives. His collaborative *The Autobiography of Malcolm X* had sold at record numbers when it debuted in 1966. Writing the story of a revered and feared African American activist while building a relationship with the man ignited Haley's Black pride as he was exposed to African and African American history. Haley, who had been born in Ithaca, New York, spent much of his childhood in the South, but after retiring from the Coast Guard in 1959, he moved to New York, where he pursued his writing career. During his Coast Guard service, he moved from a cook's position to writing public relations pieces for the government organization. After building a reputation as an interviewer of various celebrities, mostly African American ones, he was able to secure his first promising contract with Doubleday for a book on the life of Malcolm X. Following the life of an inquisitive African American man meant that Haley himself had to engage in parts of African American history about which he knew little. His own mother, who died when Haley was ten years old, had shunned talk of slavery, and his father, an agricultural

---

2. See Noliwe Rooks, *White Money/Black Power: The Surprising History of African American Studies and the Crisis of Race in Higher Education* (Beacon Press, 2006) and Fabio Rojas, *From Black Power to Black Studies: How Radical Social Movement Became an Academic Discipline* (Johns Hopkins UP, 2007).

professor, did not share much information related to Black history. Haley's exposure to studies of Black people by emerging scholar C. Eric Lincoln, as well as Haley's conversations with Malcolm, including about the minister's travels to Africa during the time when African countries were separating from colonial European rule, gave Haley insight into Black life that drew him back to childhood stories he had heard of his ancestors from his grandmother.[3] With help from at least two other writers, researchers, and editors, it would take Haley twelve years to develop and finish the story that came to be known as *Roots: An American Saga.*

For Haley, writing *Roots* was most certainly an exercise in discovery—of the self, of Africa, of Black America, and of America. Before *Roots* was available to read, Haley marketed the book as a personal journey into the history of his family. In fact, "Haley mixed archival research, oral traditions, and fiction into a narrative he described as 'faction'" (Delmont 5). Maintaining that his journey was emblematic of the lives of any Americans who had come to North America and who wanted to connect to their historical past was a way in which he built an audience. But Haley also advanced a spiritual aspect that was uniquely his. Struggling to complete the project while trying to maintain some semblance of financial balance between two divorces and supporting his children, Haley decided to take a transatlantic voyage. His goal, as expressed in this chapter's epigraph, was to try to get closer to the experience of Kunta Kinte. He goes on,

> My crossing of course was ludicrously luxurious by any comparison to the ghastly ordeal endured by Kunta Kinte, his companions, and all those other millions who lay chained and shackled in terror and their own filth for an average of eighty to ninety days, at the end of which awaited new physical and psychic horrors. But anyway, finally I wrote of the ocean crossing—from the perspective of the human cargo. (Haley 884)

For Haley, it was on water that he made major turns in his journey toward a Black identity that had purpose. His father had expressed disappointment in his eldest son's lack of professional success and often advised him to pursue a degree. Stumbling upon a writing career to stave off loneliness and boredom aboard ships for months prepared him to bring forward a story that spoke of his family, maintained Haley, and that gave voice to the "physical and psychic horrors" (884).

---

3. See Norrell and Delmont.

Delving into those horrors in the twentieth century remains relevant in the twenty-first. In the twenty-first century, in the age of President Barack Obama and the millennial Black Lives Matter movement, it is worth revisiting *Roots* in its various iterations (novel and television adaptations). Since the success of the novel, a TV series captured audiences and regaled the descendants of Africans and Europeans with Kunta Kinte's "pursuit of happiness," despite being abducted from his homeland and sold into slavery. Knowing their African ancestry sustains Kunta's descendants through unbearable challenges. Readers know that the ultimate American story is that Haley himself, the descendant of enslaved Africans and European enslavers, reclaimed the narrative of ancestry and wove a tale that won him a Pulitzer Prize and critical acclaim. Unfortunately, it also earned him a few legal battles.[4]

In this chapter, I explore Kunta's story, not as a work of fact, but as Haley's attempt to use storytelling to create one's self as an act of resistance. Haley's claim to have located his forefathers placed him—at least until his story was refuted by one threat associated with claims of plagiarism and several curious, reputable scholars—as an authority on the act of reclamation through return. As a result, Haley's novel has received little scholarly attention; regardless, "Haley's return to Africa and the subsequent recovery of his ancestor Kunta Kinte allegorizes a reclamation of a racial history. Ancestors who endured the trials of the Middle Passage function as a connective tissue linking the black race in unbroken filial interdependence" (Murray 48). In addition to charges of plagiarism, there are claims that Haley's "faction" was written not solely by Haley, but also with considerable help from others who contributed to the writing and editing. To learn a story, or at least to write one, requires historical, archeological digging up of the past. What surfaces is bound to ruffle the consciousness. Haley's claim of *Roots* as "faction" came too late and prompted damaging criticism by reporters and academic scholars. Were these attempts to invalidate the reality of slavery and the ongoing implications of the slave trade? For our purposes, I am not focused on performing an analysis of the intricate historical details of *Roots* any more than I do for any other form of storytelling in this study; my concern is with the novel's purpose. Indeed, the fact that it was his idea, that he was inspired by stories of his family history, that he was a sailor, and that he wrote most of *Roots* is not under dispute. My interest in this chapter, as with my analysis of Equiano, is to critique the work as presented proceeding from the intent that that author had, which was to expose, revisit, and ponder the meaning of the Middle Passage and the slave trade from the perspective of African peoples. To be sure, questions

---

4. See Norrell.

about authenticity of authorship aside, both men's attempts to give voice to the oppressed and not to the oppressor cannot be denied.

Until the moment of *Roots*'s publication, no other fiction writer had dared to climb into the depths of the Middle Passage and to consider what the experience meant to those who had endured it. In doing so, Haley asked those descendants of the horrible experience—those Africans and Europeans—to "remember" a historical event that was wedged in the subconscious and lingered at the heart of white supremacy. Just a few years after the bombings of Black churches and race riots in major American cities, and during America's celebration of its founding, *Roots* offered a counter-narrative that emerged to shine a light on slavery and Americans' controversial connection to Africa. It also brought a sense of pride to African descendants who knew too well the legacy of slavery—the loss of names and cultural practices, social discrimination, economic disparity, and so on. *Roots* tells the story of Kunta Kinte, from his birth in Gambia, Africa, to his capture and transport as a slave to Virginia. Haley gave another perspective on slavery and Black people. While Kunta's personal story ends with the loss of his only daughter, who is abruptly taken and sold to another owner, the book's attention to Kunta's descendants, ending with Haley, suggests that slavery was neither an end of nor a beginning to Black life in America. At the heart of American history is the Middle Passage as told and remembered by Haley in the voice of Kunta Kinte. Storytelling is a form of empowerment for the one telling the story. It allows the teller to have a voice and to supersede oppression, which seeks to silence, to delegitimize the experiences of the oppressed. It is an act of resistance to social death status and an affirmation of life. Further, Haley posits that the story of a people—evolving from physical birth to death and transmitted from one generation to the next—is an expression of life. In other words, telling is an expression of life. My intent in this chapter is analyzing how Haley's use of faction as storytelling acts as a form of resistance to social death. Haley's faction stands as a counter-narrative to slavery and its attempts to dissolve African descendants' past as it simultaneously illuminates ways in which enslaved Africans remained psychically joined to their origins.

Haley gives life to Kunta Kinte; he gives him words and language to use—or not—as a form of resistance to navigate his changing environment. In his work *The Sovereignty of Quiet: Beyond Resistance in Black Culture,* Kevin Quashie delineates a difference between quiet and silence in his study of the role quiet plays as a form of resistance. Quiet, argues Quashie,

> is a metaphor for the full range of one's inner life—one's desires, ambitions, hunger, vulnerabilities, fear. The inner life is not apolitical or without social

value, but neither is it determined entirely by publicness. In fact, the interior—dynamic and ravishing—is a stay against the dominance of the social world; it has its own sovereignty. It is hard to see, even harder to describe, but no less potent in its ineffability. Quiet. . . . It is a simple, beautiful part of what it means to be alive. (6)

I see Haley's Kunta as existing in the quiet but also enacting moments of silence as he reconciles his abrupt transition from a space of safety to a space of uncertainty. While quiet is a state of being, silence is an action of that being. Quashie argues that "the expressiveness of silence is often aware of an audience, a watcher or listener whose presence is the reason for the withholding—it is an expressiveness which is intent and defiant" (22). Silence may be attributed to the dead as quiet is to death. Yet, Haley artfully uses silence in his faction as a form of defiance enacted by an enslaved man who values the interior of his life—that is, the memories of his past—as he negotiates the reality of his present status.

In walking with Kunta along the story that Haley reveals to us, listeners are asked to consider the uncertainness of life and the fluidity of identity. Who is Kunta as a person immersed in a certain culture where he thinks of himself in a certain way, according to the expectations of his society's perception of manhood? When no longer in that culture, who is he? What is death, and what does it mean to live? These questions emerge out of a transmigratory movement, from Kunta's free life in Africa, through the Middle Passage, and during his time in American captivity. Moments within these movements mark tests of manhood, if not the test of humans' desires for freedom and success (in whatever ways these might be defined). Kunta's literal journey becomes a metaphor for growth and change, where his identity as a man—defined by him, in particular, as an African man in America—finds him seeking a truth about himself that is directly linked to the creator of this patrilineal story where Haley literally writes or speaks himself into being. Through Kunta, Haley explores various stages of death to expose the interior of Black life in America. Maurice Wallace observes in his study of Black manhood, "Since the public struggle to reconcile the nation's anxieties on black male bodies is also replicated with black men privately as the angst of enframement, the private will to survive the visually inflected problematics of race and manhood in American culture can ill afford to cease" (45). Haley emphasizes Kunta's will to value his own life—through his connection to Juffure, his home village—and to, at times, engage in forms of resistance that sustain him through his conversion process, from one physical, spiritual, and mental stage to another. In Kunta's efforts to maintain his African identity and Haley's attempt to reclaim one, Kunta engages in various forms of resistance. While media versions have focused on the physical forms of resistance, I am interested in Haley's depictions of verbal and nonverbal forms of communication—or Kunta's use of quiet and silence to push back against the oppressors' attempts to render him socially dead.

KUNTA IS BORN

We see Kunta in three phases of life: before the Middle Passage, during the Middle Passage voyage, and during enslavement. In these, his birth, life, death, rebirth, and presumed death emerge as he endures and survives the traumatic turns of his life. Haley returns to Africa through the birth of Kunta Kinte. Born as the first son to Omoro and Binta, Kunta Kinte is given a name in honor of his grandfather, a holy man from Mauretania, Gambia, whose prayers to Allah saved the people of Juffure, Kunta's home village, from certain death if the rain had not come and replenished the grounds and nourished the famished, dying people. According to the story told to Kunta by his grandmother Yaisa, "Allah had guided the steps of marabout Kairaba Kunta Kinte into the starving village of Juffure, seeing the people's plight, he kneeled down and prayed to Allah—almost without sleep and taking only a few sips of water as nourishment—for the next five days" (14). Establishing his ancestry in almost sacred terms, Haley uses storytelling to give purpose to himself as a male descendant of this man and the grandson who is eventually captured and thrust into the transatlantic slave trade. Baby Kunta is born into a family with a mother, father, and grandmother. There is nothing particularly grandiose, peculiar, or different other than the fact that the people of Juffure respect the descendants of the revered holy man.

Haley carefully weaves together the everyday routine of Kunta, what he sees, hears, and eats. Drawing the background of the village with details of the foliage, animals, and crops allows readers to become acquainted with a place where we can only travel by word on the page, as the setting is 1750 when the child is born into the community he comes to love.

> Birds sang everywhere. The trees and plants were explosions of fragrant blossoms. The reddish-brown, clinging mud underfoot was newly carpeted each morning, with the bright colored petals and green leaves beaten loose by the rain of the night before. (15)

Indeed, Haley's Juffure, Gambia,[5] is a paradise before the presence of violent men with white skin disrupts family units and the order of the West African community.

Death and its relationship to life emerges as a major theme very early in *Roots*. Underneath the beauty, Juffure is a place of contradictions. Singing birds and fragrant blossoms cannot cover the fact that death is always possible when there is an imbalance of nature. In the very next line, we learn the meaning of the "hungry season": when crops do not grow fast enough for people to eat and their preserves run low, hungry season signals a watch for death.

> But amid all the lushness of nature, sickness spread steadily among the people of Juffure, for none of the richly growing crops was ripe enough to eat. The adults and children alike would stare hungrily at the thousands of plump mangoes and monkey apples hanging heavy on the trees, but the green fruits were as rocks, and those who bit into them fell ill and vomited. (15)

During one of these seasons, Kunta's grandmother, the bearer of the family's history, dies. Her passing teaches him personally about death and its meaning to the people of the village. He "saw the mourners walk seven circles around Yaisa, praying and chanting as the alimamo wailed that she was journeying to spend eternity with Allah and her ancestors" (23). He would also learn that "three groups of people lived in every village. First were those you could see— walking around, eating, sleeping, and working. Second were the ancestors, whom Grandma Yaisa had joined. The third people, said Omoro, are those waiting to be born" (24). In other words, the past, present, and future reside together simultaneously. This sense of connectedness beyond physical death is what Haley attempts to understand and to impart to readers/listeners as a member of the African diaspora and as a griot—a belief that time and space as we have come to know them in measurable ways (marking time by minutes and hours and space by kilometers and miles) do not translate in the consideration of life spans. In fact, the lives he commemorates in the reimaging of a time long past connect him to that past as well as foreshadow whom he will become. Kunta will have moments when his knowledge of residing among the ancestors and those yet to be born will sustain him and help him to see his life as having purpose regardless of his physical location.

Haley himself, who plays with time in his telling of *Roots* and his retelling of Kunta's story, signals in his personal Middle Passage story that it is the

---

5. Haley was aware that Juffure was a major trading post at the time in which he set *Roots*.

simultaneous existence of the past and present that saved his life and pointed him toward the future. In "Alex Haley on the Writing of Roots," an article published in *Reader's Digest,* Haley speaks of the moment he considered slipping from the ship he had boarded to take a transatlantic voyage into the Atlantic: "I'm standing there; I guess I was half a second from dropping into the sea. . . . And I began to hear voices, which were positioned behind me. I could hear them. . . . They were conversational. And I somehow knew every one of them. Who they were. And they were saying things like, no, don't do that. No, you're doing the best you can. You just keep going" (Haley 898). He goes on to say that they were his grandmother, Chicken George, his cousin Georgia, and others, sharing his space. Haley constructs a moment when he restores the voices of his ancestors as blessing him on his journey to bring life to their names through storytelling.

As a child growing within the community of Juffure, Kunta's own identity develops as he becomes increasingly aware of gender roles and expectations. In addition to knowing women, such as his grandmother, as storytellers/family historians, he is also aware that Binta's role as his mother and a community member places her as the primary caretaker of her son before he grows a bit older and is cared for by the older women of the community. She tends to the rice, marked as a woman's job, cooks, and sews. Kunta sees her as a woman who is quick to correct him in his behavior in the home, forcing him to learn how to navigate when under careful watch. Eventually she gives birth to another son and is pregnant when Kunta and his father travel together to visit with Omoro's brothers in another village. Binta's role is significant to Kunta in his rearing and sense of self. If for no other reason, he is able to think of his own desire to receive credit for his maturation into manhood in contrast to his interactions with his mother. It is she who makes his first suit of clothing, marking his move from one stage of life into another. When she shows him public affection, in his need to seem independent and manly to his friends, he avoids her touches—whether they be to scold him, compliment him, or hug him. Binta's interactions with her son differ significantly from her husband's. In this moving moment, Haley, in the tradition of Equiano, emphasizes human bonds among African families.

Distinct differences in his father's and mother's demeanors contrast greatly, and Kunta is keenly aware of the differences. It is also during travel that Haley establishes Kunta as a man who can take advantage of quiet. While Binta is able to show her emotions, such as grief for a loved one, Omoro acts like a man. He keeps his emotions contained, but it is clear that he loves his son. This becomes clear when Kunta's father admonishes his son for trying to prevent a wild cat from taking their goat. Kunta's father warns him that his life means more than the goat. Such a proclamation of his son's value moves them beyond a mere hug but is an expression of the value of self that is foundational to Kunta's maturation and his understanding of himself.

Further, it is his father who teaches him about the importance of quiet and its relationship to freedom. As a child, when Kunta travels with his father to his uncles' village, he learns how to discipline himself by remaining quiet. There is no idle chatting, question-and-answer sessions, or bonding by verbal exchanges. There is a sense that there are two individuals with a common goal—to get to their destination safely and on time. This leaves time for personal reflection and observation. At these moments, we become aware of what Kunta is thinking, seeing, feeling, experiencing, but have no idea of his father's inner thoughts. When they walk past one village, Kunta's thoughts are of a child's excitement and his hope that "the villagers felt they had seen a young man who had spent most of his life traveling with his father along The Gambia's long trails" (96). A few years later, when he travels with his younger brother and decides that he will travel frequently and farther, his mature thinking reveals, as Quashie describes, "the full range of one's inner life—one's desires, ambitions, hungers, vulnerabilities, fears" (6). Kunta's maturation process through the hope to define his manhood has been established by the time the toubob (White men) come to Juffure. In his lifetime, Kunta will come to define, if not redefine, the meaning of freedom and its relationship to manhood.

Kunta's masculine development is formed through interactions not just with his family but with male members of the community as well. The third phase of manhood training requires him and the boys to learn what it means to work together as a brotherhood. When one makes a mistake, they all suffer with whippings. Each son of the village must learn endurance through physical training and denial of the self. Sitting still, quiet, with a bag over the head for a long period or moving about nimbly and quietly to hunt prey requires discipline. Their successes in hunting, their ability to fight in case their lives or the lives of others are in danger, place them in a position to contribute to the security of the village that is not simply their parents', but theirs as well. Kunta and his peers become responsible and they see their lives not exclusively as theirs, but in relation to the others of the community. We see Kunta as fully alive, full of promise, and enthusiastically anticipating what's next. Unfortunately, his freedom is short-lived as he is soon taken into captivity.

Kunta has enough time in Juffure, Gambia, to develop a desire for travel, to know more of the world outside his own village, like his uncles and his grandfather. Travel is exclusively masculine. It is a daring feat that requires courage and can greatly increase the knowledge of the traveler. Kunta is named for a holy man who traveled "for fifteen rains" as a student with an "old marabout . . . from village to village in the service of Allah and his subjects" (18). Grandma Yaisa speaks of his travels:

> Over dusty foot trails and muddy creeks, under hot suns and cold rains, through green valleys and windy wastelands. . . . Upon receiving his ordination as a holy man, Kairaba Kunta Kinte had himself wandered for many moons alone, among places in Old Mali such as Keyla, Djeea, Kangba, and Timbuktu, humbly prostrating himself before very great old holy men and imploring their blessings for his success, which they all freely gave. (18)

He would later come upon Juffure in time to ask Allah to save the people by providing much-needed rain. His father's brothers were travelers. They had founded their own village, which Kunta had the opportunity to visit with his father before he went through the last passage to manhood. As Kunta decided to go on an adventure to seek gold and to take along his young brother, he also decided that he would later take the pilgrimage to Mecca. While others of his peer group were planning to travel a bit outside their village, "Kunta meant to put his eyes and feet upon that distant place called Mali, where, some three or four hundred rains before, according to Omoro and his uncles, the Kinte clan had begun" (187). Haley, who had traveled as a sailor, suggests to us that Kunta has been named for travel, to exist and thrive outside the village of his birth. Haley implies that no matter the odds, he will survive the journeys, even those that he had no desire to take. Transmigration emerges as part of Kunta's being, and travel across the land is a precursor to his forced travel across the ocean. What if, like his namesake, Kunta Kinte had been called by Allah to travel to a land far away and carry on the name of his people in a new village? Regardless of the physical location, the Kinte men, Haley suggests, must acknowledge that they have a purpose wherever they are. Haley's visitation of this era allows him the opportunity to explore his own purpose. Recalling that he had an estranged relationship with his own father, was reared in the Jim Crow South, and wrote about racism and African Americans' attempts to navigate around racial disparities and limits, moving back through history and cultural memory is as much a creation of a self as it is a re-creation of the Black male self.

KUNTA'S MIDDLE PASSAGE

At approximately seventeen, after traveling on a long walking journey only twice, and then with a member of his family, Kunta Kinte is taken. Despite the increasing threat that he is fully aware of, that *those* men with white skin and their Black traitors are kidnapping men and women of surrounding villages to eat them, he does not keep up his guard. More importantly, not following the directive of not traveling alone outside the village leaves him vulnerable, alone. The number, according to the drums, of people missing had increased, even after the king tried to negotiate by selling prisoners of war and criminals. Kunta is abducted around the year 1766.

From the paradise of The Gambia to the abrupt placement in a ship made for the sole purpose of transporting human cargo, Haley presents an unspeakable nightmare, comparable to that in *The Interesting Life of Olaudah Equiano.* Kunta's literal awakening, while lying flat in a narrow space on a hard wood surface that will not accommodate his desire to sit up, makes it seem as though he is, in fact, in a state of death. Entombed. Shackled to another, he can only detect forms of life by the fact that he is chained to one he cannot see and that he hears the moans and mangled languages of others. Haley describes Kunta's condition: "Naked, chained, shackled, he awoke on his back between two other men in a pitch darkness full of steamy heat and sickening stink and a nightmarish bedlam of shrieking, weeping, praying, and vomiting" (194). Opening with a depiction of Kunta's body immersed in the waste of others suggests to readers that the "shrieking, weeping, praying" are emotions expressed in the excretions of traumatized Black bodies. Visualizing the Black male body in this state is somewhat jarring in this unfamiliar place. As Ralph Ellison and Charles Johnson have pointed out, America has often treated Black men as invisible (Claudia Rankine addresses the woman's perspective in *Citizen*). Johnson describes this experience as he passes a professor who does not acknowledge him: "He glances up quickly, yet does not acknowledge that he knows me. He has seen a black, a body, that remains for him always in the background" ("Phenomenology" 604). Haley asks readers to see Black bodies in their *in*humanity—further, to see, hear, and feel the agony of what it means to be seen only as a body that has gone unacknowledged or made invisible in a society. Without identifying the performer of the act, Johnson implies through his attention to the act that the colleague is White. Fifteen days Kunta lies in the tomb drenched in his own feces and the feces of others, enduring rat, lice, and flea bites, knowing that he will never see his home again. Knowledge of his transformation has begun.

To be sure, Kunta's abrupt removal from Juffure by the enslavers means that he is now seen as nonhuman, in sharp contrast to his life as the son of Omoro and Binta and a promising member of Juffure; he is socially dead to those whose success depends on their sense of power and supremacy. He understands this quite soon as he has heard stories about the dangerous "toubob," or those men with white skin who speak a strange language, have a strange smell, and take his kinsmen and eat them. Haley forces us to consider what it would be like to wake up in terror and to remain there. As Black male writers of the twentieth century had done this against the backdrop of violence and usually on land, Haley's site of the ship emphasizes the interiority of the body in an enclosed space. Black experience, or in this case, Black male experience, went from being personal to being public. It involves learning that an individual captive has no control over his or her body—shackling hands and feet to control and restrict movements, jabbing the body with sticks to motivate walking, forcing food into the body to keep it alive, inspecting the naked Black body to assign monetary value. Finally, branding the body signals to the "toubob" that the body belongs to him.

Haley's careful attention to the experience of one person, a young man whose name and history readers know, compels us to focus on the experience represented by Kunta. Such a focus requires consideration for the individual choices of the person and not so much for the will of the masses. Resistance is personal. Kunta goes through several stages of death, which fluctuate between resistance and survival, as he tries to deal with what, for all intents and purposes, is an unbelievable experience. Kunta resists. Before being taken aboard, he refuses to eat the food that is given to him. Second, he tries to run, twice. After attempting to leap overboard a canoe, he found that "ropes were being looped around him, and he was helpless to resist" (199). Soon, his tactic changes. Once he realizes that "he would never see Africa again" (202), he, in the quiet, indulges a desire to "kill toubob—and their black helpers!" (202). Within this space, his sense of what it was to be a man in a protective society, where he had the support of his parents, elders, friends, and other village members, shifts. Who he is in this new space is uncertain, but what is certain is that he must begin to shift his way of thinking by relying on past experience to fit the present moment. This is the Middle Passage, where the past and present collide and intersect. Relying on his manhood training and recalling that warriors need strength, he finally eats from the daily mush given to them by the captors. Survival and reasoning within the Middle Passage require psychic adjustments. Kunta initially reasons alone within himself as he is unable to effectively communicate with others. It is also here that his sense of himself as a member of a community is disrupted, and Haley will emphasize this when Kunta arrives on the plantation. For days, he and the other captives make attempts to communicate with one another by learning each other's languages and plotting a mutiny. Kunta reasons, "Part of him wanted to die, to escape all of this; but no, he must live to avenge it" (205). In other words, he desires to prove that he is more than the Black body that has become food for insects and rodents and object for the abuses of the toubob. Haley attempts to expose the rawness of humanity by exploring the human condition within the geographical space of the Atlantic during the slave trade.

Focusing on forms of communication to build bonds of solidarity dominates much of Haley's lengthy (over eight hundred pages!) reimagining. Communicating verbally with one another by trying to learn each other's language, at least enough to pull off a successful mutiny and fan embers of hope among those bonded by more than chains, becomes a method to stave off social death. Silence is another form. When the White men come into the hold, the Africans cease to communicate through verbal expression. Solidarity exists in the form of silence. The narrator describes the hold at these times: "And there was a new quality to the quietness that would fall at these times, for the first time since they had been captured and thrown in chains, it was as if there was among the men a sense of being together" (215). Resistance and their desire to live bonded them.

Death disrupts Kunta's desire. Until hope had been dashed by their failed insurrection, Kunta staves off the feeling of death that lingered among the captives. His body had already become a source of nourishment for the rats: "Their nose whiskers would tickle between Kunta's legs as they went to bite a sore that was bleeding or running with pus" (226). On deck, he sees others succumb to death in both the symbolic and social forms. They are "zombies— their faces wore a look that said that they were no longer afraid, because they no longer cared whether they lived or died" (226). Whips had no effect on them. Some simply willed themselves to die, Kunta surmised. Unlike his treatment of death in Juffure, Haley isolates the hopelessness of the moment. Kunta is not dealing with nature inasmuch as the presence of death is man-made. Who has the power in this situation? Is it Allah? Toubob? Or the individual? Haley focuses on Kunta as subject observer. Survivor. A body. Maurice Wallace's observation that "African American men have historically survived the self-alienating disjunction of race in American culture" is appropriate here as Haley reminds us that the self-alienation is rooted in the Middle Passage (5).

Physical death and social death ravish the ship. By emphasizing death, Haley illuminates the meaning of Black life. Saving the captives from drowning during a thunderstorm causes the crew to place a covering over the deck, having the effect of suffocating them and extinguishing the life from those who were so near death. We feel this through Kunta: "Kunta's nose, throat, and then his lungs felt as if they were being stuffed with blazing cotton. He was grasping for more breath to scream with. Surrounded by the wild frenzy of jerking chains and suffocating cries, he didn't know it when both his bladder and his bowels released themselves" (232). His body fights to survive and it does, even if his mind is ambivalent about survival. Surprised that he is still physically alive when they bring him to deck, he envies those whose bodies he saw being thrown overboard, for they had transitioned to another state of being. Perhaps they had gone back to Africa. As his body purged itself so near physical death, Kunta's Middle Passage conversion experience piques. It is here that we are asked to consider the impact that the Middle Passage has on the human mind, how it invaded the consciousness slowly until it became obvious to the captive that there is no escaping what has already taken place. Days of trauma have become a reality. Kunta knows that he will not go home to Juffure because there is no hope for escape or revenge, and that he can either survive the unknown destination or die.

In this state, death lingers as he languishes. Kunta lies for three days in painful anguish, dealing with an unknown alien that is taking lives. As a death in the form of a disease takes the lives of both crew and captives, Kunta fluctuates between life and death. Disease ravages the ship, and this is only possible because of the sin of white supremacy and racism. Unable to eradicate disease, he takes his frustrations out on the toubob by killing a rat: "All the rage that had bottled up in him for so long squeezed—the rat wriggling and squealing frantically—until he could feel the eyes popping out, the skull crunching under his thumb" (236). This is the first time we are aware of him killing an animal for any reason other than for food. At one point, after feeling the loss of his Wolof shackle mate who had succumbed to death, he began to wait "almost blissfully—to die and join the ancestors" (239). During this time, Kunta does not appear to speak. Only his thoughts and sense of his failing body and distorted mind dominate the narrative. He is most certainly in a state of quiet, where his fears and vulnerabilities weigh heavily and we get a sense of his conversion experience from Kunta of Juffure to Kunta the captive. His body begins to give out, making it impossible for him to feed himself as his body fights against disease, fatigue, and homesickness. But it is also during this time that he dreams of Juffure and begs Allah for one last time to see his family. At this moment, his life's lessons in Juffure become instructive:

> The past seemed with the present, the present with the future, the dead with the living and those yet to be born; he himself with his family, mates, his village, his tribe, his Africa; the world of man with the world of animals and growing things—they all lived with Allah. Kunta felt very small, yet very large. Perhaps, he thought, this is what it means to become a man. (137)

Kunta learns about seamless existence, the interconnectedness of various forms of life, and that he has a small place within this existence. Rooted deep within him is this lesson that resides not in Africa, but in the person. Beliefs in something other than the self allow the believer to feel emotions associated with living. In this case, he lives because he misses his family and longing for them helps him to remember that he is indeed alive and to resist death. Not long after this dream, he and the others see land and know the voyage is over, and he has survived. Kunta's crossing over the water, a metaphorical medium, forces him to begin his conversion. What he has learned about himself as a result of the voyage may not be immediately clear, but it is clear that he will not be the same person who left Africa. He is an extension of himself who has yet to be defined. For Kunta, the Middle Passage may exemplify a consciousness that longs for movement outside the self prescribed by restrictions. Within the Middle Passage he too is forced to feel, to understand the significance of life even if he is not yet aware of his own personal purpose. This heightened awareness will remain with him and compel him to find ways to recall what he learned from his father the day he challenged the wild cat—that the value of his body must not supersede the significance of his life.

KUNTA KINTE MEETS TOBY

Kunta's resistance shifts from the ship to the location of the Americas. His sale into the American system of slavery to some degree only means that a man from one area of the world has been physically moved to another. How he processes this movement determines his identity. Hartman's informative analysis of resistance finds that "in considering the determination and limits of practice it becomes evident that resistances are engendered in everyday forms of practice and that these resistances are excluded from the locus of the 'political proper'" (61). First, when told by another enslaved person of African descent that his name is Toby, Kunta answers the man with silence. His response is taken as ignorance, but it is, for Kunta, an act of defiance. Further, how he thinks of himself as a man, a man of Juffure, fuels his desire for movement. Just as he moved by foot from one area of The Gambia to another, he does not hesitate to do so in captivity. Movement, for Kunta, is an exercise of independence and a tenet of manhood. We may recall that when he leaves Juffure for the first time with his father, he connects his father's decision to accompany him to come along on their journey to his idea of manhood. What will his male peers say? Won't he be the first boy in his age group to undertake such a task? Later, when he leaves and takes his younger brother along with him on their journey to find gold, he sees this as an opportunity to affirm his manhood and to help his brother move toward his own status prior to the final initiation into manhood. It is in this spirit of movement and manhood that he attempts to flee captivity.

Without any knowledge of his surroundings or a viable escape plan, he runs and is captured. Three times. Finally, one of Kunta's feet is permanently amputated, having the effect of *rooting* him to the plantation and forcing him to connect to the people of the enslaved community. His idea of manhood, of passing down his name from one generation to another as a Mandinka man should, seems lost.

Quiet and silent resistance become a way of life for Kunta. The narrator, speaking for the mind of Kunta, does not process and never accepts the name of Toby. Naming has a purpose. For the enslavers, it is an attempt to break the bond to Africa, especially for those who might be newly arrived. It is also an exercise of power—an assertion of assigning an identity to one whom the oppressor has to believe, at least on a conscious level, that the slave's true self is unknown to the oppressor. Kunta stays in solitary after his foot has been maimed and his pride has been shaken. Seeing himself as an African and not as whoever the other enslaved people are, despite the fact that he and they have the same status, marks him as different. For him, enslavement is whole; it is both mental and physical. And, Haley affirms this in the statements they make to him that cause him to only gradually engage in the community while remaining a foreigner within, even after his marriage to Belle, the enslaved woman who nursed him during the time that his foot was healing. Haley's incredible isolation of Kunta from the others because he is African and different is historically inaccurate and reads as odd. Enslaved people would have been quite familiar with African beliefs and practices from their African parents and grandparents. In an effort to solidify Haley's Kunta and Haley's own connection to Africa, Haley emphasizes Kunta as a man who, despite the physical distance, never left Africa.

How Kunta chooses to engage various forms of communication in the new land allows him the space to remain in two places at once. The Fiddler teaches him the toubob language, or at least his version of it. Kunta rarely speaks to anyone, but gradually he gets more involved with the conversations. We learn at such times about the American Revolution and the construction of America in the early days based on what Fiddler is exposed to in his travels to play the fiddle and what Kunta, a coachman, hears when he takes the slave-owning doctor from one part of the area to another. His masculine identity as a Mandinka man emphasizes the interior. Quiet is a status of mind that he is known to indulge, especially when he marries Belle. He would go within himself and she would learn to leave him where he was. At these times, she understood him to be in Africa, even though she saw him in Virginia. "'He jes' go off into his Africanisms,' Bell would tell Aunt Sukey, and after a while 'Belle would rise unnoticed from her chair, quietly leave the room—muttering to herself—and go to be alone'" (435). When Kunta mentally travels back to Africa, he assumes a stance of independence that impacts his environment such that his wife becomes "unnoticed" and must acquiesce to these moments when they arise. Only at these times do we see and can we presume that he has a major, even a profound impact on his surroundings, for he certainly would not be allowed to separate himself from his owner if his services were needed. Kunta's difference from the other enslaved people in the community means that a quiet state of existence may be a form of survival and resistance, but it is also individualized. For Kunta, it is a private and protective space where he stores the memories of the distant past, and through those memories, he is able to connect to his humanness. In this sense, his transformation does not mean that he has erased the person that he was; he has become an augmented version of the old self in a new land.

Quiet is forgone when his daughter Kizzy is born. Through Kizzy, Kunta's identity as an African patriarch is solidified. She is the one who must pass on his legacy as a Kinte, but she cannot do that if he does not share parts of himself. He names her in the ways of Mandinka by telling her her name before he tells anyone else. She is sold because of her mother's decision to teach her to write to help her feel she is worth knowing what a slave shouldn't know. Kizzy takes the lessons as a form of resistance. Like her father, she believes in freedom and writes a pass for a young man who is caught. She is sold for her daring but foolish act. Kunta finally disappears physically from the narrative. We never know what happens to him after Kizzy is taken, but she keeps his story and shares it with her only son, born of rape. Haley uses her body to preserve the legacy of her father as she gives birth to a son and disappears from the narrative, which shifts abruptly to "Chicken" George and his problematic relationship with his White father and owner. In the absence of inherited land or other goods that a patriarch may be able to pass along to his descendants, the children inherit a story. Kizzy's descendants learn the name of the man who was abducted from Africa and brought to America on a big boat. They hear the pronunciation of various words. They know that they were not always enslaved.

Each time they tell the story, they engage in a journey of return. Such a journey allows for a reclamation of what may have been lost had it not been for the significance of telling a story and passing it from one generation to another. They had little to claim as their own, but the story was theirs. What was changed, altered, or lost cannot overshadow the attempt to remain rooted in an origin that includes the Middle Passage, but does not begin in it.

ROOTS ON-SCREEN: TAKE ONE

For the American imagination, Kunta's story was reinterpreted for a visual audience. Television adaptations of *Roots* focus on the display of physical dramatic and traumatizing interactions between the enslaved Blacks and their White enslavers. Consequently, resistance became increasingly measured by reactions and showed little of the everyday ways that Black people survived slavery. *Roots* in 1977 brought Blacks and Whites in *monologue* about slavery and, subsequently, the issues of racism in America. To be sure, there was no direct conversation on the screen and, probably, not in society. What White people feared, what they thought, and how they participated in slavery was not shared with enslaved people any more than what oppressed folks feared, shared, and experienced was expressed directly to their captors or "massa." Several scenes overtly speak to the audience, probe American consciousness, but allow the reality of what is—the consequences of the slave trade—to lie still, rooted deeply in America. Further, as Maurice Wallace points out, "a racial gaze on black male bodies [is] vaguely pornographic" (86). What does it mean when Black suffering is displayed for visual consumership?

Roots's appeal to readers moved from the page to the small screen when ABC broadcasted a twelve-hour adaptation of the novel on January 23 through 30, 1977, less than a year after print publication. Viewers enjoyed a cast of all-stars such as Cicely Tyson (Binta), John Amos (older Kunta Kinte), Louis Gossett Jr. (Fiddler), Leslie Uggams (Kizzy Kinte), and TV newcomers LeVar Burton (young Kunta Kinte) and Ben Vereen (Chicken George). Donald Wright remarks, "The production broke all existing viewing records: one hundred thirty million Americans—three of five living persons in the country—viewed all or parts of the series, and millions of others watched the series when it was aired in other countries" (300). Each episode ended on a note of hope. As a result, Wright notes, "Haley rapidly became a man loved by persons around the globe, regardless of race—a kind of endearing folk hero" (300).

Building on Haley's expanding reputation, episode 1 opens to still shots of Alex Haley in a classic writer's pose as he looks down at manuscript pages while sitting at a desk and other similar images. A voice-over complements the pictures by telling viewers, "Tonight we present a landmark in television entertainment, *Roots*. The true story by Alex Haley as it was uncovered in his twelve year search . . . from primitive Africa to the Old South." In keeping with the popular idea of a primitive Africa, the opening scene shows flashes of animals in the wild—hippos and cranes bask in the sunlight not far from barebreasted African women who wash clothes and carry baskets on their heads to their huts. Audiences are introduced to Haley's "truth" through Africa. In one of those huts, a woman (Cicely Tyson) screams in agony as her husband paces outside. Kunta is in the process of being born. Within seven minutes, baby Kunta's father, Omoro (Thalmus Rasulala), holds him up to the sky and calls his name, Kunta Kinte, "no one is greater to you than Allah."[6]

Kunta's name is established as important to the viewers. Numerous times he is asked by people, usually men, for his name, and when he provides it, they seem to pay attention to him. In this series we are not told why the name Kunta Kinte (played by LeVar Burton) has meaning and value to the people of Juffure. Kunta may as well stand alone in establishing himself as a man with an identity that is his, and not in association with a history. During his manhood training at the age of fifteen, Kunta volunteers to go first in his wrestling training. Viewers do not see him succeed in advancing in this area, but he receives a lesson from his teacher, who has taken notice that Kunta tries, more than his peers, to succeed in winning the wrestling match with the learned, tall, muscular teacher (Ji-Tu Cumbuka). "I can teach you many things but I cannot teach you courage. . . . You will take courage with you wherever you go." With these words, Kunta receives instructions clearly meant to sustain him through future challenges.

Kunta is taken while separated from the community to find wood to make a drum for his brother, an act that would be pleasing to his mother, who laments the loss of her son to manhood. Ultimately, his love of family is what drives him outside the protection of his people, for it is when an individual is alone that he is vulnerable to captivity. Kunta's attempt to run and the scene in which he finds himself chained, for the first time in his life, is haunting. The African men surround him, chain him, and move back to allow the camera to focus solely on the one who is alone in a state of dire distress. A teenaged Burton throws his hands and arms in a circular motion and it looks almost as though he is dancing in front of a camera that effectively slows his motions. His experience with helplessness, his waning loss of self-autonomy, becomes painfully obvious in this moment, and it might as well be the viewer who stands on an eighteenth-century African coast in chains. Not long after, viewers see Kunta and others in sturdy makeshift cages, waiting for what, they do not know. Burton may be small, and this could account for his capture, but the strong, sturdy older wrestler has been taken as well. The 1977 Kunta shows that he has lost hope quite early. When fellow captive Fanta, who was the daughter of a man played by O. J. Simpson, says that her father will find her and come, Kunta gets her to admit that her father is dead or she would

---

6. A similar scene occurs in Disney's *The Lion King*.

not have been taken. Together they experience the fact that they will no longer enjoy life with their families.

What Kunta thinks is not as apparent to us as viewers as it is to readers of *Roots*. Through intuition, the wrestler translates various situations to Kunta. For example, it is he who tells Kunta that their people will not be able to track them through the water. In this context, water becomes their enemy. His words voice the severing of the physical bond with Africa that will grow for generations to come for African descendants, that is, until Haley attempts to reconnect by writing and creating *Roots*. It began on the coast and continues in the Middle Passage. Viewers are given an opportunity to track it, to wade through the nastiness of it as they go below deck into the hold and hear agonizing hollering, see staring eyes that indicate a form of death, observe shackled ankles that have been made raw by chaffing, look away from bodies smeared with substances symbolizing vomit and excrement. At various times, crewmen indicate a "salutation to the nose," in the words of Equiano. Once the captives are brought to the deck and made to dance, viewers see mangled backs from lying on the planks and hear the pain of those bodies when water is carelessly thrown on them for cleansing.

Kunta's resistance against captivity and his absolute denial of social death status comes out of the idea that Kunta is a Mandinka warrior. It is not until captivity that he is exposed to death, for his life in Juffure has focused on movement from one stage of maturation to another. His resistance begins when Fanta tells him she is no longer a Mandinka maiden. Motivated, possibly, by an attempt to avenge her raped body, he signals a revolt. As a result, he is able to kill the vile Slater (the White first mate). For a moment, audiences may cheer for the annihilation of a morally corrupt man. Slater is a proper representative of an inhumane business, a fact that may be clear to the audience. A cannonball disrupts the uprising, reminding all that a few dead White men, even a little boy, is insufficient in stopping the lucrative slave trade. Kunta and the others are placed back in the hold to wallow in their misery and mourn the loss of their kinsmen.

Relying on physical resistance, once Kunta is sold, he attempts to run for the first time. Finding a steel object to cut through his chains, he runs and is, of course, caught. It is at this moment when what is now an iconic moment in *Roots*'s visual history is born. Kunta is tied to a whipping post and whipped until he says the name given to him by his master. The camera's focus on Kunta shows his loneliness and vulnerability at this pivotal moment. Burton's eyes bulge and brighten, he seems breathless, and finally he relents and utters the name to satisfy the bloodlust of the proud White overseer who relishes his position of power. Kunta is to accept that he is Toby and not Kunta Kinte.

Kunta runs and Toby stays. Kunta disobeys and Toby obeys. Kunta's life will be miserable and Toby's life may be a bit easier. Not having been given any history of his name, Kunta's name, for viewers, is simply his connection to his family— a connection he is unwilling to forget for the sake of American enslavers. The overseer informs the owner that a slave is not born; he is made by fear of the whip. He is correct only if he understands that a slave's physical labor does not equate to the person's submission of the mind. As time goes on and Kunta attempts to leave a third time, resulting in the severing of his foot, it becomes clear that he never forgets his African home. Ultimately, viewers know this and applaud his resilience even as he suffers the pain of losing his only daughter.

Haley did not write the screenplay. Before he finished the novel, he had sold the rights to David Wolper, who had built a reputation as a documentarian. Blacks were largely relegated to the roles of comedies such as *The Jeffersons, Good Times,* and *Sanford and Son.* There was no history of Black casts in an hour-long series, let alone several hours of African Americans being tortured by White Americans. Wolper declared to ABC that his audience was Whites, as "they make up 90% of the audience" (Norrell 161)—hence, the scenes focusing exclusively on White actors. The result was that "the television interpretation of *Roots* diminished Haley's black characters" (Norrell 164). Biographer Robert J. Norrell summarized a poll of "one thousand Americans. Half of them black and the half white, taken a month after *Roots* aired." Respondents noted that "the most memorable scenes were those of violence— the capture of Kunta, the cutting off of his foot, the rape of Kizzy. . . . 77 percent thought [*Roots*] was relevant for contemporary race relations" (169). Norrell also notes that *Roots,* the story of an African man and his descendants, prompted Americans to put their finger on the pulse of America at the bicentennial. If it changed race relations, it is not known. Regardless, Kunta's story remains in the American consciousness.

ROOTS ON-SCREEN: TAKE TWO #KUNTASKIN

On Memorial Day 2016, a new version of *Roots* aired simultaneously on three cable stations, including Lifetime (a channel focusing on women's lives), A&E, and the History Channel. It premiered after the Department of Treasury announced in April 2016 a proposal to replace President Andrew Jackson on the twenty-dollar bill with famous abolitionist and fugitive slave Harriet Tubman.[7] The new *Roots* followed the success of films and television shows

---

7. In June 2016, Republican representative Steve King of Iowa introduced a bill to stop the change, calling it racist. The bill died in committee.

about slavery, such as *12 Years a Slave* (2013), *The Book of Negroes* (2015), and the hugely popular *Underground* (premiered 2016).[8] Out of these three, *The Book of Negroes,* an adaptation of a novel, which aired on Black Entertainment Television (BET) and told the story of captivity in Africa, American enslavement, resettlement in Canada, and a return to Africa, was the only one to deal with the Middle Passage. *The Book of Negroes* could serve as a supplement to *Roots* from the Canadian perspective in the voice of a woman. And, in some ways, it was. Yet, *Roots* had more to say. Notably, the 2016 adaptation, billed as a "reimagining" of *Roots,* clearly targeted a new generation as the social and political landscape changed. More than any other version, *Roots* 2016 relied heavily on physical resistance, to the point of gratuity, to speak to the Black Lives Matter generation.

These reimaginings of slavery took place during the period in which President Barack Obama, the son of a Kenyan man and a White woman from Kansas, occupied the White House, and a racially charged presidential race narrowed in on Donald Trump, a White billionaire who had previously challenged the legitimacy of Obama as president when he falsely claimed that the Obama was born in Kenya and not in America, despite a birth certificate confirming Obama's birthplace. The legitimacy of African descendants as American, along with other non-Whites who were new to America, was at the forefront of the American consciousness as these perspectives on American history aired. Did these televised depictions of enslaved Africans and their White American enslavers speak to the divisions in the country as symbolized in political rhetoric? Or, did they simply further commodify Blacks' bodies for commercial profit?

Americans may not have an opportunity to forget about slavery, but they could forget about the Middle Passage. Steven Spielberg's *Amistad* was the only other major American film that dared to depict the Middle Passage. His 1997 film, based on the case of the *Amistad* mutiny, came at the end of the twentieth century, when many of the targeted "reimagined" *Roots* audience had been born. What did this new generation know about the Middle Passage, its connection to new depictions of slavery, and racial tensions at the heart of mass protests?[9]

---

8. A successful television series that premiered on a cable station, WGNAmerica, with a focus on the escape of seven enslaved Black people and the experiences of those left behind on the Macon plantation and the dilemma of the Whites, including the brother of the slave owner, who took part in the Underground Railroad. It was cancelled after two seasons, in 2017.

9. An informal poll that I took of fifty undergraduate students enrolled in two of my African American studies courses revealed that only two had seen one episode of the 2016 miniseries. Three students noted that they did not have access to cable. Approximately thirty students indicated that they had seen the original miniseries.

Roots 2016 differs in significant ways from the 1977 television adaptation and even more so from Haley's novel. Historians were aware that Juffure was a major British trading post in 1750, as was Haley via his research, but he chose to create a pure African setting, one under the threat of the toubob but yet to have been visited by them. He felt as though Blacks "needed a placed called Eden" (Norrell 179). In 2016, there is no such Eden. For the most part, the production team places the onus of the slave trade on the Africans themselves. While Alex Haley played by Laurence Fishburne offers a historical commentary that slavery was known in Africa, as it had been in Ancient Greek and other societies as well, the only faces we see involved in the slave trade are Black ones. Omoro patrols and fights against this with a rifle in hand, and his son is eventually taken because of his father's push against enslavement. Omoro may be an activist, an early freedom fighter, but interestingly enough, Omoro's possession of the gun shows that he is benefiting from the slave trade, reusing the "master's tools." It is not until other Africans take Kunta to the coast that we see a European face.

In the hold of the ship, the scene is similar to that of the 1977 version. Kunta (Malachi Kirby) is not alone; the strong Silla Ba Dibba (Derek Luke), whom Kunta respectfully refers to as "Uncle," has been caught as well. Silla is known to viewers as one of those who taught Kunta and his Juffure peers how to become a Mandinka warrior, which is the focus of Kunta's identity. As in the 1977 version, the elder man's voice takes the place of Kunta's own quiet voice that Haley's Kunta relies on to survive this most unbelievable ordeal. When Kunta awakes, he exclaims, "I cannot breathe," and viewers immediately recall the movement and its memorialization of Eric Garner, who gasped, "I can't breathe" as a New York police officer held him in a chokehold in 2014. Video footage of the man's death sparked protests that fueled another chapter in the Black Lives Matter movement that had been sweeping the country, most notably since the murder of seventeen-year-old Trayvon Martin on February 26, 2012, and the subsequent acquittal of George Zimmerman, a twenty-nine-year-old White Hispanic man who argued that Martin, who was unarmed and on his way back home from a store, had attacked him and that Zimmerman used his gun in self-defense. Murders of unarmed Black men at the hands of those who claimed Whiteness prompted LeVar Burton to agree with Mark Wolper (David Wolper's son) that it was time to remake *Roots,* seeing it as an opportunity to provide Americans with a look back at the historical tensions that fueled the continued attacks against Black bodies. The handling of Black men and women as cargo, only worth labor and being absent of humanity, emerges as a dominant theme in the work, even as the resistance to such treatment permeates the visual narrative and shifts it distinctly from its origins. One thing is clear: this Kunta defies the imposition of social death status frequently and consistently. Accepting their circumstances is not an option, as this version focuses on the idea of the Mandinka African warrior.

Similar to the 1977 wrestler, Derek Luke's character speaks as a supportive guide, poised to remind Kunta of his humanity. Kunta reveals to him that he has soiled himself. We see vomit on his face, his body clearly reacting to the trauma of being placed in a space that has already been marked with the feces and excrement of the other men in the hold. Kunta states, "I soiled myself, like an animal. I am ashamed." In an attempt to resist the idea that enslavement makes them animals, Silla Ba Dibba responds, "The shame is not ours. It is theirs." Resistance to the oppressors' attempts to dehumanize their captives is obvious in this moment, and it continues.

Brutal treatment contrasts with their attempts to forge solidarity among one another. Their bodies, when brought on deck for exercise, are aggressively washed and then whipped by the British (the United Kingdom's flag is prominently displayed). The gaze targets glistening Black male bodies, dark brown ones that are barely clothed. If this were permissible, the bodies would be naked and the nakedness would reveal—not shield in any way—their vulnerability to the powers who have claimed the bodies as theirs. On the deck is where lives are violently taken and physical death occurs without warning. As a show of power to the men and women, Uncle, one of the strongest, who has been calling for solidarity through singing and dancing, is used as an example. One of the nameless crewmen literally disarms him by cutting off half of his arm. Kunta then knows that his own strength and sense of self is not what he would imagine in such extreme circumstances. Social death seems possible in the space of this television narrative. Uncle all but disappears from the narrative, as if amputating his arm renders him invisible and unworthy of being seen by Kunta and the others. Quiet descends below deck in the hold, but this is not to be mistaken for resistance. We can only assume that the lack of verbal communication is akin to depression, a step toward submitting to the despair of their situation. Focus on the inner self is underplayed.

Yet, like the other versions of Kunta, this Kunta's connection to the life he knew with his parents remains prominent in his attempt to stave off social death. Dreams work in 2016 as they did not in the 1977 version or in the novel. It is possible that dreams (visual) take the place of the quiet (lack of sound; state of reflection). They represent the moments where Kunta is able to reconnect with his parents—flashbacks punctuated with isolated shots of his parents, who often appear to look right at him across the distance—the ones he ran off from on the horse after he declared his intention to go to Timbuktu. He was not able to make restitution, and this theme of a father being separated from his son will only be resolved between Kunta's grandson, Chicken George, and great-grandson, Tom, near the end of the series. Dreams of his father make Kunta restless within hours of lying in the hold. He responds with frustration by rattling his chains, a sign that he is on the verge of losing his mind, as seen in the novel. While the sound of private reasoning soothes his troubled mind in the novel, it is Uncle who tells him that Allah sends dreams of our families to guide us. Dreams can also be painful, as they are reminders of what only resides in the memory. An elder tells Kunta he dreamed of his daughters, and Kunta's response is to tell the grieving man to keep his dreams to himself. Dreams may help to remind the men that they are attached to someone, somewhere, but that loss, if they submit to the pain, can also be a gateway to social death, a state of mind that the captors hope for. Dreams also give them a reason to resist as they now know the full meaning of the lives they enjoyed as free African persons. All of this—the dreams, suffering for want of home, memories of loved ones—exists in the Middle Passage.

Fueled by memories, resistance comes in the form of a mutiny, a willingness to die and to be with the ancestors; according to the elder, "the spirit of the ancestors will tell our families that we tried to come home to them." In the absence of his uncle, the trained Kunta emerges, the one whom the producers have billed as a Mandinka warrior, even though Haley's manhood training was more about the whole thinking man and less about killing people. In fact, 2016 Kunta is taken without much of a fight. He relies on his horse for escape, which is his best option when the men point guns. Warrior, in this historical reimagining, is a metaphor for one who perseveres, until fight and flight pervade the narrative. The captives' attempt to overtake the ship is not just a man's fight, but is actually started by a woman. Women were thought to be less likely to rebel, and therefore had more freedom in comparison to the male captives. A woman kills one captor with an ax, and the men follow her actions with actions of their own. Only a cannon shot, like that in *Roots* 1977, can stop them from succeeding. By now, it has been established that Black women were/are active in social justice fights. In 2016, then, women *and* men resist slavery.

If *Roots* 1977 "diminished" Haley's Black characters, Mark Wolper attempted to correct that in 2016. The 2016 version goes on with more forms of rebellion through murder. Kunta attempts to escape at least twice when he arrives on the plantation. On one such occasion, he attempts to spear one of the captors. On another, during the mayhem of the American Revolution, he kills his overseer with a stone, an act of revenge for the man's having whipped him mercilessly until he acknowledged the name of Toby. In another scene, after Kunta's foot has been amputated for attempting to escape, Fiddler and

Kunta kill White men on the night of Kizzy's naming. Fiddler is killed, and there is no further word about the loss of life, or rather, the loss of a valuable, moneymaking slave. White enslavers are shown little mercy in the contrived 2016 Black imagination.

If the killing of Whites is an expression of the desire for resistance in the slavery era, scenes from *Roots* 2016 recall the reality of 2016 in America. In multiple interviews, LeVar Burton, an executive producer of the "reimagined" version, noted that the timing for *Roots* was not planned, but it was perfect. As in the epigraph, Burton shares with interviewer W. Kamau Bell that he sees *Roots*'s relevance to the state of America as speaking truth as scientific: "The vestiges of slavery are alive and well and have been institutionalized in American culture—in the disproportionate number of black men incarcerated, in phenomena like Driving While Black. It's like Neil deGrasse Tyson says about science: 'The great thing about science is, whether you believe it or not, it's still true!'" (qtd. in Bell). With the help of director and actor Mario Van Peebles, who directed such iconic 1990s Black urban films as *Panther* (focused on the Black Panther Party) and *New Jack City* (focused on the illegal drug industry), Burton's sentiment became reality. Whites shoot Noah, played by Van Peebles's son, multiple times in the back for attempting to flee enslavement. On Twitter, #Roots and #Kuntaskin began to trend. @Amanda_Learning posted, "Ya'll catch that 'hands up, don't shoot' moment?" Upon the depiction of emancipation in the series, popular blogger @FeministaJones tweeted, "'Liberty to Slaves.' They hated that as much as folks hate 'Black Lives Matter.'" @JustAnt1914 tweeted, "Liberty to Slaves was the original Black Lives Matter." The significance of the series to connect the slavery era to the twenty-first century was not lost on viewers. African descendants who felt as though there was a lack of convictions in high-profile cases that involved Whites killing Black men could at least feel moments of vindication through this visual narrative.

From resistance through and in quiet and silent acts to visual narratives of overt, physical resistance, *Roots* has given voice to a history that is engrained in the DNA of America. Like the tests that allow people to discover their personal history and return to an origin that is there but is not there, Kunta Kinte's story, in whatever form, continues to remind Americans of what has survived the Middle Passage—a fundamental connection to life that had been present long before the transatlantic slave trade served to disrupt family histories and attempted to sever the ties to cultural beliefs and practices. In the face of scrutiny by reporters and scholars, Haley would maintain his resolve that *Roots* had a purpose, but the criticism obscured the story's intent: "What really upset me the most was that, also by implication, it clearly sought to impugn the dignity of black Americans' heritage" (Norrell 181). Despite its flaws, Haley's faction stands not only as an appropriate and successful attempt for Black people to reclaim an African identity, but also as an example of how African descendants defied social death.

CHAPTER 3

Middle Passage Legacies in Charles Johnson and HBO's *Treme*

> You have seen how a man was made a slave; you shall see how a slave was made a man.
>
> —Frederick Douglass, *Narrative of the Life of Frederick Douglass, An American Slave, Written by Himself*

TO BE SURE, *Roots* opened the door for more writers to explore the dimensions of slavery. Prior to *Roots,* fugitive slaves or those who were alive during the slavery era had written most depictions of slavery. Margaret Walker's historical novel *Jubilee* had been published in 1966, but its focus was on slavery and the post-Reconstruction era in the South. *Roots*'s attention to the Middle Passage first introduced the journey to mainstream readers. Other writers would eventually follow Haley's lead by using research to construct novels based on their family history.

While there are now many literary texts by writers of African descent that explore the Middle Passage, my focus on the Middle Passage's connection to the South brings me to Johnson's *Middle Passage* and HBO's *Treme* in this chapter and Rhodes's *Voodoo Dreams* in chapter 4, texts highly influenced by African history in New Orleans. Most prominent of the two major bodies of water that border the city is the Mississippi River, which is responsible for bringing people of various national backgrounds to the city that has, over time, formed its identity as an international city of blended cultures, languages, and religious practices, a prime location in the Atlantic Global South. Among these groups are people of West Africa and their descendants who were traded for labor and dispersed to plantations across the state and the South. Further, the novels and television series centralize and make prominent the presence of Africa in the U.S. South, revealing the development of the African diaspora in the South.

As noted earlier, gender figures prominently in considerations of the Middle Passage. Both Johnson and Rhodes develop characters who see themselves through the lens of their parents. Knowing the intricate details of what motivates the parent's individual decisions is often not possible; therefore, the son or daughter depends on what he or she perceives as the parent's motive. As the descendant ponders why a father or mother made a certain decision or why the parent is present or not, the descendant becomes engaged in the stages of both discovery and recovery. Orlando Patterson argues that social death is the disconnect between the African descendant and the African origin. Recovery of the origin where the Black self resides, in Patterson's scenario, is impossible. Yet, contemporary representations of Black parent and child relationships suggest that recovery is possible. More specifically, in this chapter, I am interested in representations of father-and-son relationships. Recovery of the identity, the attempt to understand what has been taken, destroyed, or lost, as represented by the missing or lost parent, brings the descendant into the possession of life. Of *Roots,* David Chioni Moore observes, "The recovery of a root—as in Haley's *Roots*—serves an especially important function when a major chunk of the tangle of one's identity has been either erased or systematically denigrated" (21). Moving through the Middle Passage, returning to it to reclaim what was disrupted and distorted through the mental and physical trauma of the journey, presses upon the reader the possibility of removing the distortions to reveal a connection that is not lost but hidden. Using Johnson's novel and the series *Treme* as representative written and visual texts, I explore how a return to the Middle Passage as a geographical space and temporal space of metaphorical discovery serves as a site for the development of Black masculine identity, which emerges from the overlapping perspectives and experiences of fathers and sons, despite the threat of social death. Black sons' knowledge of the cultural and familial past allows them an opportunity not only to understand their fathers but, consequently, to understand their own purpose and value.

NEW ORLEANS: A MIDDLE PASSAGE

As a port city, New Orleans was a busy point of entry for enslaved Africans and slaves from the Caribbean. In 1719, two hundred enslaved Africans were brought to New Orleans for the first time. During the roughly fourteen-week journey, "roughly 20 percent" died (Borders 501). Relying on an extensive excavation of historical records, James Borders IV concludes:

> The Trans-Atlantic Slave Trade Database will document 107,000 enslaved Africans who were brought to Louisiana between 1719 and 1820. Of those brought to New Orleans whose regional origin is identified, 37% are Central Africans (principally Angolan and Congo), 22% Senegambians (Mandingo, Bambara, Wolof), 15% from Benin (Dahomey), 14% Sierra Leone, 9% Biafra, with the remaining 3% split between Mozambique on the East Coast of Africa and Gold Ghost (Ghana) on the West Coast. (502)

New Orleans would undeniably become an African port. By 1830, the year Johnson's *Middle Passage* is set, 56.5 percent of the 46, 085 residents of the city were African or African descendants (Borders 539).

New Orleans is a commonly used site for southern African American and African diaspora literary discourse. A city born out of its reliance on the Mississippi River, it is a setting for works of literature that deal with the sordid and horrific matters related to the slave trade at this famous port. As early as the days of the slave trade, writers recorded experiences at the New Orleans port. Harriet Beecher Stowe has Tom save Little Eva from certain death by drowning in the Mississippi River. In a touching scene, Uncle Tom is taken in by Eva's father, who is indebted to the good man for saving the life of his only, beloved child. As a result and by Eva's request, her father purchases Tom and provides him with as good a life as might be expected on a Louisiana plantation. New Orleans's appeal to writers remains.

Seeing the Middle Passage as connected to New Orleans, African American contemporary writers Charles Johnson and Jewell Parker Rhodes have chosen not only to revisit the Middle Passage but also to recast it through a combination of memory and reimagination. They were not there, but they were there[1]—at least, they would have us to go back there by inviting us to indulge their historical imagination. Through their characters' reluctant engagement with the Middle Passage, they, through a series of circumstances, find themselves involved in what becomes a transformative purging of sorts, where at the end of the experience they will find a self that is better, and more specifically, is more knowledgeable, than the self that existed before going through the passage. Indeed, it could not be helped, this transformation, for

---

1. I am paraphrasing Ernest Gaines's Grant Wiggins, who in the opening line of *Lesson Before Dying* states, "I was not there, yet I was there" (3). Grant suggests that he experienced the impact of the trial's outcome and the community's responses as if he were physically present in the courtroom although he heard about it from his relatives.

it is not difficult to believe that people who experience sheer terror and then find themselves reaching deep into their own spirit to survive must become a self other than the original self. Assigning purpose to the Middle Passage, Johnson and Rhodes excavate the possibilities associated with "embracing . . . the memory rather than being crushed by it" (Saunders 65).

As demonstrated by Olaudah Equiano, the Middle Passage elicits memories that serve as a gateway to a hybrid identity. Equiano's narrative on his capture from Africa, experiences with slavery, and journey toward freedom shows how he refuses defeat by enslavement. He instead takes advantage of the "master's tools"[2] to resurrect himself from his treatment as a socially dead person to become a new person. His narrative gives voice to the humanity of African peoples through a critique of the actions and behavior of Europeans. To be sure, conversion does not mean that remnants of a previous self are no longer in existence after transformation. Johnson, and later the characters in *Treme*, rejects the narrative of loss by focusing on the Middle Passage as a medium for renewal and ascension from one state of consciousness to another. Johnson's Rutherford Calhoun is a socially dead man because he has succumbed on a subconscious level to feelings that he is a nonperson unworthy of love, feelings he has developed since his days of enslavement. He later comes to understand himself as a man who is part of a larger history that begins long before he was born into slavery. His reclamation of the lost past converges with the hope that he can be a person of value, in effect redefining the idea of the slave as a soulless laborer.

When Johnson's *Middle Passage* debuted in 1990, it provided a unique contribution to American literature as it focused almost exclusively on the transatlantic voyage. A National Book Award winner, it would mark the first time that readers were able to see a perspective on the experience of captivity and exclusive interactions with transatlantic slavery from the United States to the coast of West Africa and back to the United States. At the heart of the depiction, it is clear that the Middle Passage is a haunted space that inhabits more than just the Atlantic Ocean. It is there, in that haunted space of lingering memories, that Johnson draws from to revisit a time that has passed, but not really. Storytelling provides the opportunity to exorcise feelings and emotions associated with the traumatic experiences of the ancestors whose voices emanate from the pages, to revisit this time in world history as well as to consider the lingering implication of the historical past in the present. In this chapter, I focus on the Middle Passage and its legacy as depicted by writers who set their work in New Orleans. More specifically, I argue that Rutherford Calhoun,

---

2. See Audre Lorde's *Sister Outsider: Essays and Speeches* (Crossing Press, 2007).

when enslaved in southern Illinois, succumbs to his owner's implication that he has no worth or purpose. Seeing himself through the eyes of his master and having been abandoned by his father years earlier, he only changes his perception of himself when he is able to "meet" his father in the Middle Passage and engage with Africans who are brought aboard the slave ship. Through engagement with them, he converts from social death and finds his identity and purpose. I argue further that Johnson's work nods to the future of New Orleans as depicted in the HBO series *Treme,* which celebrates the influences of Africa in various musical and cultural performances. *Treme*'s storyline of the Lambreauxs, a father and son who return to New Orleans after Hurricane Katrina, compels us to consider how culture can survive migrations and engagement with trauma and how African descendants rely on cultural practices to maintain their humanity. Delmond, with the help of his father, experiences conversion as he delves into the nuances of New Orleans culture and both men work to retain aspects of their pre-hurricane identities and to locate their identity in the post-hurricane city. By placing Rutherford Calhoun, a troubled son, in conversation with a contemporary father and son in New Orleans, where Johnson's novel is also set, I would like to tease out the legacy of oppression and how Black men navigate and resist it from one generation to the next.

JOHNSON'S MIDDLE PASSAGE

Joining a tradition of writers who explore New Orleans, Johnson connects the port city to the Atlantic as a location for transition and growth. According to Daniel M. Scott III, "For Johnson and for *Middle Passage*'s protagonist, Rutherford Calhoun, identity is the precarious 'middle' experience of the African American: offspring of the middle passage, refugee from an uncertain origin, subject to the marginalization of his experience, searcher of meaning" (654). Indeed, Johnson would agree: "Black fiction has always been about the crisis of personal identity, the profoundly painful effort to answer the question 'Who am I?' in a culture that constantly portrays blacks as different. . . . It's there—the quest for selfhood" (Monaghan 40). This crisis of identity is a legacy of the Middle Passage. Charles Johnson's *Middle Passage* is the story of Rutherford Calhoun, a former enslaved man from southern Illinois who moves to New Orleans, where he enjoys engaging in petty crimes. Such activities leave him indebted to Papa, a Creole gangster who makes a deal with Isadora, Calhoun's lady-friend. Without Calhoun's knowledge, Isadora pays his gambling debt and insists that Calhoun marry her as part of the deal to save his life. However, Calhoun rejects this arrangement and chooses to stow away on a ship that, he later finds out, illegally trafficks enslaved Africans from West Africa to New Orleans. During the return voyage, the ship's crew succumbs to a mutiny amongst themselves and the enslaved, as well as a mysterious storm that rips apart the ship. Calhoun records the unusual events of the ship in the captain's log, another layer in the story he tells from his perspective, which ends with his transformation into a new man. In many ways, the novel is about his movement from self-alienation toward "selfhood."

In *Middle Passage*, we find parts of Johnson, including his studies in philosophy, his belief in Buddha, and his maternal connection to New Orleans. Indeed, the novel is an exercise in return for Johnson, whose mother's side of the family traces their roots to New Orleans. Although raised in southern Illinois, Johnson's connection to New Orleans inspired him to give some treatment to the meaning of the place and return for his protagonist, Rutherford Calhoun, who seems intent on being lost in the city. Although Calhoun is the clear hero of the novel, his transition to self-definition and self-awareness occurs largely as a result of his interactions with the Allmuseri, the mythical group of Africans who are captured for transport. In an interview, Johnson is clear that the Allmuseri god is powerful and his captor, the arrogant Captain Falcon, underestimates the god's power. Johnson's depiction of the Allmuseri god and its interactions with the crewmen reflect his idea of writing. As a philosopher, he advocates for Black writers to use writing as intellectual art:

> I realized that we did not have in the tradition of Afro-American literature anything that might be called "philosophical fiction." Our writers have always been pressured to limit themselves to racial and social issues, usually defined by white and black critics in the most narrow of terms. What I'd hoped to do when I started writing novels in 1970 was "fill the gap," so to speak, by exploring those philosophical and scientific questions other black writers had blinked away, ignored, or dismissed, because I believed then, and believe even now, that they are crucial to our understanding of culture and consciousness. (Johnson, *White Books* 35)

Thus, for Johnson, Calhoun is a complex character intended to explore the universal theme of identity under extreme circumstances. Readers might see the Middle Passage as a symbolic space to explore and find their own hidden identities.

Establishing his own identity as an American writer, Johnson shunned the tradition of protest literature, popularized by Richard Wright in the 1940s, in an effort to offer an alternative to writing about Black experiences. Calhoun emerges as a man who does not wallow in racial oppression and does not succumb to a tragic end: "The negative is obvious. We have spoken a lot about it. But I think we have in some cases forgotten the remarkable triumphs of black people" (Monaghan 50). This is only made possible by the fact that Calhoun engages the Middle Passage and survives it through confrontation of his paternal and personal past. Calhoun undergoes a trial, but he is clearly destined to go through the trial and find a pleasurable outcome on the other end. His is not a trial that allows for physical strength to force an outcome. Johnson shares how he shapes the contours of his fiction: "Naturalism is pretty much tied to a late-nineteenth-century vision of the physical world and human psychology. It's fine, for example, if you want to write novels of social protest. But other visions and interpretations of the world require other fictional means" (*White Books* 38). Calhoun must use his intellectual reasoning to tap into his emotional senses to overcome the social and physical barriers that threaten to subdue him. What Johnson also implies in this statement, and this will certainly become clear at the end of the novel, is that the triumph is decidedly Calhoun's. While others, namely women, may be tangentially involved, their rise above adversity is not as glorious as Calhoun's is. For Calhoun, the Middle Passage experience not only affirms his humanity, as we might see with the characters featured in *Reimagining*, but similar to Kunta Kinte, it also functions to define his masculine identity, or his Black manhood, in a society where Black masculinity is seen as a thing in need of taming or annihilating altogether.

Calhoun, by his own account, is a vile man of disrepute. New Orleans, famously known as a party city, is the perfect place for him to do the things he has no business doing while enjoying every second of it. In many ways, the novel sets out to hold its characters accountable for their behavior. His stealing and lying are expressive of the belief imposed upon him by his morally supreme White owner that Calhoun has little worth. Having survived a childhood where he was an enslaved person, he finds himself free in New Orleans but confined by the feeling that he has little to no social worth. Stealing, lying, and manipulation allow him the power to create a self while annihilating another self, and leave him feeling so exhilarated by the experience of living so close to physical death that he has succumbed, without realizing it, to social death. By trying to escape marriage to Isadora, a good but miserable woman, he finds himself in a situation where he will have to atone for his sins by traveling through the Middle Passage. In the Middle Passage, he will learn that he loves his life and will find a reason to live as a better man.

The protagonist's attitude toward life emerges from his lack of a Black father and that father's experience as an enslaved man. According to what he learns from his estranged older brother, their father was a field hand, handsome, popular with the ladies, and "could whip a guitar like nobody's business and sing until it made grown women cry" (169). In other words, he was the original blues man, one who clung to life as best he could and made the best out of bad situations, a survivor, a lover, a good-time man. His flight or pursuit of freedom was what his youngest son could not forgive or, for the most part, understand. On this ship, his engagement with the Allmuseri god gives him an expanded perspective of his missing father. Gifting him with insight, the god allows Calhoun to learn why his father seemed incapable or unwilling to live respectfully within the confines of slavery. As a consequence of his wounded masculinity, "he couldn't look his wife Ruby in the face when they made love without seeing how much she hated him for being powerless, even with their own children, who had no respect for a man they had seen whipped more than once" (169). Calhoun did not know his father; this new knowledge can only be attributed to the fact that the knowing occurs as a result of his having confronted his past through the working of the Allmuseri god, the deity of the people the ship's captain has taken as cargo. At the time in which his curiosity leads him to meet the god—a god who has already left at least one person in a state of irretrievable shock for trying to feed him—Calhoun finds a truth about his father that leads him to understand a truth about himself. Calhoun may also understand his father from his perspective as an adult man who was enslaved as a child. They have both been relegated to social death status. At the point of knowing that his father died at the hands of slave patrollers, also known as pattyrollers, trying to escape social death status, he knows that his father chose to leave but did not choose not to return. Alternatively, at least, he did not return to his son in the physical sense. Remembering the dead causes the person in the state of recollection to invite a return; his engagement forces him to construct a beginning, a middle, and an end to his father's life. Johnson infuses the narrative such that what Calhoun remembers learning from his brother about their father evolves into knowing why the man left and what happened to him. Whether this is his imagination (of course, the entire narrative could be Calhoun's vivid imagination) or this is an experience worth believing may not matter as much as what occurs as a result. For Johnson, the Middle Passage distorts relationships as it distorts time and leaves it to the traveler to wade through the messiness to locate a truth about the self. Embracing that truth makes survival possible.

Johnson engages the collective voices that are not just that of the father, but of others whose stories ended in violence. Calhoun writes, "I heard a cross wind of sounds just below his breathing. A thousand soft undervoices that jumped my jangling senses from his last, weakly syllabled wind to a mosaic of voices, each one immanent in the other" (170). Voices and sounds carry across the novel, particularly once they land on the African coast. Calhoun also records that "moaning and sharp cries such as only Negro women can make drifted on the wind from the warehouse, where Africans living, dying, and dead were thrown together" (58). Documenting the sounds of pain and misery as they are separated from their loved ones and prepared for transport marks the first instance when Calhoun is unable to think only of himself and his situation; he becomes a participant through his observations of the cries and the meaning of those cries. As such, this moment serves as a precursor for his experience with the god whose name he will identify as Rutherford. His identity becomes one with the head of the Allmuseri as he begins to see himself as part of the African diaspora and not as a fatherless slave.

The Allmuseri god serves as a catalyst for Rutherford's search for redemption. Calhoun's anger at the loss of his father is seen through the perspective of masculinity, or at least his perception of it under the confining constraints of enslavement. Calhoun sees his father as a man whose masculinity has been assaulted and violated, causing the father to reclaim the loss through sex with women. Further, the father sees himself as being made into such a man, a consequence of his circumstances: "Looka how we livin" (169). Their living led to him feeling as though his wife and children also perceived him as "powerless." Gambling, "bedswerving," and flight were ways of coping, but also ways of having some control over his actions. If he had no control over his enslavement status, he had control over his actions within the slave community. Defying the rules of respectability was one way to rebel against enslavement. Calhoun's own experience with his owner, Master Chandler, makes clear that the man expects that his own sense of moral superiority will extend to those that he owns. Calhoun's father does not oblige. Interestingly, Calhoun restricts the story to his father's actions within the slave community and overlooks any interactions he had with the enslavers.

For his part, Calhoun rejects his father on one hand but embraces his way of living on the other. Like his father, Calhoun indulges a life of gambling and "bedswerving," as well as stealing. Such actions suggest that he is making every attempt to reject the White man who owns them in southern Illinois. Master Peleg Chandler, whom he describes as abhorring slavery, proved this by personally teaching him and his brother how to read and write, and how to critically analyze some of the most profound philosophical and classical literary texts. Despite his shortcomings, Calhoun's narrative proves that he excelled in his education. He lacked ethics and felt justified in his grudge against his brother, Jackson. His brother, who loyally tended to Master Chandler, when asked to identify what he wanted after the man's death, felt it appropriate to share the wealth of the estate with all who were owned by it at the present and in the past. Of his brother, Calhoun observes: "He was (to me) the possible-me that lived my life's alternate options, the me I fled. Me. Yet not me. Me if I let go. Me if I gave in" (112). He suggests here that there is a hidden self that is capable of acting morally right but chooses to perform morally wrong. According to Calhoun, his brother says that in him he "saw their runaway father" (113). In one man, there exists another man.

Each one of these men has been influenced by the experience of enslavement and seeks ways to define himself despite this experience. If Calhoun is a replica of his father, it is not insignificant that Calhoun sees his brother as akin to the Allmuseri in action and belief. He shares with Squibb, his drunken confidant and the ship's cook, that Jackson "could be from their tribe, for all I know," to which Squibb reminds him that means that Calhoun would be Allmuseri as well. Calhoun clarifies that he sees the Allmuseri "less as a biological tribe than a clan held together by values" (109). Once rescued from the ship's wreckage, Calhoun reveals that he wrote the log in retrospect, based on memory and, undoubtedly, some imagination. As the writer of the log, he takes license to show what changed him by casting himself as a man who transitioned from seeing himself as a person with no history he cared to remember or respect to a man who sees himself as part of a "clan held together by values" (108).

Probably as a result of having been abandoned by his father, he boards the ship as a man who has come to see himself as worthless/valueless, or, on some level, as socially dead. What he does not reveal in the story to Squibb is that Master Chandler voiced his disappointment in his protégée's actions. He writes, "If you had known me in Makanda or New Orleans, you would have known that I doubted whether I truly had anything of value to offer others" (162). This stems from an earlier time when he asked Chandler what he felt as though he could do for others; Chandler responds by asking him, "What *can* you do?" (162). Consuming the master's assault on his character, he concludes, "it made me feel as if everything of value laid outside me" (162). Chandler's power over how the fatherless boy thinks of himself is undeniable, and he is certainly aware of his influence; what he underestimates is Calhoun's capacity to rebel against him in subtle but effective ways. Following this exchange, Calhoun begins to steal Chandler's valuable possessions—certainly an attempt to assert revenge, but also an attempt to recoup the value of his life that he felt had been denied by Chandler. This is likely why when his brother, a man who found a way to define his value through service to others (even Whites who were not too evil) and to God as a preacher, shares the wealth of the estate, Calhoun is enraged. The fact that he asked a man who is in legal possession of his freedom what he had to offer to others reveals the profound feeling of

worthlessness that has lain dormant until Chandler gave it voice. Not knowing how to define his worth through character, Calhoun assumes that money
and possessions would fill the gap of value and negate his social death status.

Although Calhoun sees himself as the moral opposite of his brother,
he takes transformative steps, while traveling through the Middle Passage,
toward becoming his brother's moral equal, if not superior. Just as Jackson laid
out the clothes and combed Chandler's brittle hair, Calhoun, who is generally
loyal to no one but himself, seems to show sympathy for Captain Falcon, a
man who traffics African men and women and rapes young sailors. Falcon
is similar to Chandler in some respects; both men read extensively and take
serious study of the work that they read, presumably to make the best of their
lives. Once caught in the captain's room, Calhoun distracts from his attempts
to steal by telling of the crew's plans for a mutiny, and Falcon rewards his loy-
alty by giving him a gun and a means to use the gun. Further, Calhoun finds
himself caring for Falcon when he is confined to his quarters, a man that he
had earlier felt apprehension in conversing with in closed quarters for fear of
rape or cannibalism, or some yet unrevealed threat to his person. Once it is
established that White men have no unique claim on masculinity, as indicated
by their similarities, Calhoun and Jackson move past oppression to extend
forgiveness to their oppressors. Forgiveness is a human virtue that may serve
as a form of resistance.

Falcon, according to Johnson, is evil (Monaghan 54). Unlike Captain
Davies in *Roots,* he has no consciousness and gladly engages in the sale of
Africans. A little man, he exerts power over others as he hopes to advance
the idea or myth that he is superior. Yet, he is not superior in any stretch of
the imagination. Johnson sees Falcon's warped sense of himself as laughable:

> The Allmuseri god sits in the hold of that slave ship, *The Republic*, like a
> nuclear bomb ready to go off at any time. It resembles less a Western god
> (Jehovah or Allah) than Krishna, the shape-shifting, omnipresent deity in
> the *Bhagavad Gita*. Literally, it's everywhere at once. Captain Falcon has only
> captured one of its infinite manifestations, and the Allmuseri god is rather
> amused by that. (Williams, "Charles Johnson Discusses")

Falcon, then, contrasts significantly with the Allmuseri god that has allowed
itself to be captured and, in doing so, has allowed the White man to believe
that he is in charge. Falcon's Whiteness, his sense of himself as capable of
doing whatever he wants with whomever he wants, is a façade. He learns this
as he begins to die and to lose his power to men who are interested in killing him. His life depends only on what they are willing to believe about him.

As symbolic of what James Baldwin calls the "lie of white supremacy," Falcon is representative of American delusions. Baldwin describes it as stemming from those who "informed their children that Black women, Black men and Black children had no human integrity that those who call themselves white were bound to respect. And in this debasement and definition of Black people, they debased and defamed themselves" (Baldwin 87). Falcon is guilty of both believing in this and acting on it as truth. Through the mutiny, Johnson reveals the fragility of white supremacy by contrasting the crew's chaos to Calhoun's bonding with the Allmuseri god. Nevertheless, Calhoun's transformation allows him to see Falcon as the oppressed other and to extend his own humanity to the man who upholds the belief.

His most remarkable step in his transformation is the bond that he develops with Baleka, a young Allmuseri girl. When he first meets Baleka and tries to give her a moldy biscuit, he takes note of her mother's protective nature, which is shown when she takes the biscuit for inspection and finding it unsuitable for her daughter, gives it back to Calhoun with a look of scorn. Noting her actions, Calhoun is placed in a position to learn that even those deemed as the lowliest on the ship still retain a sense of dignity. From them, he will get another perspective, as he has from his father and brother, of how people of African descent navigate the threat of social death. An enslaved child, Baleka can receive little from her mother but lessons in how to behave, namely how to retain her humanity even at the worst time in her life. Calhoun also takes note that the mother seems drawn to him to forge a bond between him and her daughter. Seeing that he has more freedom than they, even though he is the only free Black body among their White captors, she may not be able to understand fully his position on the ship, but she understands that he possesses more power than she. Calhoun's sense of himself as a man who has loyalties to no one but himself, then, is challenged by the woman, who, in essence, asks him to think not simply of himself and his own survival, but of the child as well. Her eventual removal from the ship by falling over the side during a storm and, consequently, from the narrative leaves open his occasion to become a hero. Baleka's presence in his life as a surrogate daughter gives rise to his new identity as an Allmuseri and not just the fatherless ex-slave of southern Illinois. He becomes the father he did not have, a man who embraces his role as a parent.

Baleka and her mother are not the only women who help Calhoun in his transformation or rebirth. Isadora is a woman in need who tries to help a man in need, even if he does not see himself as a person who can be or should be helped. As critic Elizabeth Muther concludes, "The narrator uses her as a moral compass of sorts, the object female, though he both loves her in theory and finds her intolerable" (651). An arrogant man, Calhoun feels pity for Isadora. He describes her as a respectable woman, "pretty in a prim, dry, flat-breasted way," a woman who "never used make-up" and had "an inner brilliance, an intelligence and clarity of spirit." She was also overweight. Uncertain as to why he is attracted to her, he gravitates between spending time with her and finding her ways as a teacher and a woman with standards "unbearable" (Johnson, *Middle Passage* 6–7). Muther observes further, "Her grotesque body, as he renders it in justifying his escapades, carries all the marks of the cultural wounding she has suffered and he has compounded: not the marks of the whip, not the scars of slavery per se, but the wounds of maternal loss," and, I would add, paternal loss (651). Like her ragged band of cats, she is abused and vulnerable. Her father, who had beaten her mother to death, physically abused Isadora. Although Calhoun says that she harbored no "hatred" in her, her declaration to Calhoun that he was like her father is a confession that she hopes to use her respectability to change him into a man better than her father. Calhoun and Isadora, two people disappointed by the sins of their fathers, are well suited.

However, Calhoun's abandonment by his father and estrangement from his elder brother leave him vulnerable as well. Calhoun boards the ship not only to avoid a marriage that he did not consent to but also to defend his sense of masculinity. It is no coincidence that he boards a ship, a space dominated by men. To be sure, his transformation hinges greatly on the environment of the ship, where he must move from his identity as a thief and womanizer to a man of responsibility and respectability. He has a choice here; no one forces him because he is a slave or because he owes a debt to anyone. Under the circumstances of the strange weather and the mutinies, his survival could mean that he kills others to save himself or that he finds a medium ground. Calhoun learns how to negotiate as well as navigate the unfamiliar terrain that becomes his life during the countless days that he is aboard the ship. By the end of the voyage, he, by his own accord, becomes the respected friend of the White man whose identity he tried to steal and the surrogate father of a parentless girl. During the voyage, he becomes a friend of the Allmuseri and receives protection in the form of a gun from Captain Falcon. Notably, he does not use the gun. Instead, he builds a sense of rapport among the key players on the ship and uses it, as best he can, to maintain a slight level of stability until the ship finally breaks apart.

He is the hero of the adventure. Instead of Isadora saving him, he saves Isadora. Once he emerges from his cabin of the ship that saves him and Baleka and learns that Isadora has become the pending bride of his nemesis, he is clear that she is to blame for her condition. Calhoun has conveniently forgotten that she became entangled with Papa by buying Calhoun's debts to save him from the wrath of Santos, Papa's henchman. Her turn of fate, from a woman willing to sacrifice herself to force a man who is not ready to marry her to marry her, has left her vulnerable. Giving away her self-reliance to men—first Calhoun and then Papa because of Calhoun's absence—she finds herself marrying to survive, limited in power, rendered socially dead. Calhoun's new knowledge, not just of the Middle Passage experience but also of the names of the financiers, places him in a position of power. First, he is able to negotiate for Isadora's freedom. Second, he is able to endear himself to Santos as a newfound brother (descendant of the Allmuseri) and to force a wedge between Santos and Papa, a man now exposed as an individual who has been exploiting members of the diasporic community just as he has been supposedly supporting aspects of the community. Calhoun, then, establishes himself as a credit to the race, as a suitable man for Isadora, and as her savior. Yet, his transformation from man of disrepute to protector of girl and woman reveals that heroes have flaws.

As kindred spirits, both emotionally abandoned by their fathers and their mothers by death, Calhoun and Isadora's attempt to have sex after all has been settled is upset by the trauma that binds them and separates them. So limited is her description, we have no idea whether anything about Isadora's way of thinking changed as has Calhoun's. Perhaps the suggestion here is that she needed no change of consciousness or belief. Her only change is the loss of weight and her desire to give herself sexually to Calhoun. (Who'd have dreamed these depths of passion were in a prim Boston schoolteacher?) Although women of the nineteenth century were encouraged to follow the cult of true womanhood ideology, there is no evidence that women, including Isadora, had no ideas of desire. In fact, restrictions on exploring sexual desires suggest that in fact, women were sexual beings with desires which they unveiled behind their closed doors. Conversion for Calhoun becomes aversion for Isadora, whose sexual interests are rebuffed. Her own desires become secondary to his desire to cast himself as a hero. He tells her, "I thought this is what you wanted," but he decides to hold her instead. As a result, "Isadora drifted toward rest, nestled snugly beside me, where she would remain all night while we, forgetful of ourselves, gently crossed the Flood, and countless seas of suffering" (Johnson, *Middle Passage* 209). Muther argues further that Isadora, among other ways, is "bound by Calhoun's inability to understand that she, too, is under the constraints of the dominant social order" (651). In their relationship, Calhoun represents "the dominant social order." Heroes are not perfect. And whether or not we admire this hero is a question worth considering. Calhoun's relationships with women hinge on a patriarchal perspective that uses the Middle Passage experience as an occasion for a transformative way of thinking and being.

Nevertheless, ultimately, Charles Johnson relies on history and fiction to redefine the Middle Passage. Calhoun exits from the journey physically worn but spiritually renewed. He enters a selfish man but emerges as a father who is willing to love others. In turn, the Middle Passage is undoubtedly an experience that makes for new identities, if African descendants will allow it to. When Isadora tells Calhoun that he is not the same man she knew, he affirms her observation: "Sometimes without knowing it I spoke in the slightly higher register of the slaves" (194). He then goes on to describe his affection for Baleka: "If she bruises herself, I feel bruised" (195). Calhoun strongly implies that his change or conversion has as much to do with his contact with the Allmuseri as with any other part of his voyage. His discovery of the "claim of birth" that Patterson says is lost to the enslaved is only made possible by his engagement with the Middle Passage, where he is able to recover the past that he assumed had been lost. It is an exercise in exorcism that leaves him reconciled and able to move forward in opening himself to others. In effect, Johnson removes the power of the Middle Passage to limit and restrict the mind and spirit. While we are asked to believe the story that Calhoun tells, it is possible that what he sees after the journey—for example, Isadora's beauty— is an aspect that he missed before the journey. As such, her beauty is symbolic of what he does not see in himself or in being Black. Beauty, then, acts as a symbol of self-acceptance and self-awareness or rather, refusing to see the Black self through the eyes of the oppressor.

NEW ORLEANS IN MOTION

What of Calhoun, Isadora, and Baleka's descendants? Imagining that they stay in New Orleans, they will deal with forms of racial discrimination well into the twenty-first century. Among the problems that became clear in the days following Hurricane Katrina was the disproportionate level of poverty among a significant number of African American residents in the city. Yet, when the flooding displaced people from their homes, causing too many of them to seek shelter on the roofs of their houses or apartment complexes for days in the scorching August heat, people saw and felt racial discrimination in shocking forms. In part II of this study, I probe the economic and social legacy of the Middle Passage in the South, including New Orleans and Mississippi, on African descendants. Here, I will look at the legacy as portrayed in the HBO television series *Treme,* which seems to me to show contemporary attempts by

Black men to defy attempts to disrupt their ties to an African identity. *Middle Passage's* depiction of Calhoun's search for his self-worth by understanding his father's plight as an enslaved man is similarly depicted in *Treme,* in the relationship between Big Chief Albert Lambreaux and his son, Delmond, a jazz player. Moving from New Orleans to pursue his jazz career in New York causes Delmond to reassess who he is. Is he an expatriate in conflict with New Orleans and his culture as the son of a Mardi Gras Indian Chief, or is he still of New Orleans even though he is no longer in New Orleans? As the father and son build their relationship and deal with the contradictions associated with being Black in New Orleans, the celebration of culture and the city's mistreatment of citizens—for our purposes, working class Black citizens—we are reminded that they are legacies of the Middle Passage.

Through the Lambreaux, *Treme* attempts to highlight the presence of Africa and enslavement embodied in the Mardi Gras Indians, even if the focus in a television show in some ways amounts to minimizing the African presence. Scholar and documentarian Maurice Martinez joins other scholars in seeing the Mardi Gras Indians as a response to oppression that began in early New Orleans:

> The removal of enforced egalitarianism—protection by Federal troops— from New Orleans at the end of Reconstruction, coupled with the 1896 Supreme Court decision Plessy v. Ferguson, officially established racial segregation in America. One of the most resilient, truly indigenous "American," responses in the 1880's and 1890's in New Orleans from people of color was the Mardi Gras Indians, and with them, jazz. (para. 3)

Perhaps true to the political changes that inspired these cultural performances, this history was not always welcomed. In her unpublished tribute, "Requiem for a Chief: Allison Marcel Montana, 1922–2005," Brenda Marie Osbey writes of the history of Big Chief Allison Marcel "Tootie" Montana, who died at a New Orleans Council meeting in July 25, 2005, while telling of harassment he had endured from police. Osbey takes note of the pride he felt in the part he took in a history that, for him, dated back at least five generations as a Mardi Gras Indian and in the intricate design and unique beauty of his Indian suits. She states, "He died a warrior's death, fighting for respect for a cultural tradition that helps to define this city" ("Requiem" 22). By focusing on a father and son, *Treme* tries to capture the importance of preserving this cultural tradition not just for the community, but especially for the performers.

Treme opens by framing the fractured disconnectedness that characterized New Orleans communities shortly after the 2005 hurricane. When we

first meet Big Chief Lambreaux, played by Clarke Peters, he is in movement—
being chauffeured by his reluctant, disgusted daughter, who drives him over
the Mississippi River Bridge to their dilapidated home in New Orleans East.
In a state of quiet pensiveness, he moves from one part of New Orleans to
the other—searching for a viable place to live. He settles on a bar, a place he
does not own, but it is a place where his gang has had meetings to prepare
for masking. It is at these times that he works with other members to make
the beautiful costumes they wear on certain days of the year and to practice for their performances. In season one, Chief cannot begin this process
until he locates his members. After Katrina, people could not rely on mail
or phone service. Mail carriers, even if they were in the city, were prohibited
from delivering mail, given the condition of the streets and the inaccessibility
of homes. Overworked cell phones were just as inconsistent. In the age before
the growing popularity of smartphones with access to Facebook, email, and
Instagram, social media in 2005 was not as popular among African Americans as it became ten years after the hurricane. It was not unusual for people
to rely on serendipitous meetings, perhaps at restaurants, stores, funerals,
or churches, to locate one another. Many did not know the location of their
neighbors who too had been displaced from the most affected areas. Through
rumors, people learned that it is not unusual to return to their family's houses
and find bodies of dead loved ones under a large object or in the attic. New
Orleans resident and poet Kalamu ya Salaam captures this in haiku number
seven of "You Can't Survive on Salt Water": "a son returns, finds / four-month-
old bones wearing his / missing mother's dress." Salaam's attention to a return
where he finds death and not his parent is provocative. Such is the case with
Jesse, a member of the Chief's gang. Unfortunately, the Chief and Jesse's son
find the decayed body of the man underneath a boat. As a symbol, Paul Gilroy argues that "ships [for our purposes, a boat] immediately focus attention
to the middle passage" (4). Placing a Black man's body underneath the boat is
a reminder of the slave ship's hold, where death in one form or another was
certain to occur. Death lingers in *Treme*.[3] How Jesse died is not determined;
that he died is their main concern. Discovery of Jesse's body and the son's
final declaration that he has no desire to live in their house again marks what,
for the Chief, will be a truth that he cannot process or accept, that his life of
tradition may die too.

3. I will note here that although the series is named for an area of New Orleans that has
historical African influences, this story line is not set in Treme. Although a viewer may have
to be from an area of New Orleans to recognize the geographical shifts, the action of the series
moves from one part of the city to others, including the surrounding areas.

To stave off social death that could come as he processes the devastation of his neighborhood and the lack of efficient help by government officials, Chief works to bring the people together through preparation for Mardi Gras. According to a report, "it is because of residential segregation that predominantly Black communities in New Orleans were more susceptible to destruction caused by Katrina, which can be correlated to the rate of return of African American to New Orleans" (*State of Black New Orleans* 142). In New Orleans East, where Chief appears to reside, "five years after Katrina, the Lower Ninth Ward and the Little Woods neighborhood in New Orleans East were still experiencing declines of more than 10,000 people" (*State of Black New Orleans* 143). All over the city, much to the chagrin of critics, New Orleanians and people in the surrounding areas look forward to the city's coming together, for signs that tell them that the city and traditions will go on and will not be defeated by strong rain and wind and government failures. As he works with members of the community to make their Indian suits, Chief also tries to take a stand against the local government, who closed local housing projects after evacuating the residents. Feeling as though the city is conspiring to rid the city of poor Black people, he insists that the city reopen the housing areas to allow people a chance to return to the city whose Black population has been decimated. Much of what is expressed by characters in *Treme* was expressed by local residents in City Council meetings, in protests, in editorials, at work, in bars, in homes, and so on. A resident and survivor of the hurricane made a point of saying, "With the evacuation scattering my family all over the United States, I felt as if it was an ancient memory, as if we had been up on the auction block" (*When the Levees Broke*). Months after, people were still asking for assistance to find their elderly parents and their young children. Big Chief's desire to bring his community of African descendants back together was not just a fictional depiction.

Big Chief is a man who receives respect, at least in his community and as patriarch of his family. When he speaks, people defer to his judgment, and he does not hesitate to let them know when he does not agree with their ideas or opinions. After Katrina, he learns that his power of influence has limits. Taking his interests outside the community among politicians and the police department is met with resistance and animosity. After failing to get a satisfactory response from one politician to help with reopening the housing projects—a controversial idea at best, considering problems associated with generations of African Americans being confined by public housing—he stages a sit-in. The sit-in sounds well planned. He obtains the permission of one of the unit's residents to occupy her living area, has her son unlock the door, and tells his supporters to call the media and then the police. All works according to plan until the police come, gain entry, and perform their own script as opposed to the one envisioned by Chief, who assumed that he would make a victory walk in handcuffs to the car and be released on bail shortly thereafter. In her study of television as a site of resistance, Christine Acham observes of HBO's attention to Black life:

> The proliferation of HBO films about the past prior to the Civil Rights era overlooks the narratives present in contemporary American society. Many current incidents beg for visualization, a way to come to terms with the contemporary U.S. social and political environment. Racism, while at times more covert, still plays an active role in the lives of all minority groups. (178)

HBO attempts to address contemporary racism by revisiting the effects of Katrina in New Orleans—the most televised representation of racism in contemporary media before videos of Blacks being killed by police and the responding movement occupied airwaves and social media. Officers from the New Orleans Police Department, known for clashes with Mardi Gras Indians, close the curtains and beat Chief, who is then arrested for punching one of the officers. Big Chief's relationship to the community, when he critiques it, is tenuous. Yet, unlike Calhoun and Kunta, Big Chief remains defiant and does not bend to the will of the authorities that seek to control members of the community. As a result, he deals with their power. Jailed for several days, he is not released until after Mardi Gras, meaning that he is not able to participate in the sacred day of Mardi Gras and to mask, as is his tradition. His resistance to an institution with the ability to threaten, confine, and harm (if not kill) his Black body is another act in a long history. His position as a man of influence among his diminished community has no place among the police, whose position as government agents conflicts with Chief's sense of self-worth. In reality, after the City Council later voted to demolish the buildings, "resulting in 3,170 fewer public housing units in New Orleans," protestors "made accusations of racism" (*State of Black New Orleans* 149). Although the Calliope and other housing projects are never reopened, as Chief tells Darius, a young man he is mentoring, they have only lost the battle. In other ways, his show of defiance lets the officials know that he sees himself and the community from his own perspective and not from theirs.

Darius and Delmond learn many lessons from Chief, especially how the community's pride is connected to unique aspects of culture. Remaining in practice with the culture gives them an opportunity to remember and to celebrate their Blackness in a place that often sees them as a tolerable nuisance. Darius's aunt takes him to the Chief in an effort to keep him busy. Not knowing that the Chief found Darius the night before in the back room of the bar with a girl, Darius's aunt asks the Chief to give her nephew work if he has any. Darius eventually is given work sewing the Indian suits with his aunt, whom the Chief develops a relationship with, and other men in the community and the Chief's gang. Darius learns how to sew and learns of traditions associated with the Indians. Although he is not present the following year, we can assume that what he learns about culture and pushing forward to preserve culture is a lesson that will remain with him.

On the other hand, Delmond is Chief's son and has long been initiated into the culture his father loves. When we meet Delmond, he is in New York and is emerging as a new jazz trumpet player, like a young Wynton Marsalis, whom the jazz performers refer to several times. When asked to play classic New Orleans jazz, he simply refuses. Delmond is truly in danger of succumbing to social death, which threatens to annihilate his identity as a son of New Orleans. In New York, he wants to be more than a cliché from New Orleans and makes this clear to whoever will listen, but that changes. In season two, we learn his father is more than a chief and a construction worker—he is also a musician. It was he who taught his son to play jazz music and exposed him to the great musicians of New Orleans.

Delmond begins to return to his roots when he reengages with the men to prepare the Indian suits for Mardi Gras and then St. Joseph's Day. Although this Chief seems uncharacteristically unaware of African influences on the Mardi Gras Indian masking tradition, as revealed when they visit a museum, such influences are acknowledged by Mardi Gras Indians. Big Chief Tyrone Casby has described the lineage:

> Mardi Gras Indian masking reaches all the way back to Congo Square, where the enslaved people of color were allowed to express their own cultures, and it reaches back to the street parades long practiced in African-American neighborhoods during segregation. The suit, he said, "is just a facade; I'm expressing a spirit deeper than the costume." (MacCash, para. 6)

Delmond moves beyond being part of the sewing and listening and begins to study and think deeply about the traditions. During a few of his visits to New Orleans, he plays in the clubs and remembers with a deeper understanding of the culture. We see the pensive look of his eyes as he listens to local musicians play jazz in the clubs. Return is not just a physical movement for him, but it means being present, connecting with the community and the people he left behind to pursue his jazz career in New York. Eventually, he declares himself as part of the tradition and works to express his return to New Orleans culture in his music by making a compilation that features his Dad as Big Chief and other sounds of New Orleans. Interweaving music with masking allows the son to draw on the traditions passed down by the father, including his musical talents. In Wynton Marsalis's *Congo Square,* cowritten with Ghanaian Yacub Addy, he maintains that African sounds and rhythms were joined together and his *Congo Square* sought to rediscover the prominence of the African presence. In an interview, he states, "'Those folk songs and hymns the slaves learnt from their masters were the real basis, the African element was grafted on top, not the other way round,' he says very firmly, 'and this is why African and jazz rhythms developed in a different way. Listen, if you clap a marching rhythm, one-two-three-four, you can fit a swing rhythm over the top, like this'" (Hewett para. 3). Delmond's reclamation may show the relationship between conversion and return, not just to his New Orleans roots but to Africa through those roots. Always in process, he is certainly not the same person who left New Orleans, but the problems of the flood renew in him a new person and allow him to reconnect with his father. For them, New Orleans is more than a city of celebrations, although it is theirs by nature of the history that they claim despite the contemporary problems.

In 2015, the National Urban League, under the leadership of national president Marc Morial, former mayor and son of the first African American mayor, hosted a conference in New Orleans that featured panels focused on Katrina and the state of the city ten years later. In conjunction, the Urban League's New Orleans chapter published *State of Black New Orleans: 10 Years Post-Katrina,* which provides reports on the status of Black people before and after Katrina in the areas of civic engagement, the justice system, the economy, education, health, housing, and environmental injustice. Speaking on the historical treatment of African Americans through the lens of Katrina, Keith Weldon Medley observes in the report's foreword,

> The city's African American character is not defined by slavery or Jim Crow or caste. Its character has been defined by their transcending the many attacks on their humanity, battling back against them and finding the strength to live another day, raise families, and shatter the tenet of White Supremacist thought by forming a sense of community, educating the next generation and possessing a hell of a lot of faith and grit. (14)

Weldon's observation of resilience speaks well of the resistance to social death that is as characteristic of Black Katrina survivors as it is to their enslaved ancestors.

Like DNA, memories and practices are passed down from one generation to the next. New Orleans's connection to the Middle Passage is an appropriate setting to explore what links the past to the present. Social death's threat to an individual's identity and family ties is a remnant of the Middle Passage. Writers and performers explore the danger of this as they seek to mend the ruptures in the fabric that connects individuals to important aspects of their identities. The male characters in *The Middle Passage* and *Treme* emphasize how African-descended individuals define the relationship between how they see themselves and how they perceive the world around them. Embracing identity on their own terms is a personal act of resistance to social death.

CHAPTER 4

Calling Marie Laveau

> What if? What if the Ancestors intended some other purpose for us to have been brought to this part of the world, entirely apart from the European lust for profit? It seems to me that just asking that question puts us in a different position and releases a tremendous amount of energy. In honoring our own dead, as I said before, by focusing on ourselves and what the experience of slavery has meant and can't mean, even just embracing all that, somehow helps to contain the experience so that we can benefit from the memory rather than being crushed by it.
>
> —M. NourbeSe Philip (qtd. in Saunders 64)

BY SETTING their work in New Orleans, Charles Johnson and Jewell Parker Rhodes in conversation with the HBO series *Treme* illuminate the impact the Middle Passage has had on African descendants' lives. As depicted, rather than succumbing to the tragedy of the Middle Passage, the characters associated with these fictional narratives attempt to find a purpose that allows them the strength to move past tragedy. Whatever their process, it involves a change, a transformation. That is to say, could Johnson's Calhoun change to any extent without having the experiences he describes aboard the *Republic*'s travel over the Atlantic?

Set in New Orleans, Jewell Parker Rhodes's *Voodoo Dreams* imagines a purpose for the Middle Passage through the story of a fictionalized Marie Laveau and her coming of age, from a confused girl to a Voodoo Queen.[1]

---

1. This chapter evolves from an earlier essay: "Voodoo Feminism through the Lens of Jewell Parker Rhodes's *Voodoo Dreams*." *Women's Studies Journal,* vol. 41, no. 13, pp. 282–302. Brenda Marie Osbey notes of the historical Laveau: "A hairdresser by trade, Laveau was the first in what is now a long line of opportunists who saw in the religion the beginnings of a thriving tourism trade which, plied just so, could prove a continued source of personal wealth and power. It goes without saying that her clientele was made up entirely of whites who, ignorant of the religion *as* religion, sought her out for her so-called magical powers. And though she certainly never achieved anything like real wealth, to this day her name does strike wonder and awe in the imaginations of song writers, storytellers, visiting schoolchildren and the uncounted sightseers who still flock to mark their +'s on her tomb" ("Why We Can't Talk" 5).

Readers meet Marie in 1812 on her tenth birthday; she is a child who lives in an isolated town in southern Louisiana with her grandmother, also named Marie. Her grandmother is a secretive woman who will not discuss the where-abouts of her absent daughter, Marie.[2] We later learn that Marie, or Marie Laveau's Maman, was killed in New Orleans for leading a Voodoo ceremony in front of St. Louis Cathedral. The youngest Marie does not know her story; consequently, she is unaware of her legacy as a servant to the serpent-god/loa Damballah and is confused by the visions she receives and the voice she hears. Marie's grandmother takes her to New Orleans to find her granddaughter a husband, but it is in New Orleans that the young girl meets an older man (John) and a woman (Nattie) who answer the questions that she has about her missing mother, her legacy as a servant of Damballah, and her relationship to Voodoo. Rhodes's novel is the story about a teenaged girl who, in the nine-teenth century, learns to embrace her ability to navigate the worlds of supreme spirits, spirits of the dead and of the living. Her gift is to move between the worlds and her calling is to use the gift to resist oppression and to uplift those perceived as socially dead people in her community.

In conversation with Haley, Johnson, Equiano, and other African-descended writers and artists, Rhodes uses a feminist perspective to present a woman who reclaims her identity or rights of birth through her matrilineal line. In order to establish this, the Middle Passage is interwoven into Rhodes's novel as the mediating space that connects the protagonist's movement from mere survival to the empowering position of knowing. Or, in other words, she comes to understand life, especially her own in relation to others' lives, through her engagement with death. In this chapter, I argue that Marie's act of seeking her identity and finding that she is a legacy of the Middle Pas-sage—in fact, is a cultural medium between Africa and the enslaved in Amer-ica—shows a successful attempt to defy social death, but this is only made possible when she understands her possessed performance in relation to the story of her maternal past. I argue further that Rhodes casts a gaze on the Black female body as possessed and desired, and when placed against the backdrop of the Middle Passage, Marie's knowledge and understanding of her purpose requires a reclamation not only of her self but of her body as well. I am interested in how Rhodes explores the legend of Marie as a cultural per-former "to rethink the cultural tendency to read the black body, particularly the black female body, as a cultural text" (Nunes 46). Rhodes casts Marie's purpose as a priestess to illuminate the Middle Passage as a birthplace of life

---

2. The character Marie Laveau, her mother, and her grandmother are named Marie. To make distinctions, I use the family titles of Maman (Marie Laveau's mother) and Grandmère (Marie Laveau's grandmother).

for African descendants that arises out of resistance to the oppressor's attempt to extinguish the link to the life they had before captivity. Marie's conversion experience emerges from her knowledge of her connection to Voodoo and its link to Africa.

Rhodes integrates the practice and culture of Voodoo to develop her characters and theme. Voodoo is a West African–based religion. Carolyn Morrow Long concludes that Vodou of Haiti is similar to Voodoo of Louisiana, but she notes further that it is a religion distinctive of New Orleans as it is the only Afro-Catholic religion to emerge in North America. As early as 1758, African religious and magical traditions arrived in Louisiana along with the first slaves (93). While some scholars believe that New Orleans Voodoo is a mix of Catholicism and Yoruba practices, Brenda Marie Osbey argues that African beliefs and practices, and not European, remain central to New Orleans Voodoo:

> The few Catholic saints that *have* been absorbed into the religion function both in their own right and as the servants of the Ancestors. They form neither the core of our belief, nor the object of anything that might be called worship. Rather, they retain their unique identities and function primarily as servants and messengers of the Ancestors. It is the Ancestors who are the heart of the Religion and true focus of our attention because of their proximity to us. ("Why We Can't Talk" 8)

The importance of Voodoo and the influences of West African beliefs emerge as prominent themes in the novel.

Voodoo is associated with resistance toward oppressive authorities. By 1773, Louisiana court records document a case in which several enslaved people, including a Mandingo man, were tried for using a gris-gris[3] to kill their master and overseer (Long 94). Further, the Haitian Revolution started with a Vodou ceremony in 1791. Long notes, "The service was led by a priest named Boukman; a black pig was sacrificed, and the worshipers swore a blood oath to overthrow the French" (95). Hundreds of people from Haiti, including free people of color and enslaved persons, came to New Orleans during the time of the Haitian Revolution. Some of them brought their knowledge of Vodou and their desire to remain connected to their ancestors. Rhodes's descriptions are closer to Vodou practices; however, the novel captures the spirit of resistance through religious practice among the people of the African diaspora that emerges in New Orleans. Gwendolyn Mildo Hall and Ina Fandrich argue that the Voodoo practices emerged in New Orleans before the Haitians' arrival

---

3. "Gris-gris" is a word derived from the Mende language of Senegambia, referring to magical practices.

to the city and had influences from Senegambia and the Congo. Resistance is further noted by both enslaved and free persons' desire to remain connected to Africa through the practice of Voodoo. According to Hall, Louisiana voodoo was dominated by women, unlike Haitian Vodou (302).

Philip's question, quoted in the epigraph of this chapter, is queried by any number of African-descended artists, both those referenced in this study and many who are not. However, Charles Johnson appears in direct conversation with Rhodes in considering how the ancestors would not want to be "crushed" by the Middle Passage as her novel makes use of the influences of West Africa and the tragedy of the slave trade. Significantly, when Grandmère is dying and Marie is pregnant with her first child, Grandmère knows that it is time to tell her granddaughter the story of Membe, or as she aptly puts it, "the legend of yourself" (330). The story of the Maries—three generations of women born with the gift to communicate with Damballah, a water deity believed to be "father to all the gods" who "lives in springs and swamps"—begins off the coast of Africa. As a result of the transatlantic slave trade, Grandmère says, "Memories of Damballah and Africa were being lost" (331). Rhodes reframes the Middle Passage as the site necessary for the creation story that challenges Christian beliefs and gives rise to a female savior in the form of Membe. "Damballah raised his head and looked across the ocean. Ships were stealing His dark children; white men were battering and enslaving them. Damballah's children wept in the New World" (331). To bring life to the dead, Membe responded to Damballah's call to be captured by European enslavers and to go to the New World. She was chosen to "mother [his] lost children" by reviving the people's faith in Damballah and to worship him accordingly. Through the Middle Passage, her god soothed her in the hull of the ship with comforting visions. The story of Membe, a woman chosen to mother the displaced children of Africa, gives purpose and definition to the woman who followed her call to leave her place of origin. Through Membe, Rhodes wrestles with the idea that "black women's endurances have been used against them, and their bare survival is reconfigured as a strength that cannot be altered, damaged, or destroyed" (Brown 3). What happens when a Black woman resists the call to "reconfigure" strength? Grandmère explores this possibility as she also accepts the story that her mother, Membe, tells her as truth. As a result, she sees her not as her mother, but as a woman of incredible strength—so much so that she feels incapable of accepting that she is in line to carry out the wishes of the loa, Damballah. Nevertheless, Membe's true legacy is the story. Marjorie Pryse observes, "Black women have long possessed 'magical' powers and told their daughters stories" (3). Membe's engagement in these practices demonstrates the importance of Black women to survive through spiritual reverence, but survival will only occur if the daughters do not forget how they are connected to their ancestors.

Rhodes challenges Patterson's supposition that enslaved persons suffer from social death as a result of losing ties to Africa. Through fiction and history, she attempts to show a direct link through the Middle Passage as a way of resisting any cultural disruptions. Membe, in ownership of a direct connection to her African home, does not suffer from a social death, even when she is an enslaved person. Through Voodoo, Membe's religious practices are a show of cultural memories that establish a connection between Louisiana and the Dahomey of West Africa each time she shares the memory with others in the community. Rhodes not only complicates the presence of Christianity in African American history, she also complicates the Middle Passage journey by revisiting the history through the "eyes" of Marie, an African American woman who is the direct descendant of an African woman chosen to be captured and taken to America as a slave. However, being chosen gave her purpose; Membe was a woman who saw herself not as an enslaved woman, making it necessary for her to protect her daughter when the enslaver/father of the daughter came to their shack to rape her. She had told stories of their god to the community, performed miracles, passed her knowledge to her daughter, and gave her life to preserve the bloodline. Her mission had been fulfilled and through death, her life took on new meaning.

Grandmère's fear of living up to the legacy keeps her from passing the story of the women to her granddaughter, Marie, until she is on her deathbed. There is power in the story. By not telling it, she decides to leave her motherless granddaughter wandering without a history. While living in the isolated rural town of Teche, Marie longs to learn about her absent mother as she begins to resent her grandmother's unwillingness to tell her about the absent woman. Her grandmother's response is to tell her stories about her own history of oppression and sadness. Marie learns that she is of "mixed blood." More specifically, their lines are from "French royalty," an "African queen," and a "Muskogean warrior": "Mixed bloods. Our history and power" (16–17). Choosing to overlook her grandmother's insistence that their familial background is equated with power, Marie maintains her desire for tangible connections—ones that she can touch, that can touch her, and that can give her a place to leave her emotions. Consequently, she is unable to appreciate the idea of history and "lines" from the person who seems intent on keeping her from her history. While in Teche, Marie languishes in a state of "loneliness" (16), and this feeling is acute, considering she is called to serve and reside among a community of African descendants.

It is unknowing partnered with loneliness that compels young Marie to exist more often than not outside of herself as she begins to rely heavily on the voices that she hears around her. In response to her unanswered questions to her grandmother, she is given responses from an unknown source. She has a vision of a fight between two women, and Marie "somehow knew that the two women fighting were Maman and Grandmère" (18). Although her grandmother does not share with her the stories that she desires, that is, information about her mother and her mother's whereabouts, Grandmère does tell Marie about herself. At the age of nine, Marie's naïveté and youth make her unable to listen carefully to her grandmother. In addition to telling Marie about her familial lineage, Grandmère also tells her that she was born with a caul: "She saw herself, bloodied, slipping out of her mother's body, and Grandmère's frantic fingers, ripping the caul away" (18). Marie's astonishing ability to see her *self* born sets the foundation for the rest of the novel. Time and space are not boundaries for Marie simply because she is called into possession. With this gift, or curse, she is able to exist in the past and the present simultaneously. Through performances, Rhodes manipulates W. E. B. Du Bois's idea of the double consciousness, wherein an African American is born with a veil and is therefore gifted with "second sight." Du Bois informs us that it is a state of awareness that is unique to African Americans, a survival mechanism.[4] Rhodes asks readers to think of the idea literally. Marie's ability is a metaphor for a racialized experience that is made possible only through the Middle Passage. As the only vision-memory she will have of the three Maries in the physical world, readers are asked to consider the recurring cycle of birth, death, and rebirth and the cycles' relationship to water as a transitional and transformative source. Marie's birth secures the passing of Membe's legacy from mother to daughter as it emphasizes the importance of passing, from one generation to the next, the knowledge of the past itself. Knowing the purpose of second sight, rather then ignoring it, allows the recipient of the power contained within the ability to see beyond the self.

To be sure, Grandmère cannot keep Marie from her legacy. Following the confusing vision, when Marie is emotionally vulnerable and in search of answers, a "man so black he blended into the skyline" (19) touches her. It is not clear to Marie whether the man is a strange vision or a physical being, but he proceeds by "cupping the valley between her thighs, rubbing her in slow even movements" (19). Marie will later learn that her grandmother moved to Teche from New Orleans to protect her from the villainous conjurer John, a man responsible for the death of Marie's Maman. John's entrance into Teche, where

---

4. For his full explanation of double consciousness, see W. E. B. Du Bois. "Of Our Spiritual Strivings." *The Souls of Black Folk*. Chicago: A. C. McClurg, 1909.

Grandmère feels that she has a protective covering over her granddaughter, is empowered not so much by his desire to disrupt Grandmère's space as it is by Marie's desire for the unknown. If Marie is sensitive to the spirit world that appears to reach out to her through visions and whisperings, these spirits also welcome John's presence in the girl's life. As we learn later, her grandmother's plans to find a man in New Orleans to marry her and return them to Teche are thwarted by the spirits that seem intent on making sure that Marie will commit to Damballah and the plans he has for his African enslaved people.

Telling her isolated granddaughter about her family's history provides Marie with a historical identity. More specifically, the lifeline in her diverse ancestral background, according to Grandmère's story of Membe, is her African maternal roots. Rather than look backward, however, Grandmère hopes to inspire her granddaughter to look forward. As does Haley, Rhodes emphasizes power in storytelling by showing what occurs when stories remain quiet. In this case, Marie is unaware of the women's fierce fight to define themselves, to have lives that are not controlled by oppressors, even when those oppressors assume power. Marie, unlike her grandmother, was born a free woman. She is the daughter of a White man unknown to her, but her grandmother is the daughter of the White man who owned her and her mother. Living as an enslaved woman necessitated moments of resistance, especially when there were threats to the body. During her time as a slave, Grandmère loved a Native American man who was killed by her White father/master. Following that tragic event, Membe killed the White man when he came to rape Grandmère. Membe's resistance, which results in her death, teaches her daughter that her status as an enslaved person does not obligate her to accept that she cannot define her value. In other words, Membe accepts physical death to resist social death. Fearing that she cannot live up to the legacy of her mother, Grandmère flees the plantation and redefines herself in New Orleans as a free woman. From her personal experiences, she clearly hopes that Marie will have an appreciation for her freedom. She may have social freedom among the community of African descendants in New Orleans, but Grandmère is not free from her obligation to Damballah and her people.

Grandmère's eventual retreat to Teche and her reliance on Catholicism leave her vulnerable to the man she fears the most, John. Rhodes writes against colonization in the novel. Catholicism is representative of colonization. Christianity's role in the novel is merely to provide comfort to oppressed people. It is not an active religion that one can exclusively rely on to change circumstances or outcomes. In Grandmère's case, it veils. Therefore, Grandmère is not stripped of her awareness that change will come, but she does not call Damballah to provide her with a means to react responsibly to the signs that she receives from the spirits. John is aware of her vulnerability, which is exacerbated by her fear that she will lose Marie to him. To be sure, Catholicism represents colonization of the captive as Voodoo represents empowerment from oppression.

It later becomes clear that Grandmère's roots in the worship of Damballah remain too strong for her to abandon her practices. We are given a glimpse at the power that she draws from when she and Marie are threatened by Antoine, a violent White man they encounter upon their arrival in New Orleans. Marie's cries for help are immediately met with her seeing a grandmother in the process of transformation: "Marie blinked and saw a Grandmère she'd never seen before. Standing atop the wagon, her face contorted, the whites of her eyes visible, Grandmère had personified violence" (49). Grandmère's fear that she will sin—a consequence of conversion to Catholicism—by killing a White man as she had done to avenge the death of her lover extinguishes her desire to kill Antoine. Her history of killing White men, slowly, by means of calling on the death gods and enacting certain rituals, is a bold act of defiance. At that time, Grandmère was Marie, a young girl in mourning for the man she dared to love and to let love her. Their love had no respect from the man who owned her and other people, who had power, and who used it to make decisions about the enslaved, including his daughter. Her passionate pleas for the men to stop beating her lover were useless; in fact, they only served to illuminate her powerlessness. Her conversion to Catholicism is unconvincing. It was not unusual for those who remained connected to African deities to convert to Catholicism. Christian African descendants may also be African religion practitioners. While she may not regularly call on Damballah when she is in Teche, Grandmère's decision to relocate there after she converts and leaves New Orleans strongly suggests that she remains comfortable with having an attachment to the serpent god, as we know that Teche is the place of snakes.

Not long after she returns to the New Orleans area with Marie, we learn from her nemesis, Nattie, that Grandmère has been involved with conjuring. If Grandmère truly did not want to expose her granddaughter to the family's relationship with Damballah, she certainly should not have relocated to the place where people only identify her as a Damballah priestess. Rhodes casts the women as strongest when they openly acknowledge Damballah. Though the details are not provided, evidence exists that Grandmère has been using her African knowledge of healing, and not relying simply on Catholic prayers, to administer treatment to the people in her community. Marie becomes aware of this when one of her neighbors makes a statement about practices unknown to Marie: "She make a miracle. She call on the snake, lil Zombi, Dambal—" (71). The faithful man who is thankful for Grandmère's ability to act as midwife/healer/conjurer speaks of practices that Grandmère wishes to keep mysterious, unspoken. However, Damballah will not remain hidden. Finally, Grandmère becomes exposed when Nattie announces that Grandmère's lack of obedience to Damballah has caused the death and deformity of a baby, a potential member of the community. Her inability to bring forth a fully developed baby on the day that her granddaughter marries Jacques marks the end of Grandmère's place of respect in the community. The dead baby's presence suggests that the community's future is vulnerable and uncertain. It will be up to Marie to reconnect with Damballah and follow the legacy of her African great-grandmother.

Until Marie finds her place, John and Nattie's self-serving desires endanger the community. Nattie wonders why she was not chosen by Damballah to serve him. John wonders why Damballah favors women. Their jealousy and envy confirm the need for Membe's "daughters." Their cruel intentions also confirm that the power is in the knowing. Moreover, there is no other way for Marie to know who she is but for the story to have been told to her about her mother and great-grandmother by the woman who knew it best, her Grandmère. Grandmère's power remains in Membe's legacy. On her deathbed, after she has lost her granddaughter to John's influences, she realizes her error in judgment and feels compelled to empower her granddaughter with the story of the obedient and fearless woman, Membe. Grandmère's silence has made it possible for the voice of others to prevail through manipulation. When she speaks, she redeems herself and makes possible the advancement of those who are most in need of what the loa has to offer. Further, she affirms her identity as an African-descended woman and moves from beyond the shadow of oppression she has embraced. To be sure, even though she is in the process of passing into the world of the dead, her redemption results in a rebirth from social death.

Knowledge is the beginning of understanding. Marie's story is one that unfolds in various ways. Rhodes's novel is not historically factual, but the facts remain sketchy. Scholars remain baffled by who Marie Laveau was. In fact, there is some discrepancy about whether or not her father was a White planter or a free Black in New Orleans. Nevertheless, there is no indication that she left behind a diary or a memoir. To account for the fact that her historical persona is derived from written historical texts—newspapers, early nineteenth-century novels, and Works Progress Administration (WPA) interviews—Rhodes introduces interviews given by an elderly Marie to a White reporter, Louis, who was enamored by her beauty. For the most part, the narrator knows Marie intimately. From the narrator, we know what she feels when she is possessed by Damballah and when she is not possessed, what she's thinking, and what she does in response to her environment. We know her fears, her passions, and her desires.

More importantly, we learn her role as a mediator between the dead and the living. Marie's first possession finds her sharing her body with both the mother who is lost to her by physical death and the god that is unknown to her. In the novel, Rhodes focuses mostly on Marie's ability to communicate with spirits and avoids situations related to casting spells. In these possession passages, Marie transforms. During the first, her transformation controls her rather than her controlling it. She feels the presence of her mother and Damballah. She knows, without knowing how, that she is mimicking a snake and can impart wisdom to the people around her through this form. Marie's transformation appears both physical and spiritual. It is noted that "Marie slithered down from her chair. She moved through forests, crawled, and felt the earth tremble between her belly" (121). Placing her body in submission to the spirit of a deity and to that of her mother accentuates how her body is not her own and how, if she is to mature through empowerment, she will have to learn how to maintain control of her body at all times. As a person born free, she is indeed free to do so in ways that her great-grandmother and her grandmother were not, having lived as enslaved women. We must recall that this is not only the first time she connects to Damballah and, therefore, has made a major step in fulfilling her chosen legacy as Membe's granddaughter, but also that she is only sixteen years old. In Jennifer L. Griffiths's study of the impact of trauma on body and memory, she states, "Since trauma evades conscious understanding, memory becomes encoded on a bodily level and resurfaces as possession" (1). Marie is carrying the trauma that her great-grandmother was asked to carry and that her grandmother refused to carry. As such, her spirit is bonded to the history of trauma first experienced by Membe. Each transformation is a step in the conversion from a naïve girl to a community leader who must learn how to navigate trauma in service to others.

Just as the legacy of the Middle Passage is passed on from one generation of African descendants to another, so is the power that Damballah bestowed on Membe when she was called to enter the passage. As a daughter of Damballah, she is expected to give comfort to those who are in need, most of whom are slaves. Rhodes emphasizes the historical fact that many of the people who come to her are enslaved people of African descent, those who are deemed socially dead. They are so desperate for the comforts of Damballah as Marie shares them that they steal from their White owners—a crime that could bring heinous consequences—to pay for access to the advice she imparts. Her connection to Damballah places her in a position of power and influence that is recognized by the people of the Black communities and feared by John, her manipulative lover. Power is useful when the recipient has a sense of how to both access and use it. Marie is unsure of how to do either, and her performance masks her fears, but her presence on the public stage suggests to the people that they have a connection to a place that has been hidden from them by way of enslavement and lost because of the Middle Passage. For them, she represents the self that supersedes humanity and gives them a reason to suffer in the human self. Further, for the free people of color and the enslaved, she relieves the suffering placed upon them as the children of Africa in the New World. Ultimately, she gives them hope that they will all meet again in Guinea—heaven or Africa—where their spirits will be at peace.

Marie must mature into her position as the people's spiritual guide. Unfortunately, she contends with the interference of her jealous mother's spirit and her lover John. To meet the needs of the people, her body must submit to forces she does not know. During her first ceremony, after Damballah leaves her, Marie contends with her maman's possession. Accordingly, "Maman dove inside her, possessing, fitting neatly into sinews, bones, and blood" (123). Maman's possession of Marie's body is attractive to John, Maman's former lover. Intoxicated by her mother's sexual presence and desires, Marie, who has sex with her husband Jacques on only one other occasion, has an exhilarating night with John. At some point she realizes that his desire for her has been motivated by his knowledge that his Marie has co-inhabited the body of her sixteen-year-old daughter. Having been isolated for most of her life in Teche, Marie is even more susceptible to John's cunning. She will need to learn the difference between the motivations of John's self-centered possessiveness and Damballah's spiritual possessions.

John enjoys the possession of bodies, and the younger the better. A manipulative man, John is a controller, and his ability to control is not mental as much as it is bodily. He possesses an ability to defy time, in fact quite possibly in the legacy of the flying Africans (see chapter 6). The first time he has contact with Marie is when he massages her vagina in Teche. The young girl is young, impressionable, and lonely. She does not know who the man is or even how she can feel his presence, but his touch in the right place makes her eager to go to him when the opportunity presents itself. Knowing her vulnerability, he moves from a touch to sexual intercourse. While he, a man who has seduced young girls before, knows that he is engaged with the body of a confused teenager possessed by her mother's spirit, the facts do not dissuade him from moving forth. In fact, it becomes clear that this will be a pattern of calculating behavior for him.

John's control of Marie's body moves from sexual manipulation to life-threatening physical violence. As is common with abuse, he sets parameters in regard to her movements. She is not allowed to leave the house, and when she does Ribaud must accompany her. It is his job to report to John where Marie goes and whom she speaks with. In one significant scene, John rapes Marie. Later, after she walks on water, he feels humiliated by her growing power and almost chokes her to death. Of him, Rhodes remarks, "He's the puppet master, and that's why he's threatened whenever Marie does anything that seems beyond his control. He needs to have control" (Rhodes and Ramsey para. 43). John's attempt to control is reminiscent of the oppressor who sees the Black body for profit. It is not until Nattie tells him that Marie is pregnant that he relinquishes her from his grasp. John has achieved the ultimate control over her body. He knows that Marie will do what she can to bring the baby to full term, and when the baby is born, he will have access to Damballah through his daughter. His plan, then, is to control the baby as he has Marie and her mother. More specifically, he will commodify his daughter's body for the purpose of making money and to boost his ego. As the baby grows, so do Marie's knowledge and maturity, as well as her need to resist the control of her enemies.

Seeing the value of her life and her body (the whole self), she makes deliberate efforts to resist John's control. Irrespective of him, she sees herself in relation to others. For the first time since she has been servant to Damballah, Marie questions her role as a prominent figure among her people. While she is in jail, for killing a White male attacker, fellow prisoners ask her for help that she does not feel that she can provide. To make matters worse, there is a naysayer who challenges her ability to help anyone since those around them are dying. Marie's position in the jail with the suffering parallels that of her great-grandmother Membe and the woman's journey through the Middle Passage. First, as Membe was placed in chains and confined to the ship where she suffered, her great-granddaughter suffers the indignity of having been arrested for resisting the advances of a White man who presumed a right to do with her body as he willed. In this act, Marie avenges Membe, who was raped by her owner. Further, Membe knows that she cannot stop the slave trade from taking place; she has not been called to do so. Her job is to carry the message of Damballah to the "children of Africa," and it is now her descendant's calling to do the same. Physical confinement is not a barrier to them. In her moments of despair, Marie gives hope to the people in their last hours. Jennifer Griffith asserts, "Bearing witness to the suffering of another involves exposing oneself and one's potential as victim, perpetrator, or accomplice" (10). Marie tells them that they will be saved, providing them a sense of value to navigate social death status. Part of deliverance is the idea that there will be a return to Guinea. Salvation is not of this world, but Marie has not yet reached the point where she can reason what she knows intimately. She is still in the process of growth. Marie's extraordinary life represents what Kimberly Juanita Brown calls the "multiple enactments of hypervisibility black women cannot escape" (20).

Marie has certainly been in the process of maturing during the time she leaves her grandmother to live with John. Her steps in maturation are marked by moments when she gains significant knowledge; much of that knowledge is gained through acts of resistance. After her first encounter with Damballah, which leaves her vulnerable to the possession of her mother, she refuses to let Damballah enter her again. Her decision to control her body, to choose the use of her body, leaves her open to constant attacks by John, who can only profit when Marie is under the command of Damballah. Further, his deepest sexual desires are met when he feels the presence of the more experienced Maman. Marie is willing to entrust her body to Damballah, who has chosen her to help her people remain connected to Africa and to find peace with the ancestors, but she refuses the presence of her mother. Marie's Maman has other reasons to possess her daughter. Surely she can become alive through Marie when she is with John, but she can also feel empowered by resuming her position as "Voodoo Queen." Marie's decision to resist the control of her mother is a significant step toward defining her identity as it relates to her relationship to John and as she emerges as a priestess.

Marie's actions work in defiance of expectations that others may have of her. As such, her relationship with the spirit world motivates her way of thinking: she has no sense of or respect for boundaries. Her ability to move beyond boundaries of both time and space becomes apparent when she walks on water.[5] Rhodes shows what it means to expand the perspective of the Middle Passage not "as a phenomenon of constricted space and limited time" (Gates et al 9.). Marie thinks that she has to "fight her way to spirituality" to keep her life from "corruption" (Rhodes 303). Her "fight" finds peace in the response of Damballah. In her fervent prayer for Damballah to come to her during the ceremony, and while consumed by her fear that he will not, she is drawn to the depths of nearby Pontchartrain Lake, where the water deity makes his presence known. When there is a delay in her emergence, her spectators, including John, Ribaud, and Nattie, believe that she is physically dead. Gone. However, some of the enslaved see her as having transformed into the next state. To, in a sense, open

---

5. It is recorded that her nephew, Luke Turner, witnessed the historic Laveau emerge from water at the beginning of her ceremonies at Lake Pontchartrain (Fandrich 199–200). Osbey notes: "Nineteenth-century *Daily Picayune* articles about 'camps of Voodoos' on St. John's Eve; the fictions of George Washington Cable; twentieth-century inventions of Hurston and Robert Tallant; and the speculations of modern day anthropologists aside, the religion here has never included public ritual or anything resembling group worship" ("Why We Can't Talk" 3).

the gates to the next world, they begin to sing spirituals: "My Soul Walks Free. Death Awaits Me." Death in Christianity and religions of Africa and the diaspora do not allow for a belief that one is completely gone, but rather that the dead will live on in a different form. However, for those who are in attendance, this also means that Marie is not there to provide them with the service they wish, whether it is to see a spectacular performance, to keep them connected with their ancestors, or to solve one of their problems. Marie is unconcerned with these people and their wishes. She sees herself as called by Damballah and is in the process of communicating with him in ways that she has not previously. He conveys to her in an African dialect she has heard newly arrived enslaved persons speaking, "You belong to me. You always have and always will" (306). Rhodes uses water to revisit the Middle Passage in the third generation, or two generations removed, to note how the Middle Passage remains present.

In conversation with Olaudah Equiano, Rhodes helps us to consider the meaning of Equiano's observations that captives, "preferring death to such a life of misery, somehow made through the nettings and jumped into the sea" (Equiano 159). During her time in the water, Marie receives Damballah's blessing as he shows her her purpose and reward for worship and service. Marie finds herself as central among a circle of the women who have come to her in the lake. The circle is a barrier of protection for Marie, who is under the threat of a corruptible man who has no respect for Damballah or Marie. Within this circle, she feels the presence of those who are no longer with her in the physical world. There she learns that she is the heart of the women's legacy and that their home is Africa and what it represents. Africa is the place of the origin. At the origin, those who return gain a sense of knowing what has been corrupted by leaving the homeplace. If we recall that Marie longed for the love of the mother who seemingly abandoned her, she becomes overwhelmed with love when she "returns" to Africa: "Love was in the lush foliage, the cawing of birds" (306). Her reemergence is possible because her spirit has been relieved of her fears that Damballah may have abandoned her. With a lightened spirit, she can walk on water "as if it were earth" (307). If her other possessions did not allow for a renewal on some level, this "journey" to Africa by crossing the barrier of water certainly allows for a rebirth. Damballah's claim on her as his certainly releases her from John and feelings she has regarding the absence of her mother. Marie has been spoken to by Damballah and reveals, "I know who I am" (307). Barbara Christian notes, "Self-knowledge [is] critical if Black women [are] to develop the inner resources they . . . need in order to cope with larger social forces" (237). Marie's understanding about her self through this intimate experience with the spirit world gives her claim to her own calling and story. Further, this revelatory experience moves her closer toward independence from her oppressors.

Nattie's death is a long time coming. She has manipulated three generations of Maries to get closer to a god that has not called her. Her last heinous act of killing Grandmère, a woman who was her friend, to avenge Marie's "arrogance," proves that she will remain a constant threat to Marie and to her newborn daughter (406). As a form of protection and to eliminate threats to keeping Damballah and Voodoo accessible to the people, Nattie must die. Nattie's ability to conjure and her jealousy make her an enemy that serves a great purpose for Marie's evolution. Nattie's plotting with John to hurt Marie forces the maturing girl to develop ways to defend herself, drawing her closer to her ancestral spirits and forcing her to submit to Damballah as her protector.

Moving in and out of the spirit world, where she literally is consumed by the spirits of the dead in reverence for her god, means that she learns about various forms of life and death. Death is not always absolute, and water is the transformative substance to help with the passing from one world to the next, as best illustrated when she encounters her husband, Jacques, in the form of a zombie—courtesy of Nattie prior to her death. Jacques is a Creole sailor, his very existence is representative of African and European interrelations in the Atlantic Global South. In the form of an "undead" man, he represents the powerlessness that Marie tries to subvert through her work as a priestess. Marie, through her possession, learns that he feels the blows that John places on him in front of the erotic audience on Mardi Gras night as well as the shame brought on by the fact that his penis has been exposed to the audience for their pleasure. Seeking to help him fully transition, Marie tries to guide him to the water, where drowning will take him easily from the middle space where he has been bound. In other words, Jacques lingers in his own personal Middle Passage, where he is subject to the powers of others, abused, humiliated, starved. Acting as Jacques's captor, motivated by his jealousy for the love Marie has for Jacques, John stabs him in the heart. Such an act is only symbolic, as the stab to the heart is only to break the physical bond between Jacques and Marie. However, theirs is a spiritual bond. Therefore, Marie's ability to guide his spirit, during a coma-like sleep in the days to follow, from the banks of the New Orleans port east to the land of the Dahomey in Africa, past the slave ships of the Atlantic, is her final gift to him. Indeed, water figures prominently on this spiritual passage of one form of life to another, to heal and to bond back to the origin of life.

The last threat to Marie and her legacy is John, who sees his power over Marie waning, ritual after ritual. As she knows, John is a corruptible man whose only power is in controlling others by inflicting bodily harm. Although Grandmère has told Marie not to kill John, Marie reacts as a mother. John's threat to his daughter by caressing her body in a way that Marie perceives as inappropriate leaves her with few choices. She can either remain with him and hope for the best or she can eliminate him as a threat to her daughter—the legacy of the chosen. John has only one palpable fear—the pet python. While he clearly believes in the existence and power of Damballah, the serpent god, John is unable to submit to the god. Submitting to fear of the god, the tangible fear between members of the African-descendant community and Africa, illuminates his disconnect to Africa, and, by extension, his inability to serve the people of the community. Further, he is angered by the fact that "Damballah favored women" and that he had to rely on a "child" to get wealth (127). Osbey describes the role of women in New Orleans Voodoo as central:

> The religion here in New Orleans is entirely within the sphere of women, whom *we* call Mothers. Clearly, men cannot function in this capacity. They may well work as herbalists or other kinds of *traiteurs,* but lack the capacity for what is called Deep Work. Deep Work requires a cleanness which only women possess. Men can work with roots or may call themselves psychics—whatever that means—but they can never "read," do Deep Work or otherwise function as Mothers. . . . How then does one become *"a Mother?"* you ask in disbelief. It's quite simple really. You are born into a lineage of Mothers. At some point, an Ancestress, a Mother from your own line, appears to you in a dream or a vision and you are afflicted. ("Why We Can't Talk" 4)

John's thinking reveals that he feels powerless as he is dependent on Marie and a god that favors her and not him. This feeling is a formidable motivation to take power by any means. Given his past behavior and his admission that he now has some claim to Damballah through his daughter, there is no doubt that he will use his own daughter to achieve power through wealth. It is only a matter of time when he will conclude that Marie is of little value to him and dispense of her as he has Nattie. Marie's decision to use the python—a symbol of the god he has disrespected in many ways—to kill John puts an end to the threat against the woman called to be a leader among those displaced from Africa. At this point, she has proven accomplished in having secured the community of believers by eliminating their most serious threat.

Philip's question, "What if the Ancestors intended some other purpose for us to have been brought to this part of the world, entirely apart from the European profit?," is one explored by Rhodes. As the great-granddaughter of a woman called to travel the Middle Passage, Marie's sense of purpose has become clear, and it is now her responsibility to move forward as a community leader with the knowledge of her ancestors. Rhodes relies on West African religious beliefs that survived the Middle Passage and that remained among African-descendant communities in New Orleans. As does Equiano, Rhodes shows how identity is as fluid as the Atlantic water. Not knowing her history caused Marie to go in search of what was hers, allowing her to find the self that had been hidden from her because of fear. Marie sought a life that was distinctly hers, and what she found was that she had a place of belonging among a community of people who were longing for the spiritual presence that only she could bring. Social death was not an option for her. As such, she is cast as a woman with a certain kind of power of influence in the Middle Passage era, a time when women, especially Black women, were silenced. Through Rhodes, we can consider that the Middle Passage did not diminish African descendants' ability to define their self-worth on their own terms.

To say her name is the act of eliciting a certain kind of memory. In his blues song "Marie Laveau," Papa Celestin calls to the power of the memory of the infamous Black woman as he declares, "The folks still believe in the Voodoo Queen way down yonder" and the influence she has on people's beliefs.[6] Whether people see her merely as a cultural icon who appears as an intimidating figure in shows like *American Horror Story*, in fiction, and in songs like Papa Celestin's, or they see her as the object of their religious worship, prompting them to visit her grave in New Orleans, Marie Laveau was the product of the African presence in the South. Through legend, she defies forms of death.

Without question, the Middle Passage has resulted in the making of new cultural identities in the Americas. Ancestral connections remain among the stories that beg to be preserved in written or oral forms. Through their stories, Johnson and Rhodes propose to revisit, redefine, and reimagine the Middle Passage narrative by assigning purpose to trauma. *Treme* suggests to us the ways in which this continues in New Orleans. Showing links between West Africa and New Orleans allows for the opportunity to remember the history that exists in various practices even though the origins of those practices have been forgotten. Their perspectives complicate narratives about the slave trade. They suggest to us ways in which social death is not absolute, and that rebirth is possible. As such, their stories act as forms of exorcism; it is in the practice of storytelling from one generation to another that power is assigned to the word and not necessarily to the act. Consequently, the speaker/writer has control over the narrative that is told, for our purposes, the African descendants' perspective. Transformations, then, are not just personal, but communal. They are not just practices, but acts of redemption.

---

6. Lyrics of Oscar "Papa" Celestin's "Marie LaVeau" (1954) can be found on the Internet, including at www.musixmatch.com/lyrics/Oscar-Papa-Celestin-feat-The-Original-Tuxedo-Jazz-Band/Marie-Le-Veau.

PART II

LEGACIES OF THE MIDDLE PASSAGE

CHAPTER 5

Deadly Waters, Southern Blues, and Richard Wright

I'm gonna lay down my burdens
(Down by) Down by the Riverside
(Down by) Down by the Riverside
(Oh . . . Down by) Down by the Riverside

—lyrics to "Down by the Riverside" (Negro spiritual)

SEEING WATER as a metaphor for memory and history, Toni Morrison observes:

> You know they straightened out the Mississippi River in places, to make room for houses and livable acreage. Occasionally the river floods these places. "Floods" is the word they use, but, in fact it is not flooding; it is remembering. Remembering where it used to be. All water has a perfect memory and is forever trying to get back to where it was. Writers are like that: remembering where we were, what valley we ran through, what the banks were like, the light that was there and the route back to our original place. It is emotional memory—what the nerves and the skin remember as well as how it appeared. And a rush of imagination is our "flooding." ("The Site of Memory" 77)

Mississippi writers Richard Wright and Jesmyn Ward know well what Morrison refers to in this excerpt. Like writers who reimagine the meaning of the Middle Passage, they, in conversation with Morrison, use literature to depict historical moments marked by flooding in 1927 and 2005, moments that qualify as their "emotional memory" or imaginary flooding. "Water has a perfect memory." Therefore, it is not surprising to find that threats of physical death and social death are as present in historical memories of the Middle

Passage as they are in depictions of floods. Wright and Ward consider the meaning of flooded communities when the community occupants are poor and Black. What resources do they have to prepare for such a catastrophe? What resources do they have to survive? What resources do they have to be made whole again in the aftermath of the flooding? Wright and Ward reveal harsh truths in response to these questions.

As I will discuss in this chapter and the next, Wright and Ward revisit the Middle Passage as they explore the significance of destruction by water to poor Blacks in the South. Their depictions illuminate Black people's traumatic experiences as their struggles to survive the already harsh realities of life as poor Black folks in America are further complicated by unplanned major losses of what they deem precious. Like water, literature and blues express the memories of tragedy and the memorialization of lives lost. Blues may have lyrical notes to form musical scores, but it originates from a feeling, an emotion that is captured in a variety of ways. Wright and Ward attempt to express the emotion in their descriptions of Mississippi floods through their depictions of people who struggle against the label of social death imposed upon them by the government and White neighbors. Their humanity, then, is accentuated by their close familial bonds. Social death is represented by their economic instability; as working poor, their access to adequate resources before the flood was already limited. After and during their battle with rising floodwaters, their position in society becomes painfully clear.

My concern in this chapter is with how flooding and its impact on poor Black communities show the legacy of the Middle Passage. If the Middle Passage shows racism as the devaluing of Black life in favor of valuing Black bodies, then Wright's "Down by the Riverside" is a twentieth-century reminder of that history. By reimagining a historical event through the eyes of a father and husband, Wright's work shows resistance to social death in the actions of Mann, who fights to survive when the 1927 floods threaten the lives of his family. While JanMohamed sees Mann as one who has "accepted his social-death," I would argue against this, at least from my point of departure in defining social death (52). Mann may be Black in the South, but when confronted, he has not accepted the restrictions placed on him because he is Black. As with African captives, not until confronted with the threats to their lives did they need to resist. To a lesser degree, I argue further that the blues and its Atlantic Southern roots provide access to the emotions and historical memories associated with flooding and death. Ultimately, the literature and the music serve as sites of performative and literary reenactments and reengagements with death and survival.

BLACK EXPERIENCES IN THE 1927 MISSISSIPPI FLOODS

Undoubtedly, the U.S. South is largely influenced by who and what survived the Middle Passage. Although labeled as mere laborers, millions of cultural-practitioners from Africa and later the Caribbean were brought to the southern coastal port cities and distributed for sale in auctions. Congress's ban on the importation of Africans for slavery began on January 1, 1808. The 1860 U.S. Census data reveals that "4 million people [were] in bondage: slavery was concentrated along the Chesapeake Bay and in eastern Virginia; along the South Carolina and Georgia coasts; in a crescent of lands in Georgia, Alabama and Mississippi; and most of all, in the Mississippi River Valley" (Mullen). By 1877, the federal troops had pulled out of the South and *Plessy v. Ferguson* had ushered in legalization of "separate but equal" in public transportation, education, and other aspects of life in the South. Descendants of enslaved people had few choices about where they would live or how they would live if they stayed in the South, and many parts of the North and West were little better.

In 1927, the flood found a significantly poor and disenfranchised African American populace in the states mostly affected by floodwaters, including Louisiana, Mississippi, Alabama, Arkansas, Illinois, Kentucky, Missouri, and Tennessee (Mizelle 4). My focus on African descendants' experiences does not mean that people who do not claim African heritage were not affected by the floods. Floodwaters do not make choices about which lives will be taken or disrupted. However, it is clear that there is a pattern of behavior in the treatment of African descendants that leave them more vulnerable to disaster and less likely to receive help under such conditions caused by catastrophe. Testimonies from Hurricane Katrina survivors and 1927 flood reports make this painfully obvious. In his book *Backwater Blues,* Richard Mizelle traces the impact the 1927 floods had on poor African American communities. Black folks have a long history with levees, as Mizelle finds that levees were not regulated in the early nineteenth century and were built by enslaved people and Irish immigrants in an "attempt to channel the Mississippi River" (4). Regulation began in 1879 "to develop and maintain a unified federal system" (5). He agrees with other scholars that the burgeoning cotton industry, largely supported by Black field-workers, in some of the states along the Mississippi River and the threat to those areas by the floods is why the government eventually responded to people in need. If the laborers and the crops were in jeopardy, then the industry could die, having a major impact on the economy.

Unusually high rainfall caused the Mississippi River to "remember," according to Morrison, and its tributaries to rise and to breech levees. African American men were threatened and forced to patch levees, placing their lives in eminent danger from the water and from their scared White neighbors. African American writers would capture this in their literature. Black newspapers informed readers how flooding in Greenville, Mississippi, left vulnerable African Americans in even greater need. Will Percy, the son of a major cotton plantation owner, was in charge of relief affairs in the southern city. According to his diaries and other reports, he tried to evacuate Blacks who had been gathered and left on the levees in the treacherous flood, but his efforts were hindered by planters who feared that if their workers left, they would never return. Percy then used his power and privilege and reminded the citizens that they were laborers, nothing more (*Fatal Flood*). According to John M. Barry, "Will declared, 'No able-bodied negro is entitled to be fed at all unless he is tagged as a laborer'" (80). Noting the extreme inequity in treatment, he goes on to tell that in some camps, even forced laborers were paid. Under Will Percy's leadership, food was the only compensation. The documentary *Fatal Flood* gives testimony of African Americans and Whites of Greenville who recall the horrific conditions the African American residents of the city endured during the months they were forced to remain on the levees. Black-and-white footage shows the few lucky enough to have a blanket huddled under makeshift tents on wet ground in April. A commentator informs viewers that it was cold and rainy. Through the historical lens, we can only imagine their fear and frustration, for none of them knew what would happen next, how they would feed themselves or their children. During the two months of enduring their imprisonment in the camp, the White guards, reminiscent of enslavers, raped and beat their African-descended captives. To make matters worse, they were later forced to take provisions off a Red Cross boat to distribute to Whites. Leftovers were given to Black captives. One African American testifies that they knew no other way but to make Black people do the work. It's how it had always been *(Fatal Flood)*. Natasha Trethewey would capture the experience in her poem "Flood" in "Scenes from A Documentary History of Mississippi": Of a *"group of black refugees"* (italics hers) she writes, "The caption tells us, was ordered / To sing their passage onto land, / Like a chorus of prayer—their tongues" (23). Trethewey's reading of a visual documentary reminds us of other historical moments when dancing was required of the African captives by slave ship crews. From the transatlantic slave trade to the twentieth century, black bodies were expected to forgo their own needs to meet the demands of Whites in power.

Although this chapter focuses on Richard Wright, his contemporary Zora Neale Hurston in her 1937 novel, *Their Eyes Were Watching God*, provides a depiction of Tea Cake finding himself working under threat along with other Black men after the hurricane decimates the muck. For African Americans who survived the floods, there seemed a price to pay for that survival. Like their ancestors, they were treated as though their bodies did not belong to them under the rules of racism. The natural occurrence of the enormous rainfall did not make them equal in the eyes of man when it came to determining whose lives were worth saving. Historically, African Americans were left on levees while White women and children, and later men, were evacuated to higher grounds.

FLOODING BRINGS THE SOUTHERN BLUES

Jean Kempf notes, "A catastrophe is first and foremost defined by its victims" (57). The moans and complaints of the enslaved and their ancestors led to the development of new forms of music artistry. Christian O'Connell remarks,

> The blues is American music with origins within African American culture of the South, but its story has not been limited by these national or cultural boundaries. Thus, to fully understand the nature of blues historiography and the way the blues has been invented since the revival, it is necessary to acknowledge that from the middle of the last century the blues was consumed, performed, and interpreted within a transatlantic context. (63)

We might be reminded here of Robert Harms's description of the forced dancing that occurred onboard slave ships like the *Diligent* (see chapter 1). Expressions of emotional longing—the sounds of the music being played on instruments with which the sailors were not familiar, "shrieks" stemming from the loss of home and the mourning of the enslaveds' unpredictable status as slaves—would constitute the blues, in fact, might be considered the birthplace of the blues.

Returning to its Atlantic Global South origins, a genre known as flood blues best encapsulates this history for those of Black Southern communities. Flood blues speaks of the ways in which poor Blacks resist social death because if they don't, their lives will most certainly be taken by nature or by humans. Blues provides a way to share the multiple layers of emotion, grief, and perspective. Notably, as Houston Baker points out, W. C. Handy, the "father of the blues," began to construct the music genre in Tutwiler, Mississippi, in 1903. Exploring a definition of the blues, Baker offers, "Rather than a rigidly personalized form, the blues offer a phylogenetic recapitulation—a nonlinear, freely associative, nonsequential mediation—of species experience. What emerges is not a filled subject, but an anonymous (names) voice issuing from the black (w)hole" (5). Although expressed in terms of "I" and "me," the blues are communal. Baker's description of the "nonlinear," I contend, also describes the Middle Passage experience, and that experience lives in the Blues music. Acknowledging direct links to the South and its African heritage, Baker observes:

> Combining work songs, group seculars, field hollers, sacred harmonies, pro-
> verbial wisdom, folk philosophy, political commentary, ribald humor, elegiac
> lament, and much more, they constitute an amalgam that seems always to
> have been in motion in America—always becoming, shaping, transforming,
> displacing the peculiar experiences of Africans in the New World. (5)

Baker appears in conversation with Harms, Equiano, and others who provide historical description of Africans' responses with the Middle Passage. From the moment of capture until the moment of sale(s), and beyond, Africans' survival necessitated their subconscious and at time conscious willingness to shape and transform. This music is only possible as a result of the Middle Passage.

In her study of the meaning of blues and its relationship to lived experiences of African Americans, particularly as it relates to flooding, Angela Davis notes,

> The seasonal rains causing the Mississippi River to flood its banks are part
> of the unalterable course of nature, but the sufferings of untold numbers of
> black people who lived in towns and the countryside along the river were
> attributable to racism. Black people were often expendable, and their com-
> munities were forced to take the overflow of backwaters in order to reduce
> the pressure on the levees. While most white people remained safe, black
> people suffered the wrath of the Mississippi, nature itself having been turned
> into a formidable weapon of racism. (109)

Blues songs, then, document historical experiences with inequity, especially threats to Black people's lives. According to ethnomusicologist David Evans, Lonnie Johnson's "Broken Levee Blues" is credited as the first song recorded in response to the 1927 floods, just a few days after the main levee break north of Greenville, Mississippi. Johnson's lyrics, accented by the gritty sounds of his soulful guitar, testify to events that Black men endured as a result of the floods. Of Johnson, Evans observes, "He was a prolific recording artist and perhaps had a studio date already scheduled. He recorded 'Broken Levee Blues' and then also did a cover of [Bessie] Smith's song 'Back Water Blues,' which had actually been recorded before the big flood of 1927" (Evans).

What occurred in Greenville, Mississippi, was but one example of forced labor imposed on Black male residents, having the effect of separating Black families. Johnson sings, "They want me to work on the levee, that I have to leave my home. / I was so scared the levee might break out and I may drown."[1] As in Greenville, when Will Percy demanded that people, including Blacks, evacuate their homes, Blacks resisted and so did their planter bosses. Probably feeling safer in their homes than they did going to a place where they would have uncertain control over their fate, African American families protested removal. Johnson emphasizes that this is a difficult decision to make.

On one hand, staying at home allows for the possibility of certain death, for no one can really know how far and wide floodwaters will spread to reclaim their space. Johnson sings, "I'd rather leave my home 'cause I can't live there no more." On the other hand, leaving home means that people, especially the most vulnerable, must rely on Whites to provide them with the basic necessities. Black folks had enough experience to know that the latter option was quite risky, and their concerns often proved correct. Johnson describes trying to remain in his home, as opposed to staying in his house. Home refers to a place of comfort. It alludes to what is personal (mine), while "house" refers to simply to shelter.

As a Black man, Johnson is to work according to the mandates. There are consequences if he does not, and he describes the police's attempts to force him into labor. Motivated by his fear of dying while working on the levee and his right to say no to forced labor, he resists their attempts and threats. "The police say work, fight, or go to jail, I say I ain't totin' no sack. / And I ain't buildin' no levee, the planks is on the ground and I ain't drivin' no nails." The song ends on a note of defiance. Evans does not see protest in blues as overt: "One has to keep in mind that these records were made for companies that were owned by and run by whites. It would have been a little bit dangerous to come out and protest overtly, so the protest often is between the lines and sometimes it requires a bit of interpretation" (Evans). In fact, Johnson holds fast to his resistance that he will not be defined by the police. Whatever "they"—the police, who represent white supremacy and power—think of him, they will not define what he thinks of himself. Johnson's song rings as a rejection of social death.

Bessie Smith brings a woman's perspective to the impact of flooding. Though recorded before the Mississippi floods of 1927, Smith's "Back Water Blues" is one of the most well known of flood blues, and the pre-1927 recording reminds us of the possibility that flooding can disrupt lives always and

---

1. Lyrics for Johnson's songs are available at www.lyricsmania.com.

any time. Smith's interest in how Black people were treated during floods by authorities in the South inspired her to write the song. By coincidence, it was released at the time that levees were breached and thousands of African Americans in poor areas were killed.[2] Like Richard Wright and Jesmyn Ward, Smith and other blues artists give voice to catastrophe. Their work shows the connection between knowledge, experience, and memory, an important aspect of the responses to the flooding and the focus on its impact on the poor.

Smith repeats the help she must receive to evacuate her house, which is surrounded by water: "they rowed a little boat about five miles 'cross the pond." Once they arrived, the "poor girl" packed "all [her] clothes, throwed them in," and was taken away to "some high old lonesome hill," where she looked down on the house where she used to live. Juxtaposing this lyrical scene to photographic scenes—Backwater blues done call me to pack my things and go / 'Cause my house fell down and I can't live there no more (Davis 263)—Smith's "poor girl" appears in a state of reflection; she is sharing with her audience events that have already occurred earlier in the day, beginning when she woke up in the "mornin." The poor girl's response to her experiences exemplifies and illuminates a simultaneous feeling of disorientation and transition that is common in the Black literary imagination when water is used as a metaphor for change. As a catalyst for destruction, water is present at a moment of psychic trauma. We see here the fear of death by drowning in one's own house, the desperate escape to higher ground for safety, and the experience of thousands who have had similar experiences, crowded in a space away from their home. Her descriptions cause us to delve into our experiences with the loud sounds of thunder and gusty winds banging against solid, or probably in her case, not-so-solid walls and to imagine these in correlation with the movement of a slave ship. In both instances, the uncertain nature accentuates the powerlessness of humans and their inability to construct shelters that are impenetrable. Further, Black people feel their vulnerabilities. Smith ends with a gut-wrenching moan: "Mmm, I can't move no more / Mmm, I can't move no more," and succeeds in conjuring an experience of debilitating trauma to the body. This is what social death sounds like. A moan not only of the "poor girl" but of all the thousands of poor Black girls and boys, men and women, who have lamented the loss of the house they used to live in as the masses

---

2. David Evans commits to studying the origins of the famous flood song in his article "Bessie Smith's Back-Water Blues: The Story Behind the Song." He concludes that there are several beliefs, advanced by biographers and others, about what inspired the lyrics of Smith's blues. The song is (1) a fictional account or generic account "of a typical flood," (2) "drawn from her memories of some event experienced in the earlier years"; (3) a prediction of the flood of 1927, and (4) based on her observation of flooding during a 1926–27 tour.

huddle together in a relief camp on a hill, possibly the levee. According to John M. Barry, in Greenville, Mississippi, "five miles of the narrow levee were crammed with refugees, almost all of them there black, and refugees were still pouring in" (80). Barry unwittingly conjures the historical trauma associated with huddled Black bodies without a home—crowding on West African shores, walking in slave coffles, packed into slave ships.

Usually, standing on a hill represents a sense of power and privilege, a status above the masses. However, Smith subverts the image to convey a severe feeling of loss, loneliness, and hopelessness. Further, as Jean Kempf observes in her study of Hurricane Katrina coverage, "Aerial shots are classics of the floods, even of the early ones, such as the1927 Mississippi flood" (56). Kemp continues by noting that whereas photography makes "well-known places . . . unrecognizable," the place in fact is recognizable as a home to the former occupants. As such, home is ascribed a meaning. Kempf concludes that home is "the intimate, the personal, the cherished, and of course, the 'duly and difficultly earned' that are washed away by the catastrophe" (58). With the home gone, there is no place of belonging, no place for return. Such a reality is a haunting repeat of the Middle Passage, gone but not forgotten.

MANN'S BLUES IN "DOWN BY THE RIVERSIDE"

Though not known for integrating blues music into his literature, the theme of blues most certainly resonates in Richard Wright's literature. From the theme of oppression in his first published collection of short stories, *Uncle Tom's Children*[3] (1940), to his film adaptation of *Native Son* in 1951, where Bessie is recast as a blues singer, Wright most certainly remained consistently in love with African American spirituals and blues music. In fact, he is known to have visited blues clubs going back to his days living in Memphis, and later wrote the lyrics to a blues song in collaboration with Count Basie and Paul Robeson that gave tribute to Joe Louis in 1941 (Rowley 256–57). Published in 1938, Richard Wright's short story "Down by the Riverside" invokes feelings of rage, steeped in racial tensions, violence, and inequity that Wright, a native Mississippian, felt aptly characterized the home state he left as a teenager. Race and class were foremost on the mind of the writer, a Marxist, when he wrote the short stories, and they emerged as prevalent themes in his body of work following the success of *Uncle Tom's Children*. To be sure, the theme

---

3. Wright's *Uncle Tom's Children* was originally published in 1938 with four short stories. It was released again in 1940 with an additional short story, "Bright and Morning Star," and the essay "The Ethics of Living Jim Crow."

of race and class is made more prominent when Wright uses the backdrop of the infamous 1927 flood of Mississippi. In fact, if, as I argue, the blues figures into this collection, memories of the Middle Passage through his consistent use of water does just as much. Each of the five short stories shows the African American characters traversing toward or through water at moments that signify a sharp turn in the story's events. Consequently, Wright's literary engagement with the blues, his borrowing of the gospel song title "Down by the Riverside," as well as his use of various water images builds a multitextual narrative that shows conversion following the intersection of water and death.

Born near Roxie, Mississippi, in 1908, Richard Nathaniel Wright spent most of his childhood in the home of his devoutly religious maternal grandmother. In his autobiographical work, *Black Boy,* he describes a grandmother who sternly disciplined through corporeal punishment and harsh words while his mother lay ill from various strokes that left her incapacitated and unable to work for most of his childhood. It was the Jim Crow South, and Black boys who followed the rules were more likely to survive than those who did not. Wright was unimpressed with his grandmother's belief in Seventh Day Adventism, and its restrictions seemed always in a state of defiance, especially as he was often hungry. His father had abandoned his wife and two sons to fend for themselves as he decided that he would live with another woman and not provide for his sons. Feeling the burden of constant hunger, Wright would fight with his grandmother to work on the Sabbath day of Saturdays and to try to provide some funds for the family to eat. He would never finish high school, and his work would more likely than not feed from the hunger and thirst that he had for a semblance of freedom and equality in the South. Eventually, he would leave the family and do as so many Blacks did: move North for more opportunities. Wright knew what it was to live under a myriad of restrictions and to suffer from a lack of basic resources. Although Wright was not in Mississippi during the floods, but in Memphis, Tennessee, he lived the blues and his literature would portray this.

To him the South was not a safe space for African Americans. He writes in his essay "Traditional and Industrialization":

> I was born a black Protestant in that most racist of all American states: Mississippi. I lived my childhood under a racial code, brutal bloody, that white man proclaimed was ordained of God, said was mandatory by nature of their religion. Naturally, I rejected that religion and would reject any religion which prescribes for me an inferior position in life; I reject that tradition and any tradition which proscribes my humanity. (*White Man, Listen!* 55)

Wright's "Down by the Riverside" and his depiction of how the 1927 floods affect a Black man and his family illuminates the brutal, bloody racial code that said he was inferior or socially dead. Wright is considered the father of protest literature, and his *Uncle Tom's Children* takes its name from Harriet Beecher Stowe's *Uncle Tom's Cabin*. Tom, regarded as docile by some twentieth-century African American writers, including Wright and James Baldwin, was rewritten by Wright with the focus on African American characters who, although they live in the South, find no other way to live or to make a statement about the imposition of social death but through overt resistance. Wright begins *Uncle Tom's Children* with his description of an Uncle Tom:

> The post Civil War household word among Negroes—"He's an Uncle Tom!"—which denoted reluctant toleration for the cringing type who knew his place before the white folk, has been supplanted by a new word from another generation which says:—"Uncle Tom is dead!" (1)

Following his definition is a collection of short stories that redefine the post–Civil War definition of "Uncle Tom"; Wright's collection acts as a response to Stowe's novel, and thus becomes a sequel through Black perspectives. Dan McCall notes,

> In calling his book *Uncle Tom's Children,* Wright refers us to this mystic father [Uncle Tom], makes his characters the progeny of a stereotype and brings his book into the family of protest literature. These children are different. They refuse to be like a father, an object of pity. (24)

In effect, the characters in *Uncle Tom's Children* personify the description that James Cone provides us of Black Power: "It means that the Black man will not be poisoned by stereotypes that others have of him, but will affirm to the depth of his soul: 'Get used to me, I am not getting used to anyone'" (*Black Theology* 8). Wright, whose *Uncle Tom's Children* acts as a precursor to Cone's work, presents characters who personify this philosophy.

In the case of "Down by the Riverside," Mann and his family represent the disenfranchised and the Heartfields represent those who have, at least before the flood, enjoyed their societal privileges. Mann challenges their privilege when his wife Lulu's life hangs in the balance. Unable to give birth to a baby she is carrying, the family sits and waits for the brother-in-law to return with a boat, purchased with the proceeds of selling a family mule. But their desperation becomes Mann's downfall. Having only received $15 for the mule, the brother-in-law steals a boat from the postmaster general, Mr. Heartfield, who is known among the townsfolk for being a proud racist. While Mann tries to get his wife to the Red Cross hospital in town, Heartfield identifies his stolen boat and shoots at the family; Mann returns fire and fatally wounds Heartfield. Mann is eventually caught and killed after his wife dies, and he is separated from his son and forced to work as a relief laborer. "Down by the Riverside" gives perspective on the 1927 Mississippi River flood that resulted in the deaths of approximately 240 people in seven states. Published eleven years after the flood, Wright's story invites readers to relive the experience that Smith bemoans.

Mann's decisions are influenced by his interactions with people in power whose access to the power allows them to feel as though they can treat him like he is a socially dead being, a body with little to no worth except to work in service to southern Whites. Similar to Smith's girl, Mann stands at his door watching floodwaters rise and swirl around the corners of his house, waiting for a "little boat." He was offered a boat by the government, but he declined, probably because of his attachment to his house and probably because his wife is suffering from complications due to a stalled birthing process. Paul Gilroy sees the presence of ships as significant to African descendants:

> Ships also refer us back to the middle passage, to the half-remembered micro-politics of the slave trade and its relationship to both industrialisation and modernization. As it were, getting on board promises a means to reconceptualise the orthodox relationship between modernity and what passes for its prehistory. (17)

In the absence of a ship, a boat connects the flood to the Middle Passage, therefore illuminating the relationship to which Gilroy refers.

It is also possible that African Americans' suspicion of the government, which Mann will have confirmed in a few hours, make him hesitant to accept any aid from them. Wright, the writer, knows that levees were breached in order to flood poor Blacks in an effort to save the homes of affluent people. But in his scenario, as occurred in parts of New Orleans during Katrina, floodwaters do not discriminate. As an African American man, Mann has a litany of problems that he cannot solve. He has no boat to save his wife, young son, mother-in-law, and other family members, but he hopes that God will provide a way. Perhaps God does. Mann's brother-in-law brings a boat to the family that has been taken from one of the most powerful men in the city, Mr. Heartfield, a man who represents white supremacy in the form of the government. Expanding his representation of Heartfield as a government official, Wright presents barriers to Mann when Heartfield should and actually could offer help. Terrence Tucker asserts, "For Wright the clearest examples of oppressive forces that impose on African American subjectivity were whites, if not whiteness itself" (109). In reality, Mann knows immediately that if he heads to the hospital to find help for his wife, he will have to pass near Heartfield's house, and is very likely to be killed by him or any White man who sees his family in the stolen white boat. Such a desperate act in response to dire circumstances allows Wright to show, immediately, restrictions placed on Blacks' humanity and their marginalization within their community. Their social position serves to accentuate the fact that they are poor, a direct consequence of their race. Despite this, Mann is willing to take a step in conversion—to move beyond the fears ascribed by Jim Crow and to do what he can to save his family's lives. As an act of conversion, I refer to his conscious choice to resist death—both social and physical—by risking his own life to save his family.

Mann's decision to take the boat shows his refusal to accept the label of inferiority and to reject the historical narrative that has potential to leave him submissive and his family obsolete. Mann's journey echoes Equiano's use of language to describe what he saw aboard the slave ship. In one scan of a landscape, much like a camera records visual details, we see water—everywhere. But Wright forces us to feel Mann's dread as it increases with the vast darkness of night. Surrounded, almost overcome by darkness, Mann's fear of the unknown as he rows the boat leads us to recall, through our imaginations, what it must have been like to be held captive in the dark hold of a slave ship. There are no flashlights or other means of lighting the way for him as he moves against the current to save his wife in the boat that holds four passengers—his son, Pee Wee; his mother-in-law; his dying wife, Lulu; and Mann. Wright's attention to landscape details serves to highlight the meaning of racism, in its purest forms, as he knew and experienced it himself in Mississippi. Mann—his name clearly a play on the gender identifier—is desperate enough to jeopardize his entire family by placing them in a stolen white boat set against the black of darkness and that has an old mark on the side that makes it recognizable to everyone in the town who knows the racist Heartfield. Marked boats are analogous to the naming of slave ships. Therefore, Mann's decision to take possession of the boat reminds us of slave mutinies, such as on the *Amistad,* and other acts of resistance on slave ships where the captives' attempted to reclaim their bodies and return to their safe place of home. Wright overwhelms readers with racialized markers. Heartfield's response is as much to his own fear of losing power to a Black person as to his claim on the boat. When Mann encounters the Heartfields, they liberally call him a "nigger." We can conclude that regardless of class status, Mann and his family would be treated no better in this situation, and both Mann and

Heartfield are aware of the roles they play as actors in the historical drama set in the backdrop of the Jim Crow south.

Experience tells Mann that he has few choices. Heartfield tells him to give back his boat, and rather than waiting for them to comply or attempting to find out what the circumstances are for Mann taking the boat, Heartfield shoots at Mann. Knowing that his and his family's lives are in danger, Mann shoots back. In "Concerning Violence," Franz Fanon articulates the meaning of the oppressed responding to the oppressor with violence: the "'thing' which has been colonized becomes man during the same process by which it frees itself" (36). To be sure, making this choice is an expression of humanity. Who has the power in the situation is unclear in the dark. But what does become clear is that Heartfield can make no demands that Mann is willing to comply with if it means losing his life. Mann's decision to shoot rather than to give in to Heartfield's commands is a subversion of the historical record. Mann resists subjugation as best he can and asserts his right to save his life and those of his family members. In other words, he affirms his humanity, and this places him in a position of power. Tucker notes that Wright "provides an image of African American heroism that is usually reserved for whites or African Americans who save whites" (108). Wright casts Heartfield as an individual who relishes his power and position as a White man. He is able to afford the boat that Mann's brother-in-law resorted to stealing. Heartfield's social status, at least from his perspective, is determined largely by Blacks' fear of him and their willingness to acquiesce to any demands that he makes. Hartman argues, "The plurality of resistances enacted in everyday life is produced by and details the relations and the mechanisms of power" (63). Mann's problem is that he must contend with power mechanisms in a moment when he is not dealing with everyday circumstances, and as such, everyday practices will not do. Mann's fear for his life and his family's lives, as well as his desperation to keep them safe, means that he will not allow Heartfield to assume control over his ability to care for himself and his family. Heartfield wants to get his own family to safety, most certainly, but the tactics that he uses to retrieve the boat from the man he sees as a "nigger" or "nonperson" blind him to the fact that the man in the boat is, like Heartfield, a father and husband. Histories of the slave trade often found enslavers oblivious to the pain felt by those who were separated from their families. Wright's short story is an example of Morrison's idea that "all water has a perfect memory." Fears bred on bodies of water emerge in this short story about race and class in rural Mississippi.

As this exchange occurs, Lulu remains still, inanimate, silent, suggesting that her role in the short story is more focused on her body. More accurately, hers is a Black woman's body that is in the process of transitioning from life to death as her body is simultaneously an incubator for life and a coffin for the lost life. Regaining his composure, Mann moves toward the hospital and with the help of soldiers, he eventually gets his wife to a doctor, who pronounces her dead. Lulu has been silent since she was introduced. Is her silence indicative of her helplessness? Of her treatment as a socially dead being? Surrounded by water, her body will not yield to its natural state of expelling the small form inside. Birth, also associated with a breaking of the water, does not occur in the chaos of this moment. If a baby were to enter the narrative, there would be a sense of hope and change in the near future. However, Wright does not allow new life to enter into a space where there is a profound sense of hopelessness and despair. What will a Black child do in a world in which an adult cannot properly care for her in a hostile environment? Mann deals with this dilemma alone.

As the story progresses, Mann loses more and more of his family and his lack of rights as a human become even more apparent. First, he is not given time to mourn the loss of his wife or their unborn child; instead, his family is sent by the soldiers to the relief camp while Mann is forced to perform duties as a free laborer. He is assigned to work with the other African American men who have been placed on the front lines, so to speak, patching the weakening levee. Johnson's "Broken Levee Blues" finds an echo here. Of course, when it breaks, most of those who lose their lives are Black men. However, Mann is reassigned to save people, including the Heartfields, whose lives are deemed by society as more valuable than his. Ironically, Mann may have been better off had he been near the levee break and died in a forced act of service. Mann's fears that he will not survive the Jim Crow South have now been realized. He is fully aware that he will eventually be caught and killed for his bold move of using force to protect his dying family. He has committed an unforgivable act: killing a White man.

Second, he is charged with saving the lives of the Whites in the hospital where his wife was pronounced dead in a segregated area. Wright dramatizes history by showing how Black lives are only worth the labor to save White lives, especially when a catastrophe occurs. Valiantly succeeding in following orders to make a hole in the roof and then lifting both White men and women out through the hole, Mann emerges in the minds of his superiors as a man of decency. Under these circumstances, White men are willing to overlook any touches he makes to save White women. In sum, as long as their needs are met, some of the rules can be broken. But Mann remains ever aware of the rules and knows that his time is limited.

He is fully reminded of this in the fast-paced movement of the short story when he receives orders to try to save the Heartfield family. Unable to leave their flooded home and traumatized by the murder of their father by a Black man, they wait, with hope, for rescue. Their hope that their lives are considered valuable enough to save may match the level of hopelessness and powerlessness that Mann felt as he watched the water rise around his home. Though it is not stated, he knows that no one will come for him and his family. It is up to them to find a means to rescue themselves. Unlike Mann, the Heartfields had their own mode of transportation, and the means to call for backup when the first mode of transportation was taken from them. Flooding causes chaos, a societal rupture in the South. Although they have been forced to do so, two Black men are now in unusual positions of power, searching for the Heartfield's. Brinkley's position involves his ability to choose whether or not he will risk his own life to rescue anyone, especially since he has found himself in command of a motorboat. Only under unusual circumstances, where thousands of lives are in jeopardy, would it be possible, even in the world of fiction, to see White soldiers hand over a motor boat to an unknown Black man and to trust him and another Black man to save a White widow woman and her two children. Such a scenario proves the fragility of power and reveals it as a social construct as well as a strong psychological weapon. To be sure, the oppressors rely on the threat of death as an aspect of social death to serve them in precarious times.

Their confrontation shows the fears that living Jim Crow has placed in both Mann and the Heartfields. Who has power in such situations is complex, but ultimately indisputable. Mann is clearly too distrustful of the young boat driver to confide in him that a trip to the Heartfields' will seal his fate. His significant silence suggests that he has, one, given up on changing his situation and, two, does not trust that the young man will help him to escape. Possibly his reluctance is due to a feeling that he will reveal his crime to the Whites whom Brinkley willingly risks his life to save. His unwillingness to confide in the young man who is driving him toward the house where the family knows the face and name of the man who, just hours before, shot their husband/father, clinches the reality of hopelessness. They do indeed recognize him when he enters the home, and they will not forgive him, even after his act of saving their three lives. Forgiveness is an extreme act of humanity; therefore, it is unavailable to Mann.

Like in Bessie Smith's "Back Water Blues" and as recorded in history, Mann finds himself on a hill with thousands. He is unable to locate his family and remains as lonely as Smith's "poor girl" among the masses. Homeless and alone, his crimes are revealed by the Heartfields and without a trial, he is sentenced to death. However, he will choose his own ending. Tucker observes, "Wright still promotes a move towards self-actualization, generally expressed through rage" (107). We must not forget that what he did, he did out of love for his family. As they march Mann through the woods, he breaks and runs, significantly, toward the water, but he never makes it to his destination. His body is fatally wounded and he falls by the riverside. JanMohamed argues that "Mann has, according to the black spiritual that provides the title of the story and that he and his family dutifully and ritualistically sing, already agreed to lay down his sword and shield" (52): "I will lay down my burdens, my sword and shield, down by the riverside and study war no more." Yet, the song states that the sword and shield will be laid down at the riverside. It is the final act of conversion before death. Therefore, these Southern Blacks are always prepared for battle. The song conjures a feeling of peace that death has ushered in, a new experience where the stresses of the bodily form have been released and are no longer of concern. In the previous works discussed in this book, the characters survive and their conversion happens in life; Mann's happens through death.

A major question arises here: What will become of the parentless boy and his grandmother? He has inherited a homeless status in the wake of the deaths of his mother and his father, who would have, had they survived, been forced to rebuild their lives. Mann's death and his homeless status coincide. Water separates a family and serves as a medium for transition. The loss of half Mann's family marked the end of his life. His son will be left to follow, in some ways, the restricted path that his father walked in the Jim Crow South, with little hope that his life will be better. To be sure, Jesmyn Ward takes up this question in her novel.

As a character who represents Black resistance, Mann stood as best he could. His son may never know his story, but Wright's point seems to be to present the story from Mann's perspective. What happens next could not be controlled by Mann, only what occurred at the moment of his death. Lonny Johnson's "Broken Levee Blues" is Mann's song. Racism flows and ebbs throughout history in various forms, and new songs with the same spirit will be captured when the levees break in New Orleans seventy-eight years later. And when they do, African descendants will remain resistant.

CHAPTER 6

Katrina Sings the Blues in Jesmyn Ward's *Salvage the Bones*

ENTRY: SEPTEMBER 2, 2005

Being in the First Baptist Church shelter means . . . damn, the words don't want to come out of the pencil . . . that thousands of us have been abused by Nature and revenge is impossible.

—Jerry Ward, *The Katrina Papers*

Wade in the Water. Wade in the Water Children. Wade in the Water. God's gonna trouble the waters.

—Lyrics to "Wade in the Water" (Negro spiritual)

IMAGES OF Southern African Americans of various economic backgrounds wading through filthy floodwaters that had broken through levees in 2005 reminded America and the world that people of African descent have a long and peculiar history with bodies of water. Perhaps delving deep into a mass historical conscience, some media critics stated, "I thought I was looking at a Third World country." By implication, such expressions are a misinformed perception of the continent of Africa, language that not only serves to erase the history that long ago placed Africans in America and the more recent history that made them citizens (restrictions to citizenship aside) but also affirms the connection between the American South and West Africa. Transatlantic memory markers connect the past to the present. Bringing voice to the images, popular New Orleans vocalist Irma Thomas recorded her rendition of Bessie Smith's "Back Water Blues," a song about flooding. For the people of New Orleans and other parts of the Gulf Coast, the song serves as a reminder that the levees had been breached before and probably will be again.

Romain Huret in *Hurricane Katrina in Transatlantic Perspective* notes that "every disaster gave birth to narratives which paved the way to individual resilience and collective reconstruction" (6). For people who know something of the history of floods in the South, the 1927 floods still have life in historical memories passed down in song, art, and other forms. Gulf Coast residents nearly hold their breaths during hurricane season, which is June through November, the period when hurricanes are more likely to arise out of the Atlantic and follow the path of the transatlantic slave voyage over the Atlantic and, possibly, to the U.S. South. Adding to the documentaries on the 1927 floods, in his documentary *When the Levees Broke,* Spike Lee uses the commentary of scholars and survivors of Hurricane Katrina to make the connection between the storms, with a focus on the treatment of the people when government failed to assist them. Lee's visual interpretive narrative complements Jesmyn Ward's literary perspective that taps into the emotions and experiences before and during the storm from a poor Black girl's point of view. As seen in Wright's depiction of Mann and his family as well as in some of the testimonies of loss by Black survivors in New Orleans, preserving family members' lives was a major concern. The potential of the storm to kill family members who could not evacuate and the threat evacuation had to dividing family units, as stated by one woman in Lee's visual narrative, was like "an ancient memory." Covered by the press and in subsequent works of art, social death was implied by the lack of response to African descendants, who were treated as if they were incapable of human emotions, such as love for family members. Oppressive systems that rendered African descendants' emotions and ties to family unimportant inspired them to resist through their connection to their families and communities. Documentaries and literature provide examples of this.

In this chapter, I focus on the narratives of disaster told by Black survivors of the hurricane in Lee's documentary and Ward's novel, *Salvage the Bones.* Through interviews and scholars' commentary, Lee probes the meaning of death and the value of life in a post–Middle Passage South. My focus will be on the experience of death as it resonates as a major theme through the documentary clips and in 911 calls. Lee's work is part of the ongoing multilayered perspective that provides critical commentary on the impact the hurricane had on African Americans and their struggle to live and survive during a natural disaster that was viewed by millions of onlookers. Further, I argue that Ward's novel, as constructed in the new post–civil rights movement South, revisits the racism that Richard Wright documents. However, while Wright's narrative ends on a note of hopelessness, partially due to a Black man's unplanned but necessary acts of resistance, Ward's novel ends with a sense of hope that stems from the resilience of and love among members of the Batiste family and the power of the community. Depictions of the Black family in Ward's novel, like documented cases in New Orleans, show how African descendants refused to accept the narrative that they were socially dead.

There is no denying that the world experienced Hurricane Katrina through visual images of citizens of the U.S. South suffering in the agony of torrential rain, profound hunger, and unbearable thirst. Journalists from all over the world came to New Orleans and parts of southern Louisiana, and a few made their way to Mississippi and Alabama, other areas of the Gulf Coast affected by "the storm"—those small but powerful words that when uttered allow locals to mark time by life before Katrina and life after. Lee's *When the Levees Broke* gives voice to people of New Orleans and St. Bernard Parish, who tell the stories of how they survived the storm and the continuing struggles to restore their lives. What is prominent is how they dealt with facing death, and Lee documents how they processed the idea that their lives did not seem to matter at a critical time.

HURRICANE KATRINA AND THE MIDDLE PASSAGE

In episode 5 of Lee's documentary, we hear from Fred Johnson, a New Orleans community activist who took shelter in the Hyatt Regency downtown. Seeing a connection between the events and the transatlantic slave trade, Johnson observes, "The hurricane started on the West Coast of Africa . . . and ends up in the Gulf of Mexico. The spirits of the Africans in the holocaust are very disturbed by the way African American people continue to be treated in America" (*When the Levees Broke*). While religious leaders may have seen the hurricane as punishment from God,[1] Johnson subverts the narrative and places the critical eye on white supremacy and the long history of mistreatment of African descendants. What if the ancestral spirits wanted to expose racism in America? Could Johnson's quote be an answer to M. NourbeSe Philip's inquiry: "What if the Ancestors intended some other purpose for us to have been brought to this part of the world?"

Perhaps without realizing it, Johnson provides some of the most thought-provoking commentary on the reality of the situation as it unfolded. After days of being housed in the Louisiana Superdome and the Convention Center, where there was no fresh water, proper food supplies, or medial assistance, the media documented children screaming for assistance. Finally, people were moved from the Superdome to buses that would take them to places unknown—tired, deprived Black bodies herded from one space to another in the scorching heat. Johnson recalls what he witnessed:

---

1. "Pastor Hagee: Katrina Struck New Orleans Because of Homosexual Rally," 25 May 2016, www.huffingtonpost.com/2008/04/24/pastor-hagee-katrina-stru_n_98385.html.

The military created a line. . . . As they came through, the military was good and bad. Because, I guess as a trained soldier you have to see things and act like you don't see it. You are oblivious to it. And for as much pain people were carrying people and dragging and dragging bags of clothes and cripple people and people bleeding. I mean it was just horrific conditions, horrific conditions. Women's periods was down on them. They had shit on them, piss on them. Children were by themselves. You would have thought we were in a war and everyone took off running and hiding. And all of sudden they were able to flee. And I saw that and all I could do was cry and stand up there and stay helpless until I looked on the sidewalk and saw all of this water that the military had stacked up and I began to bust the cases on the water and put a bottle in everybody's hand. Just to give it some humanistic side, not a lot, but something. (*When the Levees Broke* episode 5; transcription mine)

Although this occurred in 2005, Johnson could have been describing Africans disembarking from a slave ship. Notably what resonates are two critical aspects for him. First, he brings attention to the condition of the Black bodies. Most of the people (some say 14,000, others 40,000) housed in the Superdome during the storm and after were African Americans who had been abandoned as the city broke down, taking with it electricity and water services. Five days later, by the time President George W. Bush dispatched the U.S. Army, bodies had deteriorated and minds were barely hanging on. Second, Johnson cries because he feels helpless, and as an attempt to help to restore a sense of dignity to the agonizing people, including himself, he offers bottles of clean water. Again, Philip's work echoes the sentiments of Johnson. In her poetry, especially #1 in *Zong!* she gives voice to the need for water, as the speaker makes broken utterances until, finally, the word "water" is made whole. Johnson sees his extension of the gift of water—how long had it been since each person had clean water?—as a moment of renewal and as a reminder that the hurricane survivors' lives matter as much as, if not more than, their suffering. In his study of looking at suffering, Courtney R. Baker asserts,

Underwriting the resistance to the perception of the black slave's humanity is the fact that "pain provides the common language of humanity; it extends humanity to the dispossessed and, in turn, remedies the indifference of the callous." Pain, then, can enable the materialization of an immaterial humanity that lies beyond linguistic representation. Viewed in this way, pain becomes the currency of black liberation from injustice and state-sanctioned violence. (4–5)

As people watched the suffering of Black Americans, it was inconceivable to many how the government could take so long to react to what was a clear disaster that left people unable to care for themselves. Everyone knew it. The media made sure of that. Mayor Ray Nagin's interview on WWL radio with local journalist Garland Robinette was picked up by national and international media. Listeners heard an exasperated and desperate man calling for help, and as he did so he affirmed the lack of humanity shown by national government officials:

> "They don't have a clue what's going on down here," he said. "They flew down here one time two days after the doggone event was over, with TV cameras and AP reporters, with all kinds of goddamn excuses."
>
> "You mean to tell me that [a place] where 1,000 people died and 1,000 more are dying every day, we can't figure out a way to authorize the resources that we need?"
>
> "Don't tell me 40,000 people are coming here," he said. "They're not here. It's too doggone late. Get off your asses and let's do something and let's fix the biggest goddamn crisis in the history of this country." (Walker)

Critics would bring attention to the fact that much of the Louisiana National Guard was stationed in the Middle East fighting an unpopular war while American citizens were dying. In sum, Nagin decries the government's decision to deny the people's citizenship rights. Seeing the link between African Americans' stay in the Superdome and "some monster slave ship of the infamous 'middle passage,'" Rebecca Hall argues that African Americans' citizenship rights were denied, as had been established by the Dred Scott case.[2] Yet, the Fourteenth Amendment overruled the Dred Scott case "by stating that all those born in the United States are citizens, and they are entitled to all the privileges and protections therefore" (72). Without the time to consider the reason for abandonment, community members would rally and save their neighbors by floating around in boats, abandoned refrigerators, or whatever they could to brave the water. Whenever possible, they would not accept that their lives were not important and would not rely on politicians to decide when to act. Probing the duties of the government to help its citizens, Jeremy Brecher states, "The US government did not send an army to kill people in New Orleans (at least not before Katrina struck), but those who died were surely the victims of the government's failure in its duty to protect their lives" (75).

If Nagin, an African American man, voiced the desperation of the majority of Black residents stranded in New Orleans, then former First Lady Barbara Bush expressed sentiments of the government that left them stranded. In

---

2. Although my emphasis is on the experiences of Black residents, I am careful to note that all people in the flood zones suffered.

a television interview recorded at a shelter for Katrina survivors, she stated, "And so many of the people in the arenas here, you know, were underprivileged anyway. This is working very well for them" (*When the Levees Broke* episode 3). Bush illuminated the perspective that the African descendants were socially dead, being "underprivileged anyway," and were better off displaced. Her perspective suggested that their social status had brought them to the place where they were, with nothing, not sure what would happen next. Bush's comment overlooks that some of the "underprivileged" had witnessed their family members drown or die from a lack of sustenance, that some had lost all of their belongings, and that others knew not the whereabouts of their surviving family members. Their humanity was invisible.

Lee's (re)telling of the story of African descendants serves the purpose of empowering those who could only find their power by telling their stories. Testifying is a way to show resistance to social death. In her book *The Great Deluge,* an artistic analysis on race, Hurricane Katrina, and the Middle Passage, Kara Walker writes, "We tell stories of events to allude to the unspeakable" (7). The telling of those stories takes many forms when told by people of African descent, but it is clear that their stories too often represent efforts to speak themselves into the light of life, to claim a space in a society that questions the value of their humanity.

JESMYN WARD'S HURRICANE KATRINA

Inspired by her own experience with Katrina, Jesmyn Ward serves to respond to Bush through the voice of a poor Mississippi girl. Ward presents a poor African American family in Bois Sauvage, Mississippi, from the perspective of a fifteen-year-old girl, Esch, who is the only girl in a family of three brothers. Their father, a man who has submitted to the status of social death, mourns the death of his wife, a fatal consequence of the birth of their youngest child. Drowning his sorrows in beer has become his way to cope with his survival, causing him to be absent in a home where the children have needs that he can hardly cover. Had it not been for the fact that he has inherited the land left to his wife by her family, including a makeshift house that borders the "Pit," a body of water, the family may very well be homeless—and eventually they are, after Hurricane Katrina floods the area. Through Esch's point of view, in conversation with Wright, Ward shows the connection between social death and physical death. However, Ward also maintains that redemption for survivors is possible.

Esch's mother haunts the Pit through her physical absence and her family's memories. Only eight years old when her mother dies, Esch recalls a woman who cared for her children with her touches and words of instruction. A capable woman, she could wring the neck of a hen for dinner, find hidden eggs with little effort, and pull a small shark out of their fishing pond for the evening's dinner. Her sense of herself as capable and fearless may very well have contributed to her death. After giving birth to all of her children in their home, it was the last one that drained her body of life. On her fateful night, her daughter, Esch, recalls that their father dragged her mother unwillingly to the hospital for assistance, and that was the last time they saw her alive. For her family, her life seems to have as profound an impact as her unexpected death.

As the only daughter, Esch feels the impact of her mother's absence in ways she cannot articulate. Surrounded by maturing boys and young men, Esch is theirs for a variety of purposes. In her home, she is more likely to take on domestic chores, as seen when her father orders her to wash out the bottles for the storage of water. Esch herself is pregnant, partially due to the fact that she resides between her mother's death and her own life, unsure of herself and the direction she should take to live without the counsel of her parents.

> Mothers of African-American girls are looked to for guidance and support and a host of issues. In addition to fulfilling their general maternal caretaking responsibilities, mothers of African-American girls are faced with the awesome responsibility of countering the persistent flood of negative images with which the African-American child is regularly confronted. The careful manipulation and provision of tangible and emotional support by mothers during this life stage is thought to serve as both a buffer and a guide during this period of overwhelming change. (Davis-Maye and Perry 311)

Living in the absence of her mother, Esch is left alone to figure out who she is as a young woman.

In many ways, this is a love story. It is about the love a girl has for her mother and the lack of love she has for herself. She sees herself as too dark, black, not worth much. In one of her memories of her mother, she thinks of herself in relation to the deceased woman:

> I pulled my hair back in a ponytail. It was one good thing, my odd thing, like a Doberman come out white: corkscrew curls, black, limp when wet but full as fistfuls of frayed rope when dry. Mama . . . said it was some throwback trait, and since I got it, I might as well enjoy it. But I looked in the mirror and knew the rest of me wasn't so remarkable: wide nose, dark skin, Mama's slim short frame with all the curves fold in so that I looked square. (Ward 7)

Feeling as though her hair is "good" and her dark brown body is "bad," Esch ascribes to the faltering sense that celebrates "good hair," a phrase used among African Americans that refers to hair with a texture that is not kinky. And, through her mother's perspective, Esch denigrates dark brown skin as having little value in society, as proving that the occupant of the body and the body itself is bad. Surely without meaning to, her mother reinforced negative ideas about beauty that prove harmful to her daughter long after the woman's untimely death. Scholars on self-identity argue, "The association of lighter skin with beauty and desirability means that colorism has a more significant influence on women" (Townsend et al. 274). Moving beyond the insecurities that are often found among teenagers, especially teenaged girls, Esch has no one to call her beautiful or to provide her with the guidance she desperately needs to see herself not as a pieced-together remnant of a "throwback trait" (referring to an ancestor who is not African), but as a maturing woman with a purpose in the present.

As a result of not seeing her body as worthy of respect, Esch gives her body to her male friends, mostly, she says, because it is easier not to say no. Manny's presence in her life allows her to confess her private thoughts about the person she is with these boys and why:

> He was peeling away my clothes like orange rind: he wanted the other me. The pulpy ripe heart. The sticky heart the boys saw through my boyish frame, my dark skin, my plain face. (16)

Again, seeing herself as black, ugly, boyish, and, therefore, unworthy of respect and love, Esch gives herself to Manny and other boys because they see her as a girl, but a girl without a voice. She reveals how not valuing her body motivates her to seek comfort with boys: "The girly heart that, before Manny, I'd let boys have because they wanted it, and not because I wanted to give it" (16). Seeing Manny as different, in fact as the love of her young life, she gave herself to him because she perceives him as beautiful, with skin lighter than hers, and he wanted her. Manny, her eldest brother Randall's best friend, is nineteen years old and has a girlfriend. He has skin she describes as "gold" and "pale" and a face scarred from a bad car accident. Perhaps Esch finds his scarred, imperfect body attractive, but she most certainly feels that he sees her dark brown body as worthy of a touch from his "gold" body. Unfortunately, he has absolutely no respect for her. Theirs is not a love story, and even though she does not articulate her feelings to him about his lack of respect, she makes increasing moves to try to get him to look at her to see her beyond the "girly heart."

On some level, she understands that sex should not be confused with intimacy or even result in respect. Scholars argue further, "According to objectification theory, adolescent girls become aware that their bodies are examined and evaluated by others and consequently internalize the observers' perspective. . . . This pattern could lead girls to believe that their value and self-worth are a function of their appearance and sex appeal" (Townsend et al. 274). A sense of desperation fills the pages when Esch sees Manny and is in his presence. After seeing him at her brother's basketball game with his girlfriend, whom he plays with and kisses, Esch is then followed by Manny into the girl's bathroom to have sex. This becomes a turning point, a conversion experience, as she tries to make more demands of him through an assertion of her own bodily movements. He unzips his pants and she "grabs his dick hard enough to hurt" (145). He pulls her down on him and she straddles him as they sit on a filthy toilet. This causes them to be face-to-face in a way that they have not been before: "It is the first time he grabbed me over my waist, kept his hands on me closer to my face. Touched me" (145). Although they face one another, she notices that he averts his eyes. In response Esch says, "I grab his face." Ward places this four-word sentence in its own paragraph; by doing so, she punctuates the significance of the act. The only aggression Esch shows toward a male figure in the novel is when she grabs her six-year-old brother, but she quickly apologizes. As Manny proceeds, she continues her quest. A repeat of the phrase "He will look at me" shifts her way of thinking from an act of silent desperation to an act of active assertiveness, an attempt to change the relationship and make it more into what she wants—in fact, an attempt to shift from her earlier belief that it was easier to let them have what they wanted. Her act is a statement of her want. In rejection of her desire for notice, Manny screams an expletive and pushes the small girl violently off his lap onto the dirty floor. "I think Manny saw me, and that he turned away from me, from what I carry, pulling his burnt gold face from my hands, and then I am crying again for what I have been, for what I am, and for what I will be again" (147). Esch sees herself through the eyes of others, in this case, through the eyes of Manny. He avoids eye contact with her for the rest of the novel. He does not see her; he only sees her body. He shares no mutual love and does not even respect her, as he makes clear when he denies that he is the father of her baby. She knows that he is the only one she has had sex with during the past three months. Her response is, "The baby will tell." Voice is strong among the yet-to-be-born and the dead in this novel. Finding her voice through the pending birth of her baby constitutes a rebirth for the pregnant Esch.

Manny is not the only man who does not see Esch. One has to wonder if her father were not around if the children would function the same without him. He emerges as a drunk man, and eventually Esch shares that he had a drinking problem before the death of her mother, as she recalls her mother helping him into the house on various nights. He has a strained relationship with his son Skeet, who has clearly taken to bonding with China, his dog, to fill the gap of not having a close bond with his father and of having lost his mother. The memories of Rose Batiste, or Mama, act as a medium to the past that the children cling to, but the memories leave their father feeling haunted by her loss. Surely the mother was the central figure in the family who linked the children to their father and the father to his children. With her gone, the link has been broken, and the children go on about their business caring for one another, even taking responsibility for Junior. This is most obvious when Randall accidently severs three fingers from his father's hand. Not much is said. No apologies. Only a bandaged hand and the service of bringing him soup and medication. Silence between the family members is deafening and allows for emotions to become private and, perhaps, destructive, as seen with Esch's feelings of abandonment and longing.

Succumbing to the loss of his wife, the father submits to the blues. Esch sees him almost as an extension of the blues. When he first enters the narrative, he drives into the yard and she says she can hear the blues playing on his truck's radio. He and her mother would frequent The Oak, "a blues club set on six acres of woods and a baseball diamond in the middle of the Bois" (92). Juxtaposing the condition of the baseball diamond where "black town teams" played to the raunchy blues club where people, including children, must go to use the restrooms shows the connection between oppression and depression expressed in the blues. Esch's parents go in and out of the club during the game, and she and her brother find themselves in the club to use the restrooms. Later, Esch reveals her memory of dancing to blues music during a gathering at her home. Her mother "would plug in the cassette deck radio in the kitchen, put in tapes by Bobby 'Blue' Bland, Denise LaSalle, and Little Milton" and encourage her to dance to the music while the crowd clapped. Blues, then, is a family affair. Her father's mood might best be expressed in Bland's "Stormy Monday Blues": "They call it Stormy Monday but Tuesday's just as bad / You know I'm tryin', tryin' to find my baby / Won't somebody please send her home to me, yeah" (92). Esch's father's blues is expressed in the music, and the family is as connected to the genre as they are to one another.

Blues is the backdrop of the family's economic situation and emotional depression. In the best of circumstances, the family does not have the resources for prenatal care, let alone the resources needed to feed another child. At one point, after injuring himself on jagged glass, Esch helps her brother to administer a used bandage, previously their other brother's that he has attempted to sterilize with bleach. Skeet eventually cuts the bandage and uses it to cover China's wounds following her last fight. Additionally, Randall needs knee surgery but is afraid that he may lose his chance to go to college on a basketball scholarship if he has the surgery. Doctors are only sought in extreme emergencies. To be sure, Esch's unplanned pregnancy is an emergency. In fact, it is the lack of medical resources that contributes to her pregnancy. Not knowing anyone who has birth control pills and convinced that her father has forgotten that she, in fact, is a girl, she is too afraid to tell anyone in her family about her pregnancy once she confirms it with a stolen home pregnancy test.

If Esch allowed herself to see her self through the eyes of Big Henry, she would be in a better position in terms of loving relationships. Yet, she is blinded by her lack of self-esteem, a consequence of a society that does not affirm Black girls' worth and her family's inability to tell her otherwise. Big Henry clearly loves Esch, and her descriptions of him and his actions toward her prove that she is aware of his respect and love for her. As she speaks of the boys and her reluctance to have sex with them, they come to her, all but Big Henry. He seems the only one aware of her feelings and is especially observant of how Manny treats Esch and how she reacts to the treatment. It is Big Henry who sends Junior to the bathroom to check on Esch at the basketball game. From his position on the bleachers, it is possible that he is fully aware that Manny has followed her to the bathroom and caused her harm in some way. Big Henry is also there when Manny returns. He is a big, sensitive young man who is always there when the family is in need. In fact, he is also the one who, when Mr. Batsiste's fingers are severed, grabs ahold of him, bandages the hand, and drives him to the hospital. Big Henry is a silent and almost invisible hero in the girl's life. His interest in the baby suggests the promise for the love that she has not yet identified as hers. Big Henry values her and sees her worth in a way that Manny and even her family members do not.

Esch learns to look at what she has and to find hope there. Hope, according to Davis-Maye and Perry, "is proposed to provide the internal motivation and energy that adolescents need to exercise self-care agency or self-preservation" (313). Once Esch realizes that Manny will accept no responsibility for the child she is carrying, she finds hope elsewhere. Indeed, it is Esch's choice to accept the "seed," as she refers to her pregnancy, as a welcomed presence in her life. She only thinks of abortion possibilities at one point, when she recalls the rumors she has heard at her school. These include taking a month's worth of birth control pills, throwing her body down stairs, or pressing forcibly upon her stomach. Having no access to the pills, she applies pressure to her stomach by pushing against her father's truck and noting that the result is that her stomach moves back into its curvy form. Although she allows her body to endure the violation of the boys of her community, she is unwilling to inflict harm to her body herself, suggesting that she has a level of appreciation for her body. Eventually she begins to visualize how the baby will look—perhaps like her or like Manny. These thoughts place the baby as part of her family, for she often looks at her brothers and compares them to her father, just as she compares herself to the memory of her mother.

As a recurring theme and concern among African-descended writers, familial relationships shape the individual characters of their work. Through these relationships, we understand the meaning of belonging and, by extension, how the relationships determine responses to the catastrophes that threaten not only individual lives but also familial bonds. Esch has a strong bond with her brothers; they must care for themselves in the absence of their father. It is conceivable that the baby she chooses to have will have "many daddies," as Big Henry tells her once he hears the news. Such connections make her feel bonded, even if she is aware that her mother's absence has weakened the bond she should have with her father. The baby has the promise of filling a void between mother and child and her father and her.

Birth and the promise for a future lingers. Not only is Esch pregnant by a young man who couldn't care less about her, but her brother's prized dog, China, gives birth to a litter of puppies that are unable to sustain life. Like the family, who has a strong bond among the siblings, the puppies' access to food and other valuable necessities is tenuous, as there is very little income. Through her ability to fight other dogs, China brings money to the teenaged owner. Yet, he needs to find ways to feed the dog. Stealing and cutting grass at a Catholic church with a raggedy lawn mower in the summer and weeding during the winter allow him to care for the female dog.

China gives him purpose and a sense of empowerment, vitally important for a poor, motherless adolescent male. Her ability to fight and to win provides the poor teenager with an identity that makes him feel proud and capable. Ward says of the dogs that the men in her community "fought them for honor, never for money" (265). For a person who is poor, living in a small town, honor is of the utmost importance, especially for the motherless Skeetah. When China has babies and is immediately labeled as incapable of fighting as she had before her pregnancy, Skeetah must prove that she is still capable of winning fights. She is an extension of him, as Ward suggests through her statement, "I . . . remember the dog fighting, and being incredibly fierce. After my brother died, his pit bull was a living link to him" (265). The same may be said of Skeetah. At one point, he tells Esch that he cannot lose China. Of course, the dog also reminds him of the loss of his mother, who died after giving birth to Junior on the same land where China gives birth. China represents for him an extension of himself, as he is an extension of his mother and the father with whom he shares the tension of their shared loss.

It is certain that the father must rely on his children if he is to live, for his meager attempts to do more come too late. Esch's father's desperate attempts to prepare for the hurricane are not enough. He pulls resources from the grounds of his land, a place that appears as a dumping ground, or rather a graveyard, for items that are no longer useful for anything other than scraps. In those remnants of the past, chickens find places to hide their eggs. Old boards from the chicken coops become the protection he hopes will keep them safe from the approaching category five storm that is heading toward the area. He gives clear instructions to his children as he lies in bed nursing his injured hand: board the windows, fill the gas tank, gather nonperishable food, and cook everything in the refrigerator. They have too few cans of food, no evacuation plan, and no sense of the real danger until the water comes. The Batiste family is bonded to the land that gives them history and place, even after the loss of the mother whose family owned it and passed it down from one generation to another. *Roots* sees the passing of a story to give a sense of connection to descendants. Ward's focus on the land allows her to emphasize the loss of the possessions that connect them to the land.

Despite the father's emotional absence, interestingly enough, the children call on the name of "daddy" as dangers come. First, they hear a loud crash and learn that a tree has fallen into the room that he shared with his wife. It is a shrine, a place in memoriam, a place where he embraces social death. Esch says the room has not changed since her mother's death. On the shelves are things that she has left behind; tucked in various places are pictures of the children with their mother and father. With these, Esch is able to see a connection that she is left to long for between her siblings and their father. As a symbolic move, the tree ruptures the father's unhealthy attachment to the death of his wife. This rupture begins earlier, when he loses his ring finger in his accident, a result of trying to prepare for the hurricane. He too is going through a reluctant conversion process—from death to life. As they lie on the floor of the living room and notice that the water is rising through the floor, their attempt to save themselves by moving into the attic is their only choice to avoid going out into the rain and high winds. Their dad feels his powerlessness. Secure in his memories of hurricanes past, he is unprepared for the fact that the Pit has actually flooded the area and the water is rising. Fast. He is barely able to tell his children how to proceed when he finally thinks to move into the attic, which they do, in thin clothes and no shoes, into an area that has no provisions. As the water rises, the father becomes disabled mentally (a clear sign of his social death), unable to think of how to get them to safety. He is consumed by his powerlessness.

Ward captures well the experience that too many suffered when the flood-waters rose. Actual excerpts from calls made to emergency personnel in New Orleans from people trapped in attics during Hurricane Katrina give voice to Ward's narrative:

"New Orleans police operator 165."

CALLER: "We have no ladder."

DIFFERENT OPERATOR; STANDARD RESPONSE: "Sir, there's no emergency units available at this time."

RESPONSE TO OPERATOR: "You've got to be kidding, man."

RESPONSE TO OPERATOR: "Please bro. Please. . . ."

DIFFERENT CALLER: "The water is steady rising in the attic, ma'am, and I'm gonna drown in the attic."

OPERATOR: "Can you break a hole in the attic?"

CALLER: "I tried."

OPERATOR: "The police are not coming out until the conditions get better."

Pause.

OPERATOR: "Hello."

CALLER: "Yes."

CALLER: "I can't get out." (*Trouble the Water*)

Such descriptions of Black bodies confined in enclosed spaces with fear of drowning are present in other works, such as those by Alex Haley and Guy Deslauriers. Ward engages the reality of that fear in her novel. Fearing the reality of such experiences, the sons, especially Skeetah, who declares he "ain't dying in no attic," take the lead and emerge as heroes. Their strong sense of survival and their appreciation of their lives propel them to safety. Working with her brother to make a hole in the attic to the roof, Esch, like Equiano before her, describes the sheer terror of seeing water in a different form:

It is terrible. It is the flailing wind that lashes like an extension cord used as a beating belt. It is the rain, which stings like stones, which drives into our eyes and binds them shut. It is the water, swirling and gathering and spreading all sides, brown with an undercurrent of red to it, the clay of the Pit like a cut that won't stop leaking. It is the remains of the yard, the refrigerators and lawn mowers and the RV and mattresses, floating like sleet. It is trees and branches breaking, popping like Black Cat firecrackers in an endless crackle

of explosions, over and over again and again. It is us huddling together on
the roof. . . . Daddy kneels behind us, tries to gather all of us to him. (230–31)

Katrina has no respect for the memories attached to each item. Esch sees the
contents of the yard being overtaken by the water and knows that if the water
can easily move a refrigerator and a truck, it can consume them too. Each
item is like a picked-over carcass or bare bones in a graveyard. Death awaits
them by way of the water. Esch says, "The storm screams, I have been waiting
for you" (230). For good reason, Skeet is unsatisfied with staying in the attic
and instead insists that they move from their crumbling house to the house
on the hill, formerly owned by their grandparents. The house is rooted in the
history of the Batistes. It has, like the family's presence on the land, withstood
any number of tragedies brought on by natural elements and sudden deaths.
At some point, they were able to live off the land that held a prosperous gar-
den and livestock as well as family stories told by grandmother and mother.
Stories that Esch remembers with fondness. It is not surprising that it acts as
a suitable shelter for them to wait for the storm to pass.

But movement from one house to the other requires skill and ability. It
also requires trust. They must work together as a family to move from the
roof, to the trees, to the top of the old house. Junior is holding on for dear
life to his big brother Randall and Skeet is holding on to his beloved dog
China while his sister carries a bucket filled with puppies. Their father, barely
balancing himself with his one good hand, reluctantly follows his children
through the storm. We see here the future of the family taking lead to move
beyond the past. Water's presence facilitates this movement as it subverts the
past and future in the present moment. Ward provides readers with a scene
that shows the sheer rawness of humans fighting against raging natural elements: "The hurricane enfolds me in its hand. I glide. I land on the thickest
branch, the wood gouging me, the bucket clanging, unable to breathe, my
eyes tearing up" (232). Water separates their lives from physical death. If their
father went day by day as if he were not only socially dead, but seconds away
from a physical death, his fight to stay with his children, to see them to safety,
awakens in him a new sense of life. Water washes away more than buildings
and other material objects.

The moment of change occurs when her father pushes her into the water
below them upon learning that his daughter is pregnant. His act of trying
to grab her with his good hand before she reaches the water is, like his lax
parenting, a gesture that comes too late to save her from falling. "The water
swallows, and I scream. My head goes under and I taste it, fresh and cold
and salt somehow, the way tears taste the rain. Who will deliver me? And the

hurricane says sssssshhhhhhhh" (235). As Junior clings to Randall and their Daddy clings to his own life, this leaves her brother to choose between his dog and his sister. Skeet sees his sister and chooses her, marking the first time any of the brothers extend themselves to her. When he saves her, he saves himself and affirms the importance of the family by preserving their bond and securing the hope of their future, represented by her pregnancy. They will never be the same, and all will embrace the baby that Esch is carrying and presumably begin to make her a priority as a young woman, and not merely as an extension of themselves and as a substitute for their dead mother.

For Ward, the novel has influences drawn from her family and childhood in Mississippi, but it is not autobiographical. Ward recalls, "My family and I survived Hurricane Katrina in 2005; we left my grandmother's flooding house, were refused shelter by a white family, and took refuge in trucks in an open field during a Category Five hurricane" (266). Yet, the novel is set in the South and racism rears its ugly head in a variety of unspoken but obvious ways. While for the most part, the family has very little contact with the Whites in the area, as seen in Wright's short story, it is clear that there are very distinct lines between the races and that the haves are White and the have-nots are Black. This becomes clear when the children try, twice, to burglarize their nameless White neighbors. The first time Skeet devises a plan to break into the shed and steel medicine for China. When the owners return and their dog chases the children, Ward revises the narrative of the roles dogs have played in hunting people of African descent in America, especially in the South. The power is subverted when the dog chases Esch and Skeet to their family's land, where China takes control of the situation and injures the dog, sending him back to his owner. A second time occurs when Randall asks his sister to go with him to take food from the house. They are unable to access the property and conclude that there is probably no food left there for them to take. Randall's engagement with the house illuminates the poor condition of the family. He aggravates his weakened knee by kicking into the boarded windows, which are sturdier than the pieces they find to board their own windows. Although the school will pay for his surgery, his fear that he will miss his chance to go to college, his ticket out of the small southern town, and his only conceivable chance to improve his socioeconomic status keeps him playing through the pain.

One of the more interesting exchanges with Whites is when Big Henry, Skeet, and Esch come upon a couple who have had a fairly bad accident. Not understanding how anyone from the area would drive fast on that section of the road, Skeet concludes that they must not be from there. However, when the man wanders to the window and insists that he knows Skeet from the work that he does in the Catholic church's graveyard, he knows that the person is in fact from the area and that Skeet is not as invisible to his White neighbors as they are to him. Their presence illuminates how financially poor the Batistes are and the lack of access they have to health care, meaning they are more likely to die than their White counterparts. Skeet is terrified of death, as seen when the group comes upon the gruesome wreck. It is that heightened level of fear that propels him to risk his and his sister's safety to break into the shed and, later, to announce that he "ain't dying in no attic." Perhaps too young to submit to social death status as has his father, he must show him how to live by affirming the value of his life. Clearly suffering silently from the loss of their mother, a fact he admits to his sister as they wait for Katrina to come and go, he does whatever he can to stay alive and to keep his family intact. Skeet's connection to the home intersects with his deep love for his family.

After the hurricane, the meaning of home shifts dramatically. They do not expect government help or a rescue. Wandering among the debris that represents the remnants of their hometown suggests to them that moving forward will not be easy but confirms that each one cannot do it alone. Jean Kempf quotes a caption from the *Times Picayune* newspaper of New Orleans: "Unbelievable debris, unbearable sadness, unrelenting need for water are among the things Hurricane Katrina deposited in Gulfport, Miss." (58). But Ward revises this narrative, even though the caption more closely resembles her own experience. Big Henry and his mother open their home to the Batiste family; however, Skeet resists the idea that he is homeless. If the house is not available for living, then his family's land is a good alternative. In so doing, he redefines the meaning of home and sees himself as attached to space rather than the place.

Esch's pregnancy ushers in a new era for the family, in which they will rely even more on one another to survive as their father begins to move past his state of mourning. Unlike their father, the children rejected social death; basketball playing, dogfighting, and sex give them purpose and make them feel alive. After the hurricane, the father assures his daughter that she has his support. With his support, Esch can now find the hope that has waned since the death of her mother. Ward's Mississippi narrative answers Wright's by presenting Esch's pregnancy as a revision of Lula's and her unborn child's death. Davis-Maye and Perry conclude, "Hope is likely a necessary feeling to possess when one exists in an environment that devalues one's worth and promotes negative images of whom it is one will become—an African American woman" (326).

There is no doubting that the Middle Passage continues to influence how African descendants are seen in America and other parts of the world. As legacies of the Middle Passage, African Americans, from one generation to the next, stand against the idea that they are socially dead. Traumatic experiences prove transformative to oppressed peoples and perhaps to their oppressors, to some extent, as well. It is in the midst of threats to their lives and those of the ones they love that people become acutely aware of their desire to live, causing them to find reasons to embrace life, regardless of the challenges. From the Middle Passage as a metaphor emerge two important facts. First, physical death and social death have taken on meanings that imply that there is little space between beginnings and endings; only hope separates the two. Second, transitional states are temporary. Perhaps Jerry Ward articulates it best. While existing in a state of exile, depression, and fear, he writes, "I am no longer who I was on August 28, and I do not applaud what I am becoming. I hope the scars are not permanent" (16). Ward's experience is not simply his own; it is ours.

CHAPTER 7

Telling of Return and Rebirth in Marshall's *Praisesong for the Widow*

One of these mornings bright and fair, goin-a take my wings and cleave the air

—"O Mary Don't You Weep"[1] (Negro spiritual)

AS SEEN in Jesmyn Ward's novel, family's connection to a home provides a place for belonging and where identity can form. A place to call home resonates as a prominent concern in the history of African descendants. As seen in chapters 5 and 6, blues songs capture what it feels like to have a home, as the singers focus on what it means to be removed from home. Blues may also speak to the loss of Africa as home. Return, then, to Africa occurs in various forms. In the age of reclamation, where commercials entice Americans to take DNA tests and engage in ancestral research to build a profile of their background, we can do what Alex Haley claimed to have done and find our own hidden selves. Take, for example, recent shows that do just that. The most well known is PBS's *Finding Roots*, hosted by professor of African American studies Dr. Henry Louis Gates Jr., whose team of researchers relies on public records and DNA testing to construct stories for famous people. Featured guests almost always discover something quite interesting, usually evidence that there are some kernels of truth in a story that had been passed down to them about a daring ancestor. DNA tests provide a way to return. Such tests may tell them which people of Africa match their DNA. Once placed in Africa, descendants might be able to make claim on a location, adopt cultural practices, or identify a language and perhaps religious or spiritual beliefs.

---

1. See #134 of the United Methodist Hymnal or hymnary.org/hymn/UMH/134.

These tests do not give a name or a personal history, as Haley attempted to do with his work, but they provide some clues to a historical identity that was distorted by the transatlantic slave trade. Indeed, seeking this information may constitute a form of resistance to the history that renders descendants nameless and placeless.

Myth assists with return. Some contemporary African-descended writers, such as Paule Marshall, have responded to the trauma associated with the slave trade by using the myth of the flying Africans (enslaved Africans who possessed the ability to free themselves from slavery by flying back to their African homelands) to assert empowerment over oppression and to "reconceptualize the meaning of the Middle Passage" (Diedrich et al. 8). In another variation of the Flying African myth, Marshall in *Praisesong for the Widow* writes of the Ibos who resisted enslavement by walking on water back to Africa. Wendy Walters observes, "Although the 'Ibo Landing' story does not contain flying, it is similar in many respects to several versions of the Flying African legend. Both stories contain specially-empowered enslaved Africans who leave slavery and travel back to Africa by 'super human' means" (19). Contemporary writers, like those who originally told the stories that reemerge in their novels, explore ways to come to terms with complexities that have risen from the details surrounding the transatlantic voyage. On one side is Africa—the original home ravaged by European settlers. On the other side is the new home, in this case the Caribbean and the U.S. American South—areas of the Atlantic Global South—for enslaved Africans and the location for torment. However, what occurred between the old home and the new home few people dare to consider. It is in this psychological escape, rooted in memories of the past that are too distant to the descendants of those who survived such voyages, that an oral tradition emerges.

In an interview, critically acclaimed Geechee filmmaker Julie Dash, known for her film *Daughters of the Dust,* discusses the idea of myth and its relationship to storytelling with feminist scholar bell hooks. Together, the two women identify several aspects of myth. One, "myth is part of every culture"; two, "myth is very important to maintain a sense of self and to move forward in the future"; and three, myth allows writers to "take factual information and infuse it with imaginative construction" (Dash 32). Marshall demonstrates two forms of myth: mythic memory and liberation myths. Mythic memory is "what is remembered" as well as what is told (Dash 30).

Recasting fact as myth provides a medium useful in liberation from forms of oppression. In *Praisesong,* belief in the flying or walking-on-water African provides a way to resist oppressions stemming from the Middle Passage. Such is the case with Avey, in Marshall's *Praisesong,* who must reconnect with her historical memories to redeem herself from the symbolic death she has come to accept. Marshall's texts intersect with the theme of death as a historical occurrence that affects the future of the deceased's relatives. In these novels we find "'spiritual metamorphosis, symbolic death, and rebirth' that will develop these 'raw souls' through their metaphysical 'striving'" (Washington 34). Avey Johnson faces the "resolution/reintegration of grief" resulting from the physical death of a loved one or the symbolic death of a relationship, followed by a resurrection of a self (McNeil 185). Marshall's characters find that death is a gateway to new life as it also symbolizes freedom, renewal, and knowledge.

Until the transatlantic slave trade was abolished in 1807 and the importation of enslaved people to the United States ended in 1808, 12.8 million Africans were transported over the Atlantic to various locations in the Caribbean and the Americas. Approximately 10.6 million survived, while others were cast overboard or died from any number of other causes (Rediker 3).[2] Those people deemed as powerless and socially dead nonpersons responded in a variety of ways. During the slave trade era, stories regarding flying Africans and those who could walk on water emerged. Those featuring flying Africans varied. Some believed that only a certain group of Africans possessed this ability, and once it was discovered, they were no longer taken from Africa. Other stories involve engagement with a ritual that would allow the enslaved person the ability to fly. What is common in these stories is the fear of salt as a deterrent. Walters believes that salt is a metaphor for European captivity, as the mineral was commonly used by Europeans and not by West Africans. Warnings to resist salt suggested that the connection, the ability to return spiritually if not physically, would be hindered by the indulgence of the colonizers' ways. References to salt suggest only one aspect of resistance to oppression in the forms of colonization and slavery. Of course, the idea that humans, particularly enslaved people, could remove themselves from slavery when they chose to by returning to their place of origin threatens the power of the people who had devoted considerable time and money to making a profit from the capture and sale of the enslaved African. It is plausible to believe that the oral myths themselves were formed to give hope to those who believed that return—in one form or another—was possible. Walters observes, "The legend of the Flying Africans, in all its variations, is ultimately about this ability to transcend one's condition" (Walters 5).

Africans' ability to fly has meaning to the storyteller and to the listener that not only works as a counter-discourse to the physical state of slavery but also emerges as a way to present oppressed people as spiritual beings.

2. For updated statistics, see the Trans-Atlantic Slave Trade Database at www .slavevoyages.org.

Consider the song "O Mary Don't You Weep." A song that is commonly sung at funerals, its lyrics clearly show the relationship between flying and dying. The phrase "going to take my wings and cleanse the air" speak of life as a state of confinement. Further, the "taking of wings" points to the achievement of a state of freedom through transcendence. Flying Africans defy enslavement and social death status through storytelling and song. As such, the myth revises the narrative of enslavement as well as the narrative of death. It suggests that death is only the final state of the transformation as death can occur as a mental and spiritual state during life for a person deemed a slave. Borders are crossed through storytelling and through faith. Lorna McDaniel observes in relation to the physical movement that "the sea (or a body of water) represents the obstacle against return and is used as the symbol of deterrence in much of the lore" (30).

WALKING ON WATER IN *PRAISESONG*

In *Praisesong for the Widow,* Avey communes with the dead. Marshall's novel begins with a woman who has been in the process of escape for at least twenty years. Escape has been her way of coping with the death of her marriage, a tragedy that occurs long before her husband actually dies. The novel centers on the life of Avey (Avatara) Johnson, a middle-aged African American widow who has achieved upper-middle-class status in New York, but has cast aside her cultural heritage that was taught to her during childhood visits to the South to attain this status. Every year, she and her middle-class friends take cruises, but when the novel begins, Avey, while on one of these yearly cruises, yields to a sudden and inexplicable need to disembark the ship and to return "home" to her house. Yet, she finds herself alone on the island of Grenada, where she meets Lebert, the ancestral figure who convinces her to visit his home island of Carriacou to engage in the traditional festivities. The purpose of going on the excursion, in Lebert's words, is "to bathe in Carriacou water and visit 'bout friends. And to fete—dance, drink rum, run 'bout after women" (Marshall 164). Without really knowing why, Avey accepts the man's invitation. And, her acceptance will be her move toward "going home" like her African ancestors, if you will, affirming her lost cultural identity and moving from the social status she and her husband embraced.

Transcendence through contact with water—that is, the Middle Passage, walking on water—emerges as a bridge between mythic memory and experience. Shanna Benjamin has argued that the "mythic backdrop" allows Marshall to "delve into the psychological and spiritual desires of black women" (50). Dash's

elements of myth—as related to culture, self-identity, and factual imagination—are central in analyzing the importance of the walking-on-water myth
that Aunt Cuney presents to the chosen girl, Avatara/Avey. For it is in this
myth that Aunt Cuney hopes that her niece will develop a "sense of self and
move forward" by delving into her "psychological and spiritual desires." Yet,
when the novel begins, we find Avey in a state of confusion. Dash and hooks
provide insight into the significance of Aunt Cuney sharing with her niece the
walking-on-water myth as a form of storytelling. Through their relationship,
Marshall shows that myth and memory are inextricably bound to haunted
spaces, including, for our purposes, the Middle Passage and, by extension, Ibo
Landing in Tatem, South Carolina.

Marshall relies on mythic memory, passed down from one woman to
another, Aunt Cuney to Avey and eventually promised to Marion, another
female relative of the next generation, to confront the Middle Passage and
redefine it as more than a site of trauma, but as a site of survival where resistance to oppression emerged through storytelling that traveled to the South.
As a result of sharing the memories, myth also serves as a tool for liberation.
My concern in this chapter is with analyzing how Marshall's character Aunt
Cuney, a southern woman, revises traumatic facts as a liberating myth. Relying on myths—specifically stories of Africans who used extraordinary abilities
to defy enslavement and determine their freedom—I argue that Marshall's
Aunt Cuney's intent is to present a counter-discourse to the Middle Passage
experience in an effort to reset the lens from victimization to empowerment.
This counter-discourse results in redefining beliefs associated with death.
Avey herself has succumbed to social death, a consequence of denying the
claim to birth gifted to her by her southern aunt. By retelling the walking-on-
water story, Marshall reveals how Black southern women's use of storytelling
in the form of mythic memories can empower and liberate not only the storyteller but also the designated listener. As seen throughout Middle Passage,
engaging in this practice places the storyteller (parent/ancestral figure) and
believer (child/descendant) in the position to challenge forms of social death
as they embrace life.

Probably because Paule Marshall is the daughter of Barbadian immigrants
who settled in New York, scholars of *Praisesong* focus on what occurs when
Avey travels to the Caribbean and finds herself led to join in the Big Drum
ceremony, a conglomeration of dances that represent the national and cultural
identities of the participants. As a result, scholars overlook the significance of
the first leg of her journey, which occurs in South Carolina, the place where
she is gifted with the story that provides her with an identity and a purpose
and where she is privy to West African cultural practices and rituals that have

been preserved in her southern Black community. My focus is on how Aunt Cuney's storytelling elucidates Marshall's emphasis on how mythic memory acts as a bridge between Africa, the Middle Passage, the Caribbean, and the coastal southern region of the United States. Marshall relies not on the flying African myths that are more prevalent in the Caribbean, but on the myth associated with Africans in the South as the foundational mythic memory for Avey's return to her roots. Wendy Walters informs, "Marshall has stated that the collection of Gullah folktales from the Georgia Sea Islands found in *Drums and Shadows* formed the basis of *Praisesong for the Widow*" (19). Because the descendants of those brought to the Sea Islands, located off the coast of Georgia and South Carolina, have retained many West African cultural practices, as seen in linguistic patterns, storytelling, dancing, song, religious practices, and so on, the islands have been the setting for literary production by people of African descent. Marcus Rediker reveals that slave ships transported Africans from "six basic regions of Africa: Senegambia, Sierra Leone/the Winward Coast[,] the Gold Coast, the Bight of Benin, the Bight of Biafra, and West Central Africa (Kongo, Angola)" (3). A significant number of those "went to South Carolina and Georgia" (Rediker 3). Marshall may have also known about the account of Roswell King, an overseer at a Georgia plantation, who chronicled the arrival of enslaved Africans, thought to be Ibo, who were considered intolerable of enslavement. Timothy Powell states that in May 1803, after enduring the Middle Passage, a group of enslaved Ibo--probably a commonly used moniker for enslaved people--who had been brought to Skidaway Island off the coast of Georgia engaged in a rebellion as they were being moved by their new owners to St. Simons Island. As a result, two White sailors and the overseer died trying to swim to shore. It was these rebellious Africans, King records, who "took to the swamp" or "committed suicide by walking into Dunbar Creek" (Powell para. 3). In a story more similar to Marshall's, Igbo Landing is identified as

> duh place weah dey bring duh Ibos obuh in a slabe ship an wen dey git deah, dey ain lak it an so dey all staht singin and dey mahch right down in duh ribbah tuh mahch back tuh Africa, bu dey ain able tuh get deah. Dey gits drown. (McDaniel 33)

Drums and Shadows, a collection of Federal Writers' Project (FWP) interviews of former slaves, documents Black narrative versions of this historical event. Refuting any idea of suicide, one resident provided his truth: "Wallace Quarterman of Darien, when asked by an FWP interviewer to verify the history of the Ibos on St. Simons who walked into the water, replied, 'Aint you heard about them? . . . They rise up in the sky and turn themselves into buzzards and fly right back to Africa'" (Powell 255). Quarterman admitted that he had not witnessed the flight, but said, "Everybody know about them. . . . I know plenty what did see them, plenty what was right there in the field with them . . . after they done fly away (Powell 255). Satisfied with the testimony and witness of the collective, Quarterman does not need to see to know.

Inspired by these stories, Marshall, as I will discuss, deals with the meaning of death as a form of resistance to a life of oppression. Further research reveals that it was not uncommon for enslaved Africans to seek a path of return over the nearest body of water, as Works Progress Administration records show. According to Stephanie Smallwood, another "testimony" from an ex-Georgia slave reveals that "Africans from the Bight of Biafra (Ibos) who were intending to take their lives 'would mahch right down in duh ribbuh tuh mach back to Africa'" (186). Marshall's work emphasizes the act not as suicide, but as a return home. Notably, what occurs at Ibo Landing suggests a relationship between death and power.

Aunt Cuney proves instrumental as a spiritual guide for her niece as she appears to Avey in her dreams, or in her subconscious memories. Traveling through her memories, Avey recalls her visits with Aunt Cuney. Marshall succeeds in providing an Edenic scene in her description of Avey as a child who participates in the "ritual" of following her great-aunt Cuney twice a week to Ibo Landing, where she tells her niece the story of their ancestors, passed down from Aunt Cuney's grandmother. For four summers, starting when she was seven years old, Avey, named Avatara by her aunt after her aunt's grandmother, follows her through "the wood, dark even on the sunniest day because of the Spanish moss hanging in great silver-gray skeins from the oaks, [which] was a place filled with every kind of ha'nt there was, according to the children she played with in Tatem" (Marshall 33). A place where rituals take place and hauntings of the past occur, Tatem represents for the child a home. While the story could be told from any location, the visit of the haunted space, where the child is part of a historical performance requiring her to walk to the setting's origin, suggests a call for her to submit. Avey must go to the place, feel the sun, see the trees and other aspects of the nature that symbolize the past. The trees, the sun, the water do not forget the past, as Toni Morrison has stated in "Sites of Memory," and Avey is asked to submit to the significance of these ancestral memories.

Shanna Benjamin and others have found that Marshall relies on her knowledge and study of African cultures to write *Praisesong*. When a child, Avey observes African cultural practices, namely singing and dancing, preserved by the people of Tatem. As she passes through this time in her memory, Avey recalls the story of her auntie who had left Tatem's only church after she was caught "crossing her feet in a Ring" and was ordered to leave the circle (Marshall 33). Her act of lifting her feet to cross them, according to Courtney Thorsson, is an offense as "constant contact with the ground is essential to connection with the ancestors, who are part of the earth" (645). Though Aunt Cuney had stopped attending church regularly and was too proud to attend the Shouts, she would stand, sometimes with Avey, to observe the movement of the people. Avey recalls it as a movement where the worshippers

> were propelling themselves forward at a curious gliding shuffle which did not permit the soles of the heavy work shoes they had on to ever once lift from the floor. Only their heels rose and then fell with each step, striking the worn pineboard with a beat that was as precise and intricate as a drum's and which as the night wore on the Shout became more animated could be heard all over Tatem. (Marshall 34)

Art Rosenbaum's description of the Ring Shout confirms Marshall's description of the dance ritual that was once widely practiced in Sea Islands and southeastern costal communities:

> Worshipers move in a counterclockwise circle, following the directions of a lead singer. They do a distinctive shuffling step in which the back foot does not pass the front foot, which would be considered dancing. (The preachers of the Great Revival strongly condemned secular dance, so the ring shout was carefully redefined as not-dancing.) Worshipers use a separate group of shout songs that have a typically African melodic shape and are as distinctive as the step. (178–79)

It is a dance that requires solidarity with the community as it also acknowledges the ancestors. Further, its songs involve repetition through call and response, suggesting the need to remember, or at least acknowledge a connection to an unknown origin and to share that connection with other members of the community. Clearly unable to divest herself of the dancing ritual that allowed her to remain connected not only with the community but also with the community's African heritage, Aunt Cuney continues to share the knowledge of this dance with her grandniece, who finds herself haunted by the suppressed memory of it over thirty years later.

Prominent in the story is the exercise of agency—whereas an enslaved person chooses liberation, particularly from social death, through a form of resistance. Accordingly, the Ibos, whom Aunt Cuney says were "pure born

Africans," disembarked from the ship and within two minutes they took "a look around. . . . Stud[ied] the place real good" (Marshall 37). Once they saw everything that was going to happen from that day up until the present, they turned back around and reportedly "walked on back down to the edge of the river and kept on walking right on out over the river. . . . Left the white folks standin' back here with they mouth hung open and they taken off down the river on foot. Stepping and Singing" (39). They did this, according to the myth, despite the fact that their ankles, wrists, and necks were bound with iron. Aunt Cuney and the Ring Shouters pay homage to the Ibos, or "pure born Africans," who survived the Middle Passage. Jon Spencer notes of the Ring Shout, "It empowered those who possessed it to endure abject slavery by temporarily elevating them out of the valley of oppression" (67). If the body is not present or capable of performing labor, then the slavery system is at a loss of both profit and control. In effect, there is a disruption of the power structure. To be sure, through physical death, they chose life, but not under the rule of their captors.

Myth requires a measure of faith. Through the enslaver's perspective, there was a mass suicide. Descendants use myth to reinterpret the fact. Rather than telling a story where misery was at the forefront and the enslaved were victimized, the Ibo Landing story, widely told by people of the Sea Islands, according to filmmaker Julie Dash, did not speak of death. The idea that people could walk on water immediately conjures the biblical story of Jesus, who walked on water, and when he was asked by Peter to help him to walk as well, indulged his request. However, Peter's lack of faith resulted in him falling into the water and calling for Jesus to save him from drowning. When the child, Avey, asks her aunt why the people didn't drown, her aunt challenges her lack of faith by referencing the biblical story and asking if she would ask the same of Jesus and His ability. Cheryl Wall observes, "The truth here, Aunt Cuney teaches, is likewise spiritual rather than factual" (187). As readers, we might ask if the Ibos' ability to walk on water is more in reference to their spiritual prowess and not a reference to their physical abilities. This reversion from body to spirit, a literal transformation by which they were able to see ahead and know the future, challenges beliefs that only the body can enjoy freedom. The telling of the story serves to empower the listener centuries later, and it is especially important to note that women, as with Rhodes's *Voodoo Dreams,* are the ones chosen to pass down the story. Venetria Patton observes, "It is this notion of resistance that is meant to empower those who may not have flown, but who can cling to the possibility, and thus not be encumbered by mental shackles" (66).

Aunt Cuney learns it from her grandmother, Avatara, who was an enslaved woman, and Cuney passes it to her great-niece, the next girl in line, and then

Avey will pass it to the daughter, Marion, who refused to die when Avey tried to abort her pregnancy years earlier. When her grandniece reaches seven, Aunt Cuney orders her nephew to bring his only daughter to Tatem in August, where she gifts the child with the story. Seven, a symbolic year referring to wisdom, is also the year that, for at least one month, she is known only as Avatara. According to Wall, the name, "derived from the Sanskrit, carries the meaning of passing down or a passing over" (187). Responding to the significance of her name—the meaning of which she would recall each time she hears it if it were not for the fact that she shortened her name to Avey—Aunt Cuney makes every effort to impress upon her grandniece a sense of pride by sharing with her a story that, though incredible, invokes in the reader and teller racial and cultural identity and empowerment, especially during the time of Jim Crow when Avey is a child. As a descendant of these people, she has forgotten that she has the ability to determine her own place in the world. In his study of flying Ibos in literature, including *Praisesong*, Fred Metting notes, "The ability to recall, through oral narrative, tales of escape and resistance provided the slave community with psychic freedom, a cultural protection from domination" (148). Yet, as she gets older, she loses sense of her self through the repression of this mythic memory and the power of its legacy. As Courtney Thorsson notes, "The further Avey strays from Tatem, the further she is from a cultural nationalism or diasporic consciousness that allows her to feel at home" (645). She proceeds through life as if she is unaware that her aunt had named her for her grandmother because she was "sent." Marshall insists that stories must be retold from one generation to another, and when the stories are not told and mythic memories are disrupted and suppressed, those who are intended to benefit from these stories experience a cultural dis-alignment.

Despite this knowledge, Avey is unaware that she has been lost in her own proverbial Middle Passage. Her moment of loss begins on Halsey Street, a space where the past and present collide, allowing for the future to emerge. It is at once a place where Avey and her husband celebrate who they are and where they eventually develop a fear of who they can be. Marshall captures its complexity: it was as if "the street along which they are fleeing is not straight as they had believed, but circular, and that it has been leading them all the while back to the place where they were seeking to escape" (83). The same might be said of mythic memories—as a circular movement that leads back to the place of origin. To be sure, Halsey Street is analogous to slave ships, where cultures intermixed and the trauma of survival took root, making room for the emergence of mythic memories. As eloquently captured by Barbadian poet Kamau Braithwaite, who manipulates oral and written forms to memorialize trauma: "& the sea between us yields its secrets . . . into sheets of sound / that bear our pain" (6). Similarly, the cramped apartment on Halsey Street bore, like the ships that crossed the Atlantic, secrets and pain. During their earlier years on Halsey Street, Jay would return home tired after working one of his two jobs and "he would lower his tall frame into the armchair, lean his head back, close his eyes, and let Coleman Hawkins, the Count . . . work their magic" (94). This Jay emerged as a "self that would never be seen down . . .was open, witty, playful and outrageous" (95). Langston Hughes's poetry is quoted several times throughout the novel, almost as an incantation, to serve as a reminder of the lineage of African Americans and their relationship with water as depicted in the Ibo Landing story and implied in Hughes's poem "The Negro Speaks of Rivers": "I've known rivers, . . . I bathed in the Euphrates when dawns were / young" (125). These links, says *Praisesong*'s narrator, "put them in possession of a kind of power" (125). Hughes's poem, as in the Ibo story, affirms the link between people of African descent in America as he acknowledges the migratory movement that caused the disconnect and need for myth to realign the disruption. And, Avey's ties to the South remain near as she and her husband take yearly trips to Tatem, where they remember the story that Jay, who was born in Kansas, declares he believes. Affirming a connection to Tatem, Jay referred to it as "'down-home' life . . . [and] he would look forward to the trip to Tatem each summer even more than she did" (116). At this point, they embrace life as African descendants and show no interest in social death.

In conversation with hooks and Dash, Marshall illuminates how "myth is very important to maintain a sense of self and to move forward in the future" (Dash 32). However, children and their growing expenses threaten Avey and Jay's financial stability and make room for the seeds of doubt and fear to grow and push the couple away from what they once enjoyed to a place that they despised. Halsey Street's working class occupants, some of whom fight in public, make the Johnsons' apartment, where they danced to jazz music, recited Hughes, and spoke of Tatem, begin to feel like a "cramped apartment where the linoleum had worn through to the floorboards" (91). It was also the place where Avey, pregnant with their third daughter, Marion, became depressed: "It seemed the china bowl which held her sanity and trust fell from its shelf in her mind and broke, and another reason for his lateness began to take shape in her thoughts with the same slow and inevitable accretion of detail and the child in her womb" (91).

Unspoken but felt, both Avey and Jay see the pending birth of the unplanned baby that Avey is carrying at the time as the last step in ensuring that they will live a life of poverty. Rather than communicate their fears to one another, shame, guilt, and feelings of powerlessness take hold, prompting Avey to accuse her husband of having an affair. Avey's accusation demonstrates that her identity has been distorted and how she sees her husband and how he will come to see her marks a transformation initiated by fear and shame of fear. Her behavior is so shocking it is reminiscent of an African American woman on Halsey Street whose public behavior embarrassed the Johnsons. Jay asks her, "Do you know who you sound like?" His question marks the death of the relationship for that question is answered by swearing off all that they identify as Black—the dancing and singing to jazz music, visits to Tatem, and the recitations of African American poetry. Black becomes a mark of shame for the two as they are immediately reminded of the turmoil caused by the public fighting of their neighbors, the Black man and woman whom they see tormenting each other far too frequently, and the brutal beating of one of them by the police. Wall finds that they became driven by a "fear of conforming to racist and sexist stereotypes" (Wall 96). For our purposes, their fear is of social death, which comes in the form of feeling the oppression associated with racism and sexist stereotypes. To avoid this fate, they focus on the material needs and are no longer able to remember the importance of their ancestral past and the ways in which the past inspired their purpose. For Avey, her self-imposed exile in the North and her refusal to visit Tatem Island when she is an adult leave her vulnerable and cause her to shield herself behind a mask of upper-middle-class comfort that recasts her as Black-less. She is a woman with no past that she cares to remember. Once Avey and Jay stop engaging in cultural practices, they begin to simply survive and not to live. Better put, they become disempowered as they give in to a form of social death.

Before fear overtook her, Avey was a dreamer. That was, until she was overwhelmed by images of the civil rights movement. The knowing narrator reports that Avey "seldom dreamed. Or if she did, whatever occurred in her sleep was always conveniently forgotten by the time she woke" (31). Blocking her dreams, or at least the memory of them, began when her dreams became a constant replay of images that were played on the evening news, more specifically, those associated with the deaths of Black people. After the 1963 bombing of the Sixteenth Street Baptist Church in Birmingham, Alabama, she dealt with the fear of losing her own daughters in the blast, like the four Black girls who died in the bombing, victims of the fight against social death status. Avey, probably like so many other mothers in the United States at the time, has a nightmare: "searching frantically amid the debris of small limbs strewn around the church basement she had come across those of Sis, Annawilda and Marion"; this dream haunts her on the Sunday her daughter, Sis, was to have recited James Weldon Johnson's poem "The Creation," his rendition of the Genesis story (31). Finally, "Avey Johnson had ceased dreaming after that" (31). These dreams are an extension of memories formed by trauma and her post-traumatic response to the violent experiences they conveyed. Interestingly, she formed a subconscious barrier not only to having nightmares, but to having dreams that may have brought her a sense of pleasure or peace. All of her dreams, it seems, are pathways that lead her to consider the significance of losing loved ones.

Notably, the next dream that she recalls features her aunt. Long after the woman's death and that of her husband, she is brought back to her time as a child with the aunt who took her to Ibo Landing and shared with her the story of the walking-on-water Ibos. There Aunt Cuney was "standing waiting for her on the road that led over to the Landing. A hand raised, her face ridden beneath her wide-brimmed field hat" (32). Marshall's careful use of language proves informative as well as provocative. At this juncture, when Avey intends to disembark the cruise ship at the next dock, the decision to do so is inspired by this dream where she sees the woman "standing waiting" near the landing. Aunt Cuney is waiting for her because, prompted by Avey's mother's disbelief in the meaning of the visits, Avey had "rid herself of the notion" by the age of ten. Marshall is clear here: it is not the story that Avey rejects as truth, but the "mission she couldn't even name yet but felt duty-bound to fulfill" (42). Avey is dressed to attend a luncheon hosted by her husband's lodge and she decides that she is not going to dispose of her suit, hat, gloves, and fur stole to follow the woman on an "obstacle course" (40). Even in her subconscious, she is willing to allow materialism to prevent her from enjoying spiritual and cultural practices. In a symbolic move, the woman, who tires of waiting for her grandniece to heed her call to come and follow her, grabs Avey's fur stole and pulls. The tussle over her prized possession, a symbol of prominence and financial success, perhaps even her turn from respect for the land that her Aunt Cuney had so revered in the South, evolves into a fistfight between the two. In the fury is a show of disrespect for her elder that leaves Avey feeling haunted for three days.

Dreams are instructive, especially when they are of the dead. Aunt Cuney's visit of her grandniece in her subconscious opens the door between memories of the past and experiences of the present, between the living and the dead, between the unresolved and the unforgettable. As she moves forward in delving into her subconscious through an excavation of her memories—the joy and the pain associated with each—she also recalls her life with her husband, before and after the change on Halsey Street. Dreams of the dead, Kelly Bulkeley writes, "reassure people that even though death has physically separated them from their loved ones, they are still connected to their loved ones emotionally and spiritually, and they will always be" (181). In this case, dreams also show that memories do not simply disappear, but continue to exist in the subconscious.

Notably, the dream also features Avey's husband, a man whom the widow had lost her connection with on the night of their argument on Halsey Street. Jay's decision to stay with his wife, at least some version of him, moved the couple into a state of grief, as they mourned his abandonment of their relationship, her inability to correct the offense she had committed by accusing him of having an extramarital affair, and their unwillingness to articulate the fear that they would succumb to the worst of Halsey Street. Haunted by the reality of the situation long ago, it takes form in the last words that Jay issues to his wife: "Do you know who you sound like, even who you look like?" Overshadowed by the unspoken, unexplored burden of the night and the meaning of their exchange, Avey feels no real sadness about his death. In many ways, Jay had died years before. What she must do is forgive herself and her husband for submitting to death out of fear.

By the time she meets Lebert, she is residing in a space haunted by the dead and dominated by memories that have been given life by myths. Avey must confront her personal memories to liberate herself from the hauntings. Keith Cartwright observes, "The creolized Gullah culture of South Carolina provides the music and myth by which Avey is compelled to dare transition in the Caribbean" (132). It no longer remains as a mythic memory that she shared with her husband, who said that he believed it. Aunt Cuney's gift to her grandniece was to give Avey a connection to her African identity and roots in U.S. southern culture by sharing the beliefs and practices of Tatem. Consequently, Avey's move away from myth means that she is unable to maintain her cultural grounding. Further, since the mythic memory was given to Avey, it was her responsibility to remain rooted in the power of the memory. Her move away from it begins before the pivotal argument the two have in the kitchen. It begins when she allows doubt to cloud her belief in the myth. What she does not know is that it is not the myth itself that she is to accept, but the meaning of the myth to the enslaved people who told it. This lack of an acknowledgment means that she redefined oppression through her desire to attain material stability.

Without question, her exposure to the myth and challenge to believe it prepare her for the transformative moment she has at the crossroads. Crossing to empower is evident in the presence of Lebert, a Papa Legba figure. At the beginning of the chapter where he emerges, there are two epigraphs. The first, an incantation used to begin Voodoo ceremonies, is a request for Papa Legba to remove the barrier between the worlds of the living and the dead. In this case, the widow's symbolic veil will no longer shield her from the memories that connect her to the dead. The other is a quote from poet Randall Jarrell: "Oh, Bars of my . . . body, open, open" (Marshall 148). Combined, the two inform any participants to prepare themselves for the presence of water—crossing it and bathing in it—as it will become instrumental in conversion, transformation, and rebirth. Lebert, a living link to the culture that he still respects and reveres, knows what Avey does not, that her desire for home is a desire to reclaim the heritage she has consciously forgotten. Because of this, Lebert "possessed ways of seeing that went beyond mere eyesight and ways of knowing that outstripped ordinary intelligence" (172). Like the Ibo, he "saw how far she had come since leaving the ship and the distance she had yet to go" (172). He will take her on a reverse migration—from her U.S. identity to an African-based one—over the waters of Carriacou, to reclaim the cultural heritage she has suppressed and help her cast off her socially dead persona.

Contact with water in the post–Middle Passage world calls to African descendants to reconnect through confrontation. Marshall moves in a non-linear movement from memory—ancestral and childhood—from the coastal South, to New York, to the experience of the Middle Passage, and finally to the Caribbean, and back to Tatem. Avey calls back to the Ibo ancestors by remembering their Middle Passage experience. While lying in a semiconscious state in the deckhouse of the boat, she "had the impression . . . of other bodies lying crowded in with her in the hot, airless dark, a multitude packed around her in filth and stench. Their moans rising and falling. Their suffering in a cramped space" (209). Again we are reminded that "the image of the ship—a living, micro-cultural, micro-political system in motion—is especially important for historical and theoretical reasons. . . . Ships immediately focus attention on the middle passage, on the various projects for redemptive return to an African homeland" (Gilroy 4). While Avey is aboard, she becomes violently ill where the two currents meet. Those who have not made the trip before, have a reaction similar to Avey's. Her contemporary perspective, then, recalls the experiences described by Olaudah Equiano in his narrative, *The Interesting Narrative of the Olaudah Equiano or Gustavus Vassa* (1789). Marshall suggests that the other passengers have not only gone through the currents before but willingly make the journey or engage the memory on some level continuously. They are aware that the Middle Passage is always present. Avey finds herself as close to social and physical death as she has ever been.

Monica Shuler notes that after the transatlantic journey, cleansing with water was often performed. Cleansing at this juncture marked a new phase for the enslaved person as the person was being prepared for sale. Rosalie Parvay enters to perform the cleansing ritual. In her confused state, notes the narrator, Avey sees a woman during the course of the night who she thinks could be "any number of different people," or any number of "passed-on" women, including her mother, the nurse at the hospital where she had her children, and her great-aunt Cuney. Rosalie, the daughter of Lebert, becomes a midwife, a mother, and a guide, and her role will be to prepare Avey for her final stage of acceptance by cleansing her. Significantly, Rosalie reminds her of the nurturing women whom Avey remembers at times of passage. By no coincidence, Avey remembers being bathed as a child by Aunt Cuney during the time she is bathed by Rosalie.

Avey has been baptized and her rebirth will begin. Eventually, she joins the dancing at the Big Drum, "a sign of respect to the ancestors" she has ignored for many years; reclaims the name of her birth, Avatara; and passes the story and heritage of the Ibos down to her grandchildren, and anyone else she can tell (Schuler 172). Dancing figures prominently in Marshall's novel as introduced by Aunt Cuney. Her love of the Ring Shout and defiance of it by "crossing her feet" in favor of dancing in possession of the Spirit and in worship of the Lord is a memory, a feeling, that Avey relished well into adulthood. As a child, she became fascinated by the Ring Shout worshippers: "It was not supposed to be dancing, yet to Avey, standing beside the old woman, it held something of the look, and it felt like dancing in her blood," inspiring her to perform it in the darkness (Marshall 34). If "crossing the feet" was not allowed, stepping certainly was. As Rosenbaum notes, "Worshipers use a separate group of shout songs that have a typically African melodic shape and are as distinctive as the step" (179). In this, it appears directly connected to the mythic memory, when the Ibos were seen, singing and stepping. From here, Avey dances as she did to African American jazz musicians with her husband on Halsey Street: "She was the better dancer, and sometimes partway through a number he would spin her off to dance by herself, and standing aside watch her footwork and the twisting and snaking of her body with an amazed smile" (123). In Carriacou, the widow's "Praisesong" is expressed in the Big Drum dance, which is the amalgamation of the histories, cultures, and memories that have informed her life since she was first introduced to the Ibo Landing myth by her aunt. In fact, her choice to join the Big Drum, where she does the Ring Shout dance of her youth, or the Carriacou Tramp, also redeems her aunt, who had been ousted from the dance by her community years prior. Barbara Christian concludes that the Big Drum ceremony "combines rituals from several New World African societies: the Ring Dances of Tatem, the Bojangles of New York, the voodoo drums of Haiti, the rhythms of the various African peoples brought to the New World" (Wall 82). To be sure, similar to the oral mythic narratives, the dances act as a performative counter-discourse to trauma associated with the Middle Passage. They also prove how such rituals and performances can free the participants from memories of oppression as they stand and remember those who have passed on.

Before they began stepping and shouting on their way back to Africa, the Ibos looked back and saw a history that had yet been lived, namely slavery, the emancipation, and "everything after that right on up to the hard times of today" (Marshall 38). More specifically, each time the story is told, the "hard times of today" refer to the moment in which the storyteller shares the story. It is a story—that is, the legacy of the meaning of the story—Avatara will pass on to her daughter, Marion, whom she will encourage to pass on to the children she teaches. Christian notes further, "Self-knowledge [is] critical if black women [are] to develop the inner resources they . . . need in order to cope with larger social forces" (237). Marion, the daughter who had inherited a rebellious spirit of the Ibos, as demonstrated when she attended the 1963 March on Washington, felt the need to save inner-city youth and to proclaim pride when her mother revealed her activism on her job years before.

Avey's summers in Tatem with her aunt are the beginning of a journey toward self-definition and cultural acceptance. Once she realizes and accepts the meaning of the Ibo Landing myth and stands in a state of liberation, she can be trusted to take up the role left vacant by Aunt Cuney and Avatara by passing the story down. Elizabeth McNeil observes, "Through her protagonist's initiation journey and participation in the endless circle of the communal Big Drum/Ring Shout, Marshall intimates to her reader that ritual reunion with an elemental physical and spiritual source of self is possible" (192). Mythic memories allow for the recipient of the memory to remain connected to the culture that the memory represents. Without the passing on of these memories from generation to generation, the descendants would be forced to look at the trauma of the Middle Passage solely through the eyes of the oppressor, but there was resistance to this way of seeing.

From Olaudah Equiano to Alex Haley to Paul Marshall, return on some level is possible, even if it is to simply repeat the story of the past. Equiano's mere survival, the fact that one survived, provides opportunity for stories that subvert the meaning of enslaved people being forced to cross over water and also shows how many resisted social death. African-descended writers have shown the possibility of using storytelling to revise historical narratives and to assign power to the subjects of the story whose voices were muted by an inability to write their own story at the time of capture and transport. An ability to return "home" by flight or by walking over water is an expression of the desire to embrace or to preserve life in one form or another. Paule

Marshall uses myth to bind the past and the future, the Americas to Africa. Through storytelling, those who accept that death has no respect for boundaries also become empowered.

African-descended writers and artists engage in a complex dialogue that helps to explicate the purpose of the history that we know as the Middle Passage. It cannot be helped. Humans, by nature, are curious; therefore, to wonder why Africans were treated as they were requires a creative approach. Such a perspective allows their descendants to make valiant attempts to cope not just with the history but with the reality of it. Finding purpose in trauma is an amazing feat. Through their collective voices and creative expressions, writers, artists, and performers represent those people of Africa and their descendants who have maintained, and continue to do so, that accepting oppression is not an option.

Acts of Redemption through Forgiveness

*Remembering Charleston in the
Post–Middle Passage Era*

IN HIS NOVEL *The Coming,* Daniel Black, in conversation with Alex Haley and other African-descended writers and artists, uses third-person narration to tell the story of the captivity and transport of enslaved people from Africa to Charleston, South Carolina. When they arrive in the port city, one by one they are taken from their space of confinement and then sold until there is no one left to tell their story. Like many before him, Black relies on an appeal to the emotions. He describes the smells, the condition of the confined spaces, and the look of the captives after days of confinement. He also shows their conversion experience, their attempts not to be defeated and not to give up hope, their recognition that if their humanity is not respected by the ones who have taken them, then they must retain respect for themselves and for one another. How each person feels about himself or herself cannot be controlled by the captors.

Black begins by establishing the humanity of the "we." His communal, ancestral voice tells of the diversity of the people. He informs readers/listeners that they had various beliefs and practices in their communities. Contributing to the vitality of the community, there were those who held posts as farmers, healers, warriors, and so on. Shying away from imagining a perfect people, the narrator(s) are sure to state that they did not do all of what they were supposed to do, that they did not treat each other as well as they should have, that they did not honor their gods as often as required. They were human and humans have their faults, but did they deserve the treatment they would come to know at the hands of other humans?

They tell a historically inspired story of what they suffered from shore to shore. Men and women endured rape by crewmen. They witnessed the fatal stabbing of a newborn baby. They suffered through whippings with things they had never seen before. They bore the humiliation of lying in one another's excrement. They struggled with hunger pangs and the desires for the food of home.

And through it all, with little physical strength, they resisted their treatment. Not knowing where they would be taken, knowing only that they wished to return home, they found various ways to let their captors know that they may have their bodies, but they would not have their minds or spirits. As a result, very few of the three hundred African captives made it to their destination of Charleston. Before the ship docked, some chose death rather than submitting to an uncertain future. Some jumped overboard into the "Great Mother," while others either willed themselves to die quietly or found ways to kill themselves in the hold. They willed themselves "into the next realm." There was no burial, but Black asks us to imagine a return to their homeplace, where their ancestors would welcome them.

Those who could not resist through death chose other ways. Some revolted. Unfortunately, as often occurred, the revolts were not successful. In another way, they sang or hummed. In still another, they simply chose to live. Seeing their lives as valuable, they decided that they would survive:

> Now we wanted to live. For those who had died and who'd been forced to die. For those back in the motherland who had taught us the value of life. For children we would birth in a new world. . . .—we wanted to live! To speak the truth, one day, about a people too strong to be destroyed completely. (57)

Resistance for the living comes in the form of naming, a way to be seen and known among those who have little to give to one another. By the time they make it to the holding pen in Charleston, they have come to form a bond. There is one theme that remains consistent among the captives and that is saying the names of those who are lost. At times, they give names to the ones whom they do not know, and the names have meaning. At other times, they say the names they know as belonging to the lost person. Naming has a purpose. It humanizes the person whom the captor has tried through heinous, unspeakable acts to dehumanize. It makes obsolete the assigning of numbers associated with a body. Second, naming is the way in which a person is remembered as having an identity. Naming is an act of resistance.

Besides the name, there is one other aspect of *The Coming* that seems hauntingly instructive and poignantly familiar. There are a few paragraphs dedicated to a young, "pale boy" who looks on in agony at the captives in Charleston. Despite their own experience, Black humanizes them further as they extend understanding and hope to the boy. They can tell from his "begging eyes" that he "was not one of them"—that if "he'd had his way, he would set us free" (83). As an extension of understanding, they cast no blame on the boy: "Even in our misery, we saw the beauty of his heart" (83). In a few words, Black strips away all that we have read, imagined, and experienced to tell of a possibility that may only be rendered by forgiveness and hope. The captives go further, to "hope he would someday heal diseases in the hearts of his people" (84). While they cannot control what the boy does in the future, they can control their response to him, and they do. Their act of forgiveness, brought by understanding, places them in a position that the captives have come to believe is impossible, for only human beings possess the capacity to look at an individual and to extend forgiveness.

Capturing tragic moments of the past, Black could not know that he was looking toward another tragic moment in the history of Charleston. On June 17, 2015, at Emanuel African Methodist Episcopal (AME) Church in Charleston, where African-descended parishioners were meeting for their weekly Bible study, in walked a young White man. Following the Bible study, the people joined hands with the young stranger to say their culminating prayer and he, Dylann Roof, pulled out a gun and opened fire. When he was done, eight people were dead (a ninth transitioned during surgery). Charleston, a city haunted by its legal, historical treatment of Black bodies, as described by Black and documented by historians, would stand in shock by the incident, and so would the rest of the country.

Roof, a twenty-two-year-old white supremacist, was known to family and friends to make disparaging comments and threats about African Americans. A news story revealed that Joey Meek, a twenty-year-old White man, knew about Roof's intentions: "Meek hung out with Roof off and on in the weeks before the June 17 shooting." A day after the shooting, Meek told the Associated Press that Roof had drunkenly complained to him that "blacks were taking over the world," asserting that "someone needed to do something about it for the white race" ("Shooting Suspect" para. 6). In addition to ignoring the threats, Roof's friends and family also turned a blind eye and deaf ear to the implications of his extensive knowledge of race history. According to one report, a Facebook photo featured Roof wearing a black jacket decorated with an apartheid-era South African flag (McLaughlin). He also seemed to target the church because of its history. In 1822, Denmark Vessey, one of the church's founders, had planned a slave revolt, causing authorities to investigate the church.[1] It was clear that like those whom Roof killed, he too was a legacy of the Middle Passage. When the police caught Roof in North Carolina, they charged him with thirty-three counts of hate crimes.

Roof took the lives of nine African descendants, some of whom were likely directly linked to the slave trade that was prominent in Charleston. We know their names:

1. Tywanza Sanders (twenty-six) was a recent graduate of Allen University.
2. Rev. Clementa Pinckney (forty-one) was the church's pastor and a member of the state legislature. He was married and had two daughters.
3. Rev. Sharonda A. Coleman-Singleton (forty-five) was a high school speech therapist and track coach. She was married with three children.
4. DePayne Middleton-Doctor (forty-nine) was a minister, the mother of four daughters, and a college enrollment counselor.
5. Cynthia Hurd (fifty-four) was a regional manager at Charleston County Public Library.
6. Myra Thompson (fifty-nine) taught Bible study at the church and was also a mother.
7. Ethel Lance (seventy) had worked at Emanuel AME for thirty years and was a retired city worker. She was a mother and a grandmother. She was also the cousin of Susie Jackson.
8. Rev. Daniel Simmons (seventy-four) had been pastor at Greater Zion AME Church, but at the time of the shooting he was on the ministerial staff at Emanuel AME.
9. Susie Jackson (eighty-seven) was a longtime church member and a grandmother.

Survivors of the tragedy would later give voice to what it meant to face death. Cynthia Taylor, one of three survivors, protected herself and her granddaughter by lying on top of the girl while playing dead. Felicia Sanders, who also survived by playing dead, lost her son, Tywanza, in the attack. Motivated by her Christian beliefs, she would later extend an act of grace to Roof.

---

1. See the church's website for more information: www.emanuelamechurch.org/churchhistory.php.

Like many across the country, I felt that a sacred line had been crossed. Through my own act of resistance to the fear that Roof tried to inflict on Black folks, I joined with the disoriented and angry at church. The next day, June 18, 2016, Rev. Alphonso E. McGlen, pastor of the Bethel African Methodist Episcopal Church in Greensboro, North Carolina, a city known for its history of activism, held a prayer vigil. All were welcomed. Local government officials, Black and White Christians, police officers, and others sat in the pews, sang songs, and joined in prayer for the victims and the nation. At the microphone, many begged others to move past their feelings of sadness and anger by remembering that we worship a God of love. Speakers also urged one another to be politically active and to pray for one another. "We are of one faith as children of God," said one. Speaking against racism, another said, "If you say you love the Lord, then you've got to love me."[2] It would become the refrain of the evening for most speakers, including those who were from Charleston and knew well some of those who had been killed. Rev. McGlen stood and spoke with honesty. He admitted that he was mad. Many of us understood. He admitted that he was tired of racism and hatred. We understood that too, but he said he was working toward forgiveness in the name of God and told us to do the same.

At Roof's hearing, two days after the shooting, members of the slain family members expressed forgiveness for Roof, who stood stone-faced and motionless in a separate room, where he watched the proceedings on-screen. News media outlets recorded the responses as some commentators also expressed shock.

> Bethane Middleton-Brown, whose sister was killed on Wednesday, told Roof, "For me, I'm a work in progress and I acknowledge that I'm very angry. We have no room for hate. We have to forgive. I pray God on your soul."
>
> "You took something very precious away from me," a family representative [Nadine Collier, Lance's daughter] for Ethel Lance, the 70-year-old grandmother who died in Wednesday's massacre, told Roof on behalf of Lance's loved ones. "I will never talk to her ever again. I will never be able to hold her again. But I forgive you and have mercy on your soul. You hurt me. You hurt a lot of people, but I forgive you." (Oh)

A year later, she would be quoted as saying, "Forgiveness is power. It means you can fight everything and anything" (Smietana). After Roof had taken so much, family members and friends of those killed refused to become victim to

---

2. During the event, I posted quotes on Twitter (@DrTTGreen).

his violence by surrendering to his act of hatred. The family led us all toward healing and pointed us in the direction of conversion. If they could do that, why couldn't we? In 2016, Roof would listen to survivors and the family members of survivors speak of what they had lost. Their testimonies would lead to his conviction.

Forgiveness, as Collier makes clear, is an act of resistance. It empowers as much as it is an act of power. It is simply human.

WORKS CITED

Acham, Christine. *Revolution Televised: Prime Time and the Struggle for Black Power.* U of Minnesota P, 2004.

Afro-Pessimism: An Introduction, 12 Mar. 2017, *Racked & Dispatched,* rackedanddispatched.noblogs.org. Accessed 17 July 2017.

@Amanda_Learning. "Ya'll catch that 'hands up, don't shoot' moment?" *Twitter,* 2 June 2016, 7:30 p.m., twitter.com/Amanda_Learning/status/738547198481158144.

Athey, Stephanie. "Poisonous Roots and the New World Blues: Rereading Seventies Narration and Nation in Alex Haley and Gayl Jones." *Narrative,* vol. 7, no. 2, May 1999, pp. 169–93.

Baker, Courtney R. *Humane Insight: Looking at Images of African American Suffering and Death.* U of Illinois P, 2015.

Baker, Houston. *Blues, Ideology, and Afro-American Literature: A Vernacular Theory.* U of Chicago P, 1984.

Baldwin, James. "On Being White . . . and Other Lies." *The Cross of Redemption: Uncollected Writings.* Knopf Doubleday, 2011.

Barry, John M. *Rising Tide: The Great Mississippi Flood of 1927 and How It Changed America.* Simon & Schuster, 1997.

Bell, W. Kamau. "The Star of the Original 'Roots' Explains Why the Remake is Must-Watch Television." *Mother Jones,* May/June 2016, www.motherjones.com/media/2016/05/history-roots-2016-remake-levar-burton-kamau-bell/. Accessed 26 June 2016.

Benjamin, Shanna Greene. "Weaving the Web of Reintegration: Locating Aunt Nancy in Praisesong for the Widow." *MELUS,* vol. 30, no. 1, Spring 2005, pp. 49–67.

Black, Daniel. *The Coming: The Novel.* St. Martin's, 2015.

Borders, James, IV, editor. *Making Time and Making Place: An Essential Chronology of Blacks in New Orleans Since 1718.* Kindle ed., Beckham Publishings, 2015.

Brathwaite, Kamau. *Middle Passages.* New Directions, 1993.

Brecher, Jeremy. "Katrina Poses the Question: What are the Duties of Governments to Their People?" *Hurricane Katrina: Response and Responsibilities,* edited by John Brown Childs, New Pacific Cruz, 2005, pp. 73–75.

Brown, Kimberly Juanita. *The Repeating Body: Slavery's Visual Resonance in the Contemporary.* Duke UP, 2015.

Bulkeley, Kelly. *Dreams of Healing: Transforming Nightmares into Vision of Hope.* Paulist, 2003.

Carretta, Vincent. *Equiano, the African: Biography of a Self-Made Man.* U of Georgia P, 2005.

Cartwright, Keith. "Notes Toward a Voodoo Hermeneutics: Soul Rhythms, Marvelous Transitions, and Passages to the Creole Saints in Praisesong for the Widow." *Southern Quarterly,* vol. 41, no. 4, Summer 2003, pp. 127–43.

Christian, Barbara. "Trajectories of Self-Definition: Placing Contemporary Afro-American Women's Fiction." *Conjuring: Black Women, Fiction, and Literary Tradition,* edited by Marjorie Pryse and Hortense Spillers, Indiana UP, 1985, pp. 233–48.

Collins, Patricia Hill. *Black Feminist Thought.* Routledge, Chapman and Hall, 1991.

Cone, James. *Black Theology and Power.* Harper and Row, 1989.

———. *The Cross and the Lynching Tree.* Orbis, 2011.

Dash, Julie. *Daughters of the Dust: The Making of an African American Woman's Film.* New Press, 1992.

Davis, Angela. *Blues Legacies and Black Feminism: Gertrude "Ma" Rainey, Bessie Smith, and Billie Holiday.* Pantheon, 1998.

Davis-Maye, Denise, and Tonya E. Perry. "Momma's Girl: The Significance of Maternal Figure Support in the Development of Hope for African American Girls." *Journal of Human Behavior in the Social Environment,* vol. 15, no. 2/3, 2007, pp. 307–28.

Delmont, Matthew F. *Making Roots: A Nation Captivated.* U of California P, 2016.

Diedrich, Maria, Henry Louis Gates Jr., and Carl Pedersen, editors. Introduction. *Black Imagination and the Middle Passage.* Oxford UP, 1999, pp. 5–20.

Dixon, Melvin. "The Black Writer's Use of Memory." *History and Memory in African-American Culture,* edited by Genevieve Fabre and Robert O'Meally, Oxford UP, 1994, pp. 18–27.

Douglass, Frederick. "What to the Slave is the Fourth of July?" *American Soul: The Contested Legacy of the Declaration of the Independence,* edited by Justin Buckley Dyer, Rowan & Littlefield, 2012, pp. 63–67.

Equiano, Olaudah. *The Interesting Narrative of the Life of Olaudah Equiano or Gustavus Vassa. Norton Anthology of African American Literature,* edited by Henry Louis Gates Jr. and Nellie McKay, W. W. Norton, 1997, pp. 138–64.

Evans, David. "Singing the Blues about 1927's Delta Floods." Interview by Noah Adams. *NPR Music.* 23 Sept. 2005, www.npr.org/templates/story/story.php?storyId=4860785. Accessed 24 Sept. 2017.

Fatal Flood. Directed by Chana Gazit and David Stewart. Alexandria, VA: PBS Home Video, 2005.

Fandrich, Ina J. *The Mysterious Voodoo Queen, Marie Laveaux: A Study of Powerful Female Leadership in Nineteenth-Century New Orleans.* Routledge, 2005.

Fanon, Franz. "Concerning Violence." *The Wretched of the Earth.* Grove Weidenfeld, 1961.

Feelings, Tom. *The Middle Passage: White Ships/Black Cargo.* Dial, 1995.

@FeministaJones. "'Liberty to Slaves.' They hated that as much as folks hate 'Black Lives Matter.'" *Twitter,* 31 May 2016, 6:16 p.m., twitter.com/FeministaJones/status/737815119703515136.

Gaines, Ernest. *A Lesson Before Dying.* Vintage, 1993.

Gates, Henry Louis, Jr. *The Signifying Monkey: A Theory of Afro-American Literary Criticism.* Oxford UP, 1988.

Gilroy, Paul. *The Black Atlantic: Modernity and Double Consciousness.* Harvard UP, 1993.

Gray, Herman. *American Crossroads: Cultural Moves: African Americans and the Politics of Representation.* U of California P, 2005.

Griffiths, L. Jennifer. *Traumatic Possessions: The Memory in African American Women's Writing and Performance.* U of Virginia P, 2009.

Guthrie, Marisa. "Roots Reborn: How a Slave Saga Was Remade for the Black Lives Matter Era." *The Hollywood Reporter,* 25 May 2016, www.hollywoodreporter.com/features/roots-reborn -how-a-slave-897055. Accessed 26 June 2016.

Haley, Alex. *Roots: The Saga of an American Family.* Vanguard, 2007.

Hall, Gwendolyn Midlo. *Africans in Colonial Louisiana: The Development of Afro-Creole Culture in the Eighteenth Century.* Louisiana State UP, 1992.

Hall, Rebecca. "We Have Lost Our Citizenship Again: Katrina's Aftermath: The New Dred Scott." *Hurricane Katrina: Response and Responsibilities,* edited by John Brown Childs, New Pacific Cruz, 2005, pp. 70–72.

Harms, Robert W. *The Diligent: A Voyage through the Worlds of the Slave Trade.* Basic, 2002.

Hartman, Saidiyah V. *Scenes of Subjection: Terror, Slavery, and Self-Making in Nineteenth-Century America.* Oxford UP, 1997.

Hayden, Robert. "O Daedalus, Fly Away Home." *Allpoetry.com,* allpoetry.com/O-Daedalus,-Fly -Away-Home. Accessed 14 July 2017.

———. "Middle Passage." www.poetryfoundation.org/poems/43076/middle-passage. Accessed 14 July 2017.

Hewett, Heather. "At the Crossroads: Disability and Trauma in 'The Farming of Bones.'" *MELUS,* vol. 31, no. 3, Fall 2006, pp. 123–45.

Hewett, Ivan. "Wynton Marsalis Interview: It Don't Mean a Thing If It Ain't Got Swing." *Telegraph,* 12 July 2012, www.telegraph.co.uk/culture/music/worldfolkandjazz/9376790/Wynton -Marsalis-interview-It-dont-mean-a-thing-if-it-aint-got-swing.html. Accessed 26 Sept. 2017.

Huret, Romain, and Randy J. Sparks. *Hurricane Katrina in Transatlantic Perspective.* Louisiana State UP, 2014.

JanMohamed, Abdul R. *The Death-Bound-Subject: Richard Wright's Archeology of Death.* Duke UP, 2005.

Johnson, Charles. *Middle Passage.* Atheneum, 1990.

———. "A Phenomenology of the Black Body." *Michigan Quarterly Review,* vol. 32, no. 4, 1993, p. 604.

@JustAnt1914. "Liberty to Slaves was the original Black Lives Matter." *Twitter,* 31 May 2016, 6:16 p.m., twitter.com/JustAnt1914/status/737815157540163586.

Kempf, Jean. "Picturing the Catastrophe: New Photographs in the First Weeks after Katrina." *Hurricane Katrina in Transatlantic Perspective,* edited by Romain Huret and Randy J. Sparks, Louisiana State UP, 2014, pp. 50–70.

Lambert, Raphaël. "The Slave Trade as Memory and History: James A. Emanuel's 'The Middle Passage Blues' and Robert Hayden's 'Middle Passage.'" *African American Review,* vol. 47, nos. 2–3, Summer/Fall 2014, pp. 327–38.

Long, Carolyn Morrow. *A New Orleans Voudou Priestess: The Legend and Reality of Marie Laveau.* UP of Florida, 2006.

Lowe, John. *Calypso Magnolia: The Crosscurrents of Caribbean and Southern Literature.* U of North Carolina P, 2016.

———. "Wright Writing Reading: Narrative Strategies in Uncle Tom's Children." *Modern American Short Story Sequences: Composite Fictions and Fictive Communities,* edited by Gerald Kennedy, Cambridge UP, 1995, pp. 52–75.

MacCash, Doug. "Mardi Gras Indian Big Chief Celebrates 50 Years of Masking." *NOLA.com / Times-Picayune,* 24 June 2017, www.mardigras.com/news/2017/06/mardi_gras_indians_casby _mohaw.html. Accessed 2017 July 2017.

McDaniel, Lorna. *The Big Drum Ritual of Carriacou: Praisesongs in Rememory of Flight.* UP of Florida, 1998.

Margolies, Edward. "Wright's Craft: The Short Stories." *Richard Wright: Critical Perspectives Past and Present,* edited by Henry Louis Gates and K. A. Appiah, Amistad P, 1993, pp. 75–97.

Marshall, Paule. *Praisesong for the Widow.* Penguin, 1983.

Martinez, Maurice. "Where Mardi Gras Indians Come From." *New York Times,* 1995 Feb. 23, www.nytimes.com/1995/02/23/opinion/l-where-mardi-gras-indians-come-from-673095.html ?mcubz=2. Accessed 1 May 2016.

McCall, Dan. *Example of Richard Wright.* Harcourt, Brace, and World, 1969.

McLaughlin, Michael. "Racist Manifesto Purportedly Written by Dylan Roof Surfaces Online." *Huffpost,* 20 June 2015, www.huffingtonpost.com/2015/06/20/dylann-roof-manifesto -charleston-shooting_n_7627788.html. Accessed 1 May 2017.

McNeil, Elizabeth. "The Gullah Seeker's Journey In Paule Marshall's 'Praisesong for the Widow.'" *MELUS,* vol. 34, no. 1, Spring 2009, pp. 185–209.

Metting, Fred. "The Possibilities of Flight: The Celebration of Our Wings in *Song of Solomon, Praisesong for the Widow,* and *Mama Day.*" *Southern Folklore,* vol. 55, no 2, 1998, pp. 145–66.

Mizelle, Richard M. *Backwater Blues: The Mississippi Flood of 1927 in the African American Imagination.* U of Minnesota P, 2014.

Monaghan, Peter. "White Books: Passing the Three Gates." *Interviews with Charles Johnson.* Edited by Charles Richard Johnson, Jim McWilliams, and Ethel Willis, U of Washington P, 2003, pp. 48–52.

Moore, David Chioni. "Routes." *Transition,* no. 64, 1994, pp. 4–21.

Morrison, Toni. *Beloved.* Plume, 1988.

———. "The Site of Memory." *What Moves at the Margin,* edited by Catherine Dennard, UP of Mississippi, 2008, pp. 65–78.

Mudimbe, V. Y. *The Idea of Africa.* Indiana UP, 1994.

Mullen, Lincoln. "These Maps Reveal How Slavery Expanded across the United States." *Smithsonian,* 15 May 2014, www.smithsonianmag.com/history/maps-reveal-slavery-expanded-across -united-states-180951452/.

Murray, Rolland. "Diaspora by Bus: Reginald McKnight, Postmodernism, and Transatlantic Subjectivity." *Contemporary Literature,* vol. 46, no. 1, Spring 2005, pp. 46–77.

Muther, Elizabeth. "Isadora at Sea: Misogyny as Cosmic Capital in Charles Johnson's *Middle Passage.*" *African American Review,* vol. 30, no. 4, Winter 1996, p. 649–58.

Nora, Pierre. "Between Memory and History: *Les Lieux de Memoire.*" *History and Memory in African-American Culture,* edited by Genevieve Fabre and Robert O'Meally, Oxford UP, 1994, pp. 284–300.

Norrell, Robert J. *Alex Haley and the Books That Changed a Nation.* St. Martins, 2015.

Nunes, Ana. "Disembodiments." *Imagining the Black Female Body: Reconciling Image in Print and Visual Culture,* edited by Carol E. Henderson. Palgrave Macmillan, 2010, pp. 45–58.

O'Connell, Christian. "The Color of the Blues." *Southern Cultures,* vol. 19 no. 1, Spring 2013, pp. 61–81.

Oh, Inae. "Families of Charleston Shooting Victims: 'We Forgive You.'" *Mother Jones,* 19 June 2015, www.motherjones.com/crime-justice/2015/06/families-charleston-shooting-victims-we -forgive-you/. Accessed 6 July 2016.

O'Keefe, Vincent A. "Reading Rigor Mortis: Offstage Violence and Excluded Middles 'In' Johnson's *Middle Passage* and Morrison's 'Beloved.'" *African American Review,* vol. 30, no. 4, 1996, pp. 635–48.

Osbey, Brenda Marie. "History." *All Souls: Essential Poems.* Louisiana State UP, 2015, pp. 190–95.

———. "Requiem for a Chief: Allison Marcel Montana, 1922–2005." 2005. Unpublished essay.

———. "Why We Can't Talk to You about Voodoo." *Southern Literary Journal,* vol. 43, no. 2, Spring 2011, pp. 1–11.

Patterson, Orlando. *Slavery and Social Death: A Comparative Study.* Harvard UP, 1982.

Patton, Venetria K. *The Grasp That Reaches beyond the Grave: The Ancestral Call in Black Women's Texts.* State U of New York P, 2013.

Philip, M. NourbeSe. *Zong!* Weslyn UP, 2008.

Plasa, Carl. "Doing the Slave Trade in Different Voices: Poetics and Politics in Robert Hayden's First 'Middle Passage.'" *African American Review,* vol. 45, no. 4, Winter 2012, pp. 557–73.

Powell, Timothy. "Ebos Landing." *The New Georgia Encyclopedia,* 15 June 2004, www.georgiaencyclopedia.org/articles/history-archaeology/ebos-landing.

Pryse, Marjorie. Introduction. *Conjuring: Black Women, Fiction, and Literary Tradition.* Indiana UP, 1985, pp. 1–23.

Quashie, Kevin. *The Sovereignty of Quiet: Beyond Resistance in Black Culture.* Rutgers UP, 2012.

Raboteau, Albert. *A Fire in the Bones: Reflections on African-American Religious History.* Beacon, 1995.

Rediker, Marcus. *The Slave Ship: A Human History.* Viking, 2007.

Rhodes, Barbara C., and Allen Ramsey. "An Interview with Jewell Parker Rhodes." *African American Review,* vol. 29. no. 4, Winter 1995, pp. 593–604.

Rhodes, Jewell Parker. *Voodoo Dreams: A Novel of Marie Laveau.* St. Martin's, 1994.

Roots. Aired 1977. Written by James Lee and Alex Haley, produced by David Wolper, Warner Home Video, 2007.

Roots. Aired 2016. Produced by Mark Wolper, Lionsgate, 2016.

Rosenbaum, Art. Shout Because You're Free: The African American Ring Shout Tradition in Coastal Georgia." U of Georgia P, 1998.

Rowley, Hazel. *Richard Wright: The Life and Times.* Henry Holt, 2001.

Salaam, Kalamu ya. "You Can't Survive on Salt Water." *Poets.org,* www.poets.org/poetsorg/poem/ you-cant-survive-salt-water. Accessed 12 July 2017.

Saunders, Patricia. "Defending the Dead, Confronting the Archive: A Conversation with M. Nour-beSe Philip." *Small Axe: A Caribbean Journal Of Criticism,* vol. 12, no. 2, June 2008, pp. 63–79.

Schuler, Monica. "Enslavement, the Slave Voyage, and Astral and Aquatic Journeys in African Diaspora Discourse." *Africa and the Americas: Interconnections During the Slave Trade,* edited by Jose Curto et al., African World P, 2005, pp. 185–214.

Scott, Daniel M., III. "Interrogating Identity: Appropriation and Transformation in the Middle Passage." *African American Review,* vol. 29, no. 4, Winter 1995, pp. 645–56.

Sellinger, Eric. "Aunts, Uncles, Audience: Gender and Genre in Charles Chesnutt's *The Conjure Woman.*" *Black American Literature Forum,* vol. 25, no. 4, Winter 1991, pp. 665–88.

Shockley, Evie. "Going Overboard: African American Poetic Innovation and the Middle Passage." *Contemporary Literature,* vol. 52, no. 4, Winter 2011, pp. 79–87.

"Shooting Suspect's Friend Says Dylann Roof Ranted About Race" *Chicago Tribune.* 19 June 2015, www.chicagotribune.com/news/nationworld/ct-dylann-roof-ranted-about-race-20150618 -story.html.

Smallwood, Stephanie. *Saltwater Slavery: A Middle Passage from African to American Diaspora.* Harvard UP, 2007.

Smietana, Bob. "A Year Later, Families of the Charleston Shooting Victims Still Wrestle with Forgiveness." *The Washington Post,* 17 June 2015, www.washingtonpost.com/news/acts-of -faith/wp/2016/06/17/forgiving-dylann-roof-is-taking-a-heavy-toll-on-those-left-behind-but -theyre-not-giving-up/?utm_term=.c10f8759d3c0. Accessed 26 July 2016.

Spencer, Jon Michael. "Rhythm in Black Religion of the African Diaspora." *Journal Of Religious Thought,* vol. 44, no. 2, Winter/Spring 1988, pp. 67–83.

State of Black New Orleans: 10 Years Post-Katrina. Urban League of Greater New Orleans, 2015.

Taylor, Eric Robert. *If We Must Die: Shipboard Insurrections in the Era of the Atlantic Slave Trade.* Louisiana State UP, 2006.

The Middle Passage. Directed by Guy Deslauriers, HBO Video, 2003.

Thompson, Robert Farris. *Flash of the Spirit: African and Afro-American Art and Philosophy,* Random, 1983.

Thorsson, Courtney. "Dancing up a Nation: Paule Marshall's "Praisesong for the Widow." *Callaloo,* vol. 30, no. 2, Spring 2007, pp. 644–52.

Townsend, Tiffany G., et al. "I'm No Jezebel: I Am Young, Gifted, and Black: Identity, Sexuality, and Black Girls." *Psychology Of Women Quarterly,* vol. 34, no. 3, Spring 2010, pp. 273–85.

Treme. Produced by David Simon. Home Box Office, 2011–2015.

Trethewey, Natasha. *Native Guard.* Houghton Miller, 2006.

Trouble the Water. Lessin, Tia, Carl Deal, Kimberly R. Roberts, Scott Roberts, P. J. Raval, T. W. Richman, Mary Lampson, Neil Davidge, and Naja R. Del. Zeitgeist Films, 2009.

Tucker, Lindsay. "Recovering the Conjure Woman: Texts and Contexts in Gloria Naylor's *Mama Day.*" *African American Review,* vol. 28, no. 2, Summer 1994, pp. 173–88.

Tucker, Terrence. "(Re)Claiming Legacy in the Post–Civil Rights South in Richard Wright's 'Down by the Riverside' and Ernest Gaines's 'A Gathering of Old Men.'" *Southern Literary Journal,* vol. 43, no. 2, Spring 2011, pp. 105–24.

Tweedy, Damon. *Black Man in a White Coat: A Doctor's Reflections on Race and Medicine.* Picador, 2015.

Walker, Dave. "Robinette Interview with Nagin Was Unforgettable Radio." *NOLA.com* / *Times-Picayune,* 2 Sept. 2005, www.nola.com/katrina/index.ssf/2005/09/robinette_interview_with _nagin_was_unforgettable_radio.html. Accessed 23 June 2016.

Wall, Cheryl. *Worrying the Line: Black Women Writers, Lineage, and Literary Tradition.* U of North Carolina P, 2005.

Wallace, Maurice. Constructing the Black Masculine: Identity and Ideality in African American Men's Literature and Culture, 1775–1955, Duke UP, 2002.

Walters, Wendy W. "'One of Dese Mornings, Bright and Fair, / Take My Wings and Cleave De Air': The Legend of the Flying Africans and Diasporic Consciousness." *MELUS,* vol. 22, no. 3, Autumn 1997, pp. 3–29.

Walker, Kara. *After the Deluge.* Rizzoli, 2007.

Ward, Jerry. *The Katrina Papers.* UNO Press, 2008.

Ward, Jesmyn. *Salvage the Bones.* Bloomsbury, 2011.

Wardi, Anissa Janine. *Water and African American Memory: An Ecocritical Perspective.* UP of Florida, 2011.

Washington, Margaret. "Gullah Attitudes Toward Life and Death." *Africanisms in American Culture,* Indiana UP, 1990, 152–86.

When the Levees Broke: A Requiem in Four Acts. Directed by Spike Lee. HBO Video, 2006.

Williams, John. "Charles Johnson Discusses Middle Passage at 25." *New York Times,* 10 Jul 2015, artsbeat.blogs.nytimes.com/2015/07/10/charles-johnson-discusses-middle-passage-at-25/ ?mcubz=2. Accessed 30 May 2016.

Wright, Donald R. "The Effect of Alex Haley's Roots on How Gambians Remember the Atlantic Slave Trade." *History in Africa,* vol. 38, 2011, pp. 295–318.

Wright, Michelle. *Physics of Blackness: Beyond the Middle Passage Epistemology.* U of Minnesota P, 2015.

Wright, Richard. *Uncle Tom's Children.* Edited by Arnold Rampersad. 1991 edition. HarperPerennial, 1993.

———. *White Man, Listen!* HarperPerennial, 1995.

INDEX

activism, 160, 166

afro-pessimism, 3n4

Alexander, Elizabeth, 33

American Horror Story (tv series), 106

Amistad (ship), 9, 31–32, 62, 121; film, 62

ancestors, 4–5, 9, 11, 22, 33, 38, 42–43, 46–48, 50, 54, 65, 71, 75, 88, 90, 92–94, 102–3, 105, 128, 133, 144, 147, 150–51, 158–59, 163

ancestry, 38, 42–43, 57, 67, 69, 73, 76–77, 85, 93–94

art, 2–5, 9, 11–16, 21–22, 29–30, 32–33, 39, 73, 127

Atlantic Global South, 10, 13, 68, 104, 113, 145; definition of, 11–12

Backwater Blues (Mizelle), 111

Baker, Houston, 113

Baldwin, James, 79, 119

Barry, John M., 117

Benjamin, Shanna, 150

black family, vii–viii, 4–5, 9, 13–16, 27, 46, 48–50, 59, 61, 64–65, 75, 77, 81, 84–85, 94, 119, 142

Black Lives Matter Movement, 8n5, 13, 39, 43, 62, 63

black men, 45–52, 55, 58–59, 61, 64, 72, 75; abandonment, 14, 75, 79–80, 118, 131, 137; fathers and fatherhood, 14, 42, 44, 48–49, 57, 59, 61, 64–65, 69, 72, 76, 79–80, 82–84, 110, 131–32, 134; and identity, 73–77, 79, 82–83, 85, 87, 89; and masculinity, 14, 45, 48–50, 55–56, 59, 64, 69, 74, 75–78, 80, 88, 120; relationships with sons, 48–49, 55, 59, 64–65, 69, 72, 75, 83, 88, 135, 137–38

black performers, 14

black women, 14, 30–37, 56–57, 65, 81; colorism, 133; cult of true womanhood, 81; girlhood, vii–viii, 57, 59, 79–80, 90–91, 93, 95–96, 99; grandmothers, 42, 46–48, 91, 93–96, 98, 104, 118, 140–41, 150, 152–53, 165–66; identity, 65, 82, 91, 94–95, 99; mothers and motherhood, 15, 25, 33–35, 48, 59, 69, 79, 80, 84, 91, 93–95, 98–99, 135, 155; objectification of, 134; relationships with daughters, 59, 79–80, 91–96, 100, 102, 131–33; relationship with fathers, 132, 137; representations of, 34–35, 59, 62, 65, 72–74, 79–81, 93–96; and spirituality, 93–94, 96, 100, 147–48, 150, 156–57, 160

blues, 75, 110, 117, 117–18, 135, 144; flood, 15, 113–16; as history, 114; history of, 113; and the Middle Passage, 114, 118. See also *Backwater Blues*; *Salvage the Bones*

body, 33, 34, 36, 38, 52, 53, 84, 158, 164; Esch's body, 131–37 (see *Salvage the Bones*); Kizzy's body, 57, 120, 122, 123 (see *Roots: An American Saga*); Kunta's body, 53, 54, 64 (see *Roots: An American Saga*); Lulu's body, 122–23; Mann's body, 125 (see Wright, Richard); Marie Laveau's body (character), 84, 99, 100–102, 104; treatment of, 3, 6, 9, 30, 37

Braithwaite, Kamu, 2, 33, 153

Brown, Kimberly Juanita, 93, 102

Brown, Michael, 8, 39n7
Burton, LeVar, 40, 58–60, 63, 66
Bush, George, 129–31

Calhoun (*Middle Passage* character), 73–86, 90. *See also* Johnson, Charles
Caribbean, 2, 11–12, 16, 21, 32, 38, 69, 145–46, 148–49, 157–58
Cartwright, Keith, 157
Castile, Philando, 8
Charleston shooting, 16, 162–67
Christian, Barbara, 159, 160
Christian or Christianity, 3, 9, 29, 93, 94, 96, 97, 103, 165
colonization, 2, 11, 96–97, 146
Coming, The (Black, Daniel), 162–64
Cone, James, 119
Congo Square (Marsalis with Addy), 88
conversion, 3, 6, 10, 15–16, 25, 29, 45, 54–55, 71–72, 81–82, 88, 92, 118, 121, 125, 134, 138, 158, 162, 167; definition of, 9; as resistance to social death, 9, 38
cotton, 53, 111, 112

dance, 16, 24, 38, 60, 64, 135, 147–48, 151, 154, 159
Dash, Julie, 152, 153; *Daughters of the Dust*, 145
Davis, Angela, 114
Davis, Jordan, 8
Davis-Maye, Denise, 132, 136, 142
death, 2–3, 5, 8, 12, 15, 21, 23–26, 30–31, 34–39, 45, 47, 51–54, 63, 76, 84, 95–96, 146; murder, 36–37, 39, 63, 65, 124; as resistance, 150, 152. *See also* social death
Delmont, Matthew F., 42
Deslauriers, Guy, 139
diaspora, 31, 33, 47, 69, 70, 76, 81, 92, 103, 153
Diedrich, Maria, 21–22
Diligent (ship), 23, 113
Dixon, Melvin, 29, 34
DNA testing, 16, 144–45. *See also* ancestry
double consciousness (Du Bois), 10, 95
Douglass, Frederick, 6–8, 68; *What to the Slave Is the Fourth of July?*, 7

dreams, 54, 64–65, 150, 155, 156–57. See also *Praisesong for the Widow*; *Voodoo Dreams*
Dred Scott case, 130
Drum and Shadows (interview collection), 149
drums and drumming, 38, 51, 159

ecocriticism, 11
economy, 88, 111
enslavement, 111, 152; enslaved men, 24, 72, 75, 77; enslaved women, 24, 31, 34; salt (as metaphor for), 146; slave revolts, 8–9, 24, 31–32, 163; slave trade (see Transatlantic Slave Trade)
Equiano, Olaudah, 13, 26–27, 30, 41, 50, 71, 103, 105, 114, 121, 139, 160; authenticity of, 28; *The Interesting Narrative of the Life of Olaudah Equiano or Gustavus Vassa*, 158
Evans, David, 114, 115, 116n2

Fandrich, Ina, 92, 102n5
Fanon, Franz, 122
Fatal Flood (documentary), 112
Feelings, Tom, 32–33
feminism, 90n1, 91, 145
floods, 109, 111, 113; as legacy of Middle Passage, 110, 112, 120–21; men's perspective of, 114–15, 119–25 (see Wright, Richard); Mississippi 1927, 15, 111–13, 120; as sign of conversion, 16; women's perspective of, 115–16 (see *Salvage the Bones*). *See also* blues
forgiveness, 78, 124, 157, 162, 166–67

Gaines, Ernest, 70n1
Garner, Eric, 8, 39n7, 63
Gates, Henry Louis, Jr., 21, 28; *Finding Roots*, 144
Ghana, 8n, 25, 70
Gilroy, Paul, 120, 158
Gray, Herman, 15
Great Deluge, The (Walker), 131
grief and mourning, 38, 47–48, 60, 65, 97, 113–14, 123, 131, 142, 146, 157
Griffiths, Jennifer, 30, 99
Gullah, 149, 157

Haiti, 159; revolution in, 92; Vodou, 92–93 (*see* Voodoo)

Haley, Alex, 13, 40–67, 144–45, 160–61; allegations of plagiarism, 43; biographical background, 41–42; faction, 42–43; journalism career, 41; Malcolm X (relationship with), 40–42. See also *Roots: An American Saga*

Hall, Gwendolyn Mildo, 92, 93

Hall, Rebecca, 130

Handy, W. C., 113

Harms, Robert, 23–24

Hartman, Saidiyah V., 55, 122

Hayden, Robert, 30–31, 33

healing, 2, 4–5, 9–10, 14–15, 17, 21–22, 35–36, 39, 56, 68, 74, 97, 167

Hewett, Ivan, 88

home, viii, 1, 8, 12, 13, 14, 25, 32, 45, 46, 48, 61, 63, 65, 82, 84, 85, 117, 118, 120, 121, 124, 131, 132, 153, 163; Africa as ancestral home, 28, 94, 103; connection to, 142, 144; homeland, 2, 9, 43, 145; homeless, 125; loss of, 15, 24, 51, 54, 113, 115, 116; return to, 16, 147, 150, 154, 158, 160

hooks, bell, 145, 147, 153

Hughes, Langston, 154

Huret, Romain, 126

Hurricane Katrina, 11, 14–15, 21, 82–90; Barbara Bush response, 130–31; evacuation, vii–viii, 1, 21, 82; in literature, 127; and the slave trade, 69–82, 129–30; Superdome, 1, 21, 128; on television, 72–90. See also *When the Levees Broke*; *Salvage the Bones*

Hurricane Katrina in Transatlantic Perspective (Huret), 126

Inter Coetera Bull, 2–3

Isadora (*Middle Passage* character), 72, 74, 79–82. *See also* Johnson, Charles

JanMohamed, Abdul, 3, 5, 11, 110, 125

Jarrell, Randall, 158

jazz, 14, 33, 83, 87–88, 154–55

Jim Crow, 50, 88, 111, 117–18, 121–25, 153

Johnson, Charles, 13–14, 51, 68–82, 90, 93; interview, 73; *Middle Passage*, 68–90

Johnson, James Weldon, 155

Johnson, Lonnie, 114–15, 125

Jubilee (Walker), 68

Kempf, Jean, 113, 117, 142

Kincaid, Jamaica, 33

Kinte, Kunta. *See* Haley, Alex; *Roots: An American Saga*

Lambert, Raphaël, 31

Lambreaux, Big Chief Albert, 83–88. See also *Treme*

Lambreaux, Delmond, 83, 86–88. See also *Treme*

Laveau, Marie, 14; historical, 90, 98; song by Oscar Celestin, 106. See also *Voodoo Dreams*

Lee, Spike, 15, 127–28, 131; *When the Levees Broke* (documentary), 13, 15, 85, 127–29, 131

levees, 116, 120, 125–26; history of, 111–13. See also Lee, Spike

Lowe, John, 12

MacGaffey, Wyatt, 10

Mardi Gras Indians, vii, 84–86, 104; history, 83; masking, 14, 86–87

marriage, 56–57, 74, 80, 147

Marshall, Paule, 16, 145. See also *Praisesong for the Widow*

Martin, Trayvon, 8, 39n7, 63

McBride, Renisha, 8

McCall, Dan, 119

McDaniel, Lora, 147, 149

McNeil, Elizabeth, 160

memory, 2, 5–6, 9, 11–13, 16, 26, 28–30, 33, 35, 57, 64, 70–71, 89, 94, 109, 116, 122, 126–27, 135, 137, 145, 147, 151, 155, 158; mythic, 135, 148–49, 157, 159–60

Metting, Fred, 153

Middle Passage, 2–6, 8–16, 21–22, 25–33, 35, 39, 42–44, 50–55, 68–91, 93, 95, 100, 102–6, 127, 130, 142–43, 145, 147–49, 152, 158, 160, 165; in film, 12, 16, 38, 62; history of, 23–24, 27; literature, 12–16, 21, 27–29, 30–35, 39, 40–57, 68–106; music, 11–12, 14–16, 31–33, 72; novel (*see* Johnson, Charles); on television, 13–14, 16, 40, 58–90

Mississippi, 11, 15, 82, 110, 115, 117; floods, 111, 112, 114, 118

Morrison, Toni, 109, 111, 122, 150; *Beloved*, 26, 30, 34–37; Sethe (*Beloved* character), 34–35, 37

Mudimbe, V. Y., 2

music, 2, 15, 24, 33, 38, 87–88, 110, 157; blues (*see* blues); festivals, 1; jazz (*see* jazz)

Nagin, Ray, 130

Naylor, Gloria, 33

New Orleans, vii–viii, 1, 13–15, 21, 69–92, 97, 104–6, 120, 125–28, 130, 139, 142

Norrell, Robert J., 40n1, 61, 63, 67

Osbey, Brenda Marie, 14, 27, 30, 92, 105

Patterson, Orlando, 3–6

Pederson, Carl, 21

Percy, Will, 112, 115

Perry, Tonya E. *See* Davis-Maye, Denise

Philips, Caryl, 33

Philips, M. NourbeSe, 8, 33, 37–38, 90, 93, 105, 128; *Zong!*, 30, 35–36, 129

photography, 117, 164

plantation, 22, 52, 56, 65, 68, 96, 112, 149; Sweet Home Plantation, 34

police, 83, 85, 115, 139, 165–66; brutality, 13, 63, 86, 155

Praisesong for the Widow (Marshall): Aunt Cuney (character), 148–52, 156–57, 159; dreams, 150, 155–57; Federal Writer's Project, 149–50; flying Africans, 145–47; Halsey Street, 153–57, 159–60; Ibo Landing Story, 145, 148, 151–52, 154; influences, 149; myth (meaning of), 145–47; Ring Shout dance, 151–52, 159; walking on water, 147, 152, 155 (*see also* water)

protests, 13, 41, 62–63, 85–86, 115; literature, 73–74, 119; sit-ins, 85–86

Quashie, Kevin, 44, 45, 49

Raboteau, Albert, 9–10. *See also* conversion

Rankine, Claudia, 51

rape, 24, 34, 57, 60–61, 78, 94, 101, 112, 163

Rediker, Marcus, 28, 146, 149

refugee, 72, 112, 117

resistance, 1–6, 8–11, 13–14, 16, 25–28, 31–34, 38, 43, 52, 55–58, 60–62, 64–65, 71–72, 84–86, 94; to social death, 34, 44, 53, 60, 64–65, 67, 88–89, 91–92, 94, 96, 98, 106, 110, 115, 119, 127, 147–48, 151, 160; through forgiveness, 78; through naming, 163; through physical assertion, 8–9, 24, 31–32, 60, 62, 65–66; through quiet and silence, 44–46, 48–49, 53, 55–57, 64

Rhodes, Jewel Parker, 13, 25, 68–96, 98–99, 101–3, 105–6, 152. See also *Voodoo Dreams*

Rice, Tamir, 8

Robinette, Garland, 130

Roots: An American Saga (Haley), 13, 16, 40–57, 74; 1977 television series, 13, 58–61; 2016 television series, 13, 40, 61–63; faction, 42–45, 67; Kunta Kinte, 13, 40, 42–61, 63–66; Twitter responses, 66. *See also* Haley, Alex

Rosenbaum, Art, 151

Rowley, Hazel, 117

Salaam, Kalamu ya, 84

Salvage the Bones (Ward), 15, 126; analysis of, 127, 131; and blues music, 135; Esch (character), 131–42

Schuler, Monica, 27, 159

Scott, Daniel M., III, 9

segregation, 15, 83, 85, 87, 123. *See also* Jim Crow

Sethe (*Beloved* character). *See* Morrison, Toni

Sixteenth Street Baptist Church Bombing, 155

slavery, 6, 40, 41, 43, 44, 68, 75, 76, 80, 88, 90, 111, 145, 146, 152, 160; and Equiano, 71; and Kunta Kinte, 40, 41, 43, 44, 55; resistance to, 65; television representations, 58, 62, 63, 66

Smallwood, Stephanie, 23, 25, 36, 37, 150

Smith, Bessie, 114–17, 120, 124, 126

social death, 4–9, 13–15, 28, 34, 37–38, 46, 51, 64–65, 67, 69, 71, 74, 77–78, 79, 81, 87, 89, 91, 94, 98, 101, 109–10, 113, 116, 124, 131, 138–39, 142–43, 154–55; definition of, 3–4. *See also* resistance

spirits and spirituality, 9–12, 16, 24–25, 27, 38, 68, 91, 97, 99–100, 102–4, 146–47, 152; Allah, 46–47, 50, 53–54, 59, 65, 78; Almuseri god, 73–78; Buddhism, 73; Catholicism, 3, 92, 96–97; Christianity, 3, 9, 23, 29, 92, 94, 103; Damballah, 25, 91, 93, 96, 98–105; flying Africans, 149–50 (see *Praisesong for the Widow*);

Jehovah, 78; Kongo, 10, 11, 25, 35; Krishna, 78; Ogbuide of Oguta Lake in Igboland of Nigeria, 25; possession, 99–100, 102–4 (see *Voodoo Dreams*); water goddess, 25, 28; visions, 91, 93, 95–96, 105; Voodoo (see *Voodoo Dreams*)

spirituals (songs), 117; "Down by the Riverside," 109; "My Soul Walks Free. Death Awaits Me," 103; "O Mary Don't You Weep," 144, 147; "Wade in the Water," 126

Sterling, Alton, 8

storytelling, vii–viii, 2, 5, 9, 12–13, 15–16, 26, 28–30, 37, 41, 43–44, 46, 57, 70–71, 94, 96, 106, 147–49, 160–61

Taylor, Eric Robert, 8, 9

teenage pregnancy, 132, 134, 136–37, 140–42

Their Eyes Were Watching God (Hurston), 112

Thomas, Irma, 126

Thompson, Robert Farris, 10, 25

transatlantic slave trade, 2–6, 8–13, 21–30, 32–33, 39, 41, 43, 50–54, 57, 59, 60–61, 71, 73, 146; history of, 69–70, 111; and hurricanes, 127; revolts, 8–9, 24, 31–32, 60, 65, 149; slave ships, 2, 8–9, 13, 22–28, 30–34, 36–38, 42, 51–55, 57, 60, 63–65, 72–76, 78–80, 84, 93, 113, 120, 149, 158 (see *Amistad*; *Diligent*; *Zong*); treatment of women, 33–35, 59, 63, 79

trauma, 4, 10, 14, 16, 21, 22, 23, 25, 27, 34, 36, 39, 51, 54, 58, 64, 69, 72, 81, 99, 106, 116, 117, 124, 143, 145; Halsey Street as site of, 153, 154, 160; Middle Passage as site of, 14, 35, 148; post-traumatic response, 156; purpose of, 161; traumatic experiences, 15, 22, 29, 30, 36, 46, 71, 143, 148

Treme (tv series), 14, 68–90, 71–72, 82–85, 106

Tretheway, Natasha, 112

Trouble the Water (documentary), 1n1; 911 recordings, 139

Tucker, Terrence, 121, 124

Twitter, 66, 166

Uncle Tom's Cabin (Stowe), 119

Voodoo, 14, 91–102, 104–5, 154, 157, 159; history of, 92; as resistance, 91–93, 97; and women, 105. *See also* Haiti; *Voodoo Dreams*

Voodoo Dreams (Rhodes): Bayou Teche, 94–95; Grandmere (character), 91, 93–98, 104; John (character), 91, 95–96, 98–106; Maman (character), 91, 93, 95–96, 100, 102; Marie Laveau (character), 90–106; possession, 95, 98–99, 102–4; walking on water, 101–3 (*see* water)

Wall, Cheryl, 152, 153, 155, 159

Wallace, Maurice, 45, 58, 149

Walters, Wendy, 149

Ward, Jerry, 143

Ward, Jesmyn, 15, 109–10, 116, 125–27, 131–32, 134, 137–42, 144. See also *Salvage the Bones*

Wardi, Janine, 35; *Water and African American Memory: An Ecocritical Perspective*, 11

water, vii–viii, 2, 4, 8–12, 15, 21, 24, 35, 42, 48, 50, 55, 60, 71, 95, 112, 126, 129, 140; as cleansing, 158; as healing, 104; as lifegiving, 11, 25, 34, 37; as metaphor for change, 116, 118, 125; as metaphor for memory, 26, 34, 42, 109; as symbol for death, 12, 14, 21, 34, 37, 42; as symbol of birth, 123; as symbol of motherhood, 25; as symbol of the sacred, 25–28, 38; walking on, 145–47

white supremacy, 2–3, 6–7, 15–16, 24, 38–39, 44, 54, 79, 115, 120, 128; and violence, 5–6, 8, 16, 23, 32, 35–37, 60–61, 65

Wright, Michelle, 22

Wright, Richard, 5, 15, 73, 109–10, 112, 116, 117n3, 120–14; *Black Boy*, 118; *Down by the Riverside*, 11, 15, 117–25; *Native Son* (film), 117; *Uncle Tom's Children*, 117, 119

Zong (ship), 8, 37

BLACK PERFORMANCE AND CULTURAL CRITICISM

VALERIE LEE AND E. PATRICK JOHNSON, SERIES EDITORS

The Black Performance and Cultural Criticism series includes monographs that draw on interdisciplinary methods to analyze, critique, and theorize black cultural production. Books in the series take as their object of intellectual inquiry the performances produced on the stage and on the page, stretching the boundaries of both black performance and literary criticism.

Reimagining the Middle Passage: Black Resistance in Literature, Television, and Song
    TARA T. GREEN

Conjuring Freedom: Music and Masculinity in the Civil War's "Gospel Army"
    JOHARI JABIR

Mama's Gun: Black Maternal Figures and the Politics of Transgression
    MARLO D. DAVID

Theatrical Jazz: Performance, Àṣẹ, and the Power of the Present Moment
    OMI OSUN JONI L. JONES

When the Devil Knocks: The Congo Tradition and the Politics of Blackness in Twentieth-Century Panama
    RENÉE ALEXANDER CRAFT

The Queer Limit of Black Memory: Black Lesbian Literature and Irresolution
    MATT RICHARDSON

Fathers, Preachers, Rebels, Men: Black Masculinity in U. S. History and Literature, 1820–1945
    EDITED BY TIMOTHY R. BUCKNER AND PETER CASTER

Secrecy, Magic, and the One-Act Plays of Harlem Renaissance Women Writers
    TAYLOR HAGOOD

Beyond Lift Every Voice and Sing: The Culture of Uplift, Identity, and Politics in Black Musical Theater
    PAULA MARIE SENIORS

Prisons, Race, and Masculinity in Twentieth-Century U. S. Literature and Film
    PETER CASTER

Mutha' Is Half a Word: Intersections of Folklore, Vernacular, Myth, and Queerness in Black Female Culture
    L. H. STALLINGS

CPSIA information can be obtained
at www.ICGtesting.com
Printed in the USA
BVHW03s0848021018
528968BV00015B/19/P

ML   12/2018